STERNE, THE MODERNS,
AND THE NOVEL

Sterne, the Moderns, and the Novel

THOMAS KEYMER

OXFORD
UNIVERSITY PRESS

OXFORD

UNIVERSITY PRESS

Great Clarendon Street, Oxford OX2 6DP

Oxford University Press is a department of the University of Oxford.
It furthers the University's objective of excellence in research, scholarship,
and education by publishing worldwide in

Oxford New York

Auckland Bangkok Buenos Aires Cape Town Chennai
Dar es Salaam Delhi Hong Kong Istanbul Karachi Kolkata
Kuala Lumpur Madrid Melbourne Mexico City Mumbai Nairobi
São Paulo Shanghai Taipei Tokyo Toronto

Oxford is a registered trade mark of Oxford University Press
in the UK and certain other countries

Published in the United States
by Oxford University Press Inc., New York

© Thomas Keymer 2002

The moral rights of the author have been asserted
Database right Oxford University Press (maker)

First published 2002

British Library Cataloguing in Publication Data

Data available

Library of Congress Cataloging in Publication Data
Keymer, Tom.
Sterne, the moderns, and the novel/Thomas Keymer.
p. cm.
Includes bibliographical references and index.
1. Sterne, Laurence, 1713–1768. Life and opinions of Tristram Shandy, gentleman. 2.
Literature publishing—England—History—18th century. 3. English fiction—18th
century—History and criticism. 4. Serialized fiction—England—History and criticism. 5.
Serial publication of books—History—18th century. 6. England—Intellectual life—18th
century. 7. Satire, English—History and criticism. I. Title.
PR3714.T73 K49 2002   823'.6—dc21   2002033695
ISBN 0–19–924592–4

1 3 5 7 9 10 8 6 4 2

Typeset by SNP Best-set Typesetter Ltd., Hong Kong
Printed in Great Britain
on acid-free paper by
Biddles Ltd, Guildford and King's Lynn

For

PRUDENCE, TOBIAS, *and* BENJAMIN

Acknowledgements

THIS BOOK HAS been in the making, alongside other projects, for almost a decade, helped on its way by the generosity of many individuals and institutions. For the initial impetus, I am grateful to Hilary Laurie, who invited me to edit *A Sentimental Journey* for the Everyman series, and to the Master and Fellows of Emmanuel College, Cambridge, where a visiting fellowship enabled me to prepare the edition while starting to conceive this study. In the same year, the York conference on Laurence Sterne in Modernism and Postmodernism provided a timely and congenial forum for debate, and friendships forged there with Geoff Day, Judith Hawley, Mel New, Tim Parnell, and Peter de Voogd have been crucial to my thinking since then. I am grateful to the late Kenneth Monkman and his fellow trustees of Shandy Hall for inviting me to deliver the Laurence Sterne Memorial Lecture for 1995, which contained the germ of Chapters 3 and 4, and to Tim Parnell for inviting me to join his panel at the Tenth International Congress on the Enlightenment at Dublin in 1999, at which an early version of Chapter 6 was presented. The opportunity to test out both these papers in the *Shandean* has been invaluable, and in taking them further I have been greatly helped by constructive feedback, published and informal, from readers of the journal. The bulk of Chapter 5 began life as a paper for the Macpherson Bicentenary Conference at Oxford in 1996, and different versions were published in Fiona Stafford and Howard Gaskill (eds.), *From Gaelic to Romantic: Ossianic Translations* (Amsterdam: Rodopi, 1998), and in Melvyn New (ed.), *Critical Essays on Laurence Sterne* (New York: G. K. Hall, 1998). I am grateful to the publishers and editors of both volumes, and to Peter de Voogd of the *Shandean*, for permission to rework this earlier material here.

The book was completed thanks to a handsome award under the AHRB research leave scheme, and many colleagues at St Anne's College and the English Faculty helped to make the leave feasible. My college teaching was expertly covered by Nick McDowell and Paddy Bullard, and Kate Williams was a resourceful and ever-reliable research assistant, with support from the News International Fund. Throughout the whole process, my thinking has been informed by suggestions, responses, and information generously provided by more scholars than I am able to list here, including Anne

Bandry, René Bosch, David Fairer, Andrew Gibson, Paul Goring, Richard Jones, James McLaverty, Susan Manning, John Mullan, Claude Rawson, Shaun Regan, John Richetti, Betty Rizzo, Adam Roberts, Peter Sabor, Marcus Walsh, Karina Williamson, and the readers for the Oxford University Press. Anyone working on Sterne owes an immense debt to the work of Melvyn New, and I count myself especially lucky to have been able to subject my thinking over the years to his sceptical yet supportive interrogation, as well as to that of Tim Parnell, whose reading of *Tristram Shandy* has influenced me more than he knows. Prudence Robey, and latterly Tobias Keymer and Benjamin Keymer, have made the years in which this book took shape a great and growing joy. Having intended to dedicate it to the first—I see more reasons for doing it to all three.

Contents

List of Illustrations

Abbreviations

Amelia	Henry Fielding, *Amelia*, ed. Martin C. Battestin (Oxford: Clarendon Press, 1983); references are to book, chapter, and page
Card	John Kidgell, *The Card*, 2 vols. (1755); references are to volume and page
CH	Alan B. Howes (ed.), *Sterne: The Critical Heritage* (London: Routledge, 1974)
Clarissa	Samuel Richardson, *Clarissa*, intr. Florian Stuber, 8 vols. (New York: AMS Press, 1990); references are to volume and page
EMY	Arthur H. Cash, *Laurence Sterne: The Early and Middle Years* (London: Methuen, 1975)
ETB	*The Life and Memoirs of Mr. Ephraim Tristram Bates* (1756)
GEL	*The George Eliot Letters*, ed. Gordon S. Haight, 9 vols. (New Haven: Yale University Press, 1954–78); references are to volume and page
JA	Henry Fielding, *Joseph Andrews and Shamela*, ed. Douglas Brooks-Davies, rev. and intr. Thomas Keymer (Oxford: Oxford University Press, 1999); references are to book, chapter, and page
Letters	*Letters of Laurence Sterne*, ed. Lewis Perry Curtis (Oxford: Clarendon Press, 1935)
LY	Arthur H. Cash, *Laurence Sterne: The Later Years* (London: Methuen, 1986)
PO	James Macpherson, *The Poems of Ossian and Related Works*, ed. Howard Gaskill, intr. Fiona Stafford (Edinburgh: Edinburgh University Press, 1996)
PR	Laurence Sterne, *A Political Romance*, intr. Kenneth Monkman (Menston: Scolar Press, 1971)
SCG	Samuel Richardson, *Sir Charles Grandison*, ed. Jocelyn Harris, 3 vols. (London: Oxford University Press, 1972); references are to volume and page
Sermons	*The Sermons of Laurence Sterne*, The Florida Edition of the Works of Laurence Sterne, vols. 4–5, ed. Melvyn New (Gainesville, Fla.: University Press of Florida, 1996). References are to the sermon number, followed by the page number in the Florida edition; thus '*Sermons*, 23.214' refers to sermon no. 23, p. 214
SJ	Laurence Sterne, *A Sentimental Journey through France and Italy and Continuation of the Bramine's Journal: The Text and Notes*, The Florida Edition of the Works of Laurence Sterne, vol. 6, ed. Melvyn New and W. G. Day (Gainesville, Fla.: University Press of Florida, 2002)

TJ   Henry Fielding, *Tom Jones*, ed. Martin C. Battestin and Fredson Bowers, 2 vols. (Oxford: Clarendon Press, 1975); references are to book, chapter, and page

TS   Laurence Sterne, *The Life and Opinions of Tristram Shandy, Gentleman: The Text*, The Florida Edition of the Works of Laurence Sterne, vols. 1–2, ed. Melvyn New and Joan New (Gainesville, Fla.: University Presses of Florida, 1978). References are to Sterne's original volume and chapter numbers, followed by the page number in the Florida edition; thus '*TS* 5.16.446' refers to vol. 5, ch. 16, in the original, and p. 446 in the Florida edition

TS Notes Melvyn New, with Richard A. Davies and W. G. Day, *The Life and Opinions of Tristram Shandy, Gentleman: The Notes*, The Florida Edition of the Works of Laurence Sterne, vol. 3 (Gainesville, Fla.: University Presses of Florida, 1984)

Introduction

ALMOST TWO DECADES after the great *Pamela* vogue of 1740–1, the publication of *Tristram Shandy*'s opening volumes in the winter of 1759–60 had a similarly galvanizing effect on the novel genre—on its formal conventions, its commercial presence, its status as a cultural force. The elderly Richardson was alive to see it happen, and his remarks on the occasion seethe with the bitterness of eclipse and unwilled abdication. A virtuoso in his day of literary innovation and promotion, Richardson knew that his ascendancy was over, but could not welcome the new era that *Tristram Shandy* seemed to herald, or even create. 'Unaccountable wildness; whimsical digressions; comical incoherencies; uncommon indecencies; all with an air of novelty, has catched the reader's attention': Richardson affects to be quoting an acquaintance here, but the tone is all his own. Perhaps he detected a strain of parody in Sterne that seemed to implicate his own techniques, and he clearly resented a display of formal and rhetorical pyrotechnics alongside which his own innovations looked staid and stale. What irks him above all, however, is the completeness with which *Tristram Shandy* had made itself synonymous with modernity and fashion, at once exploiting and reinforcing a culture now vacuously fixated on novelty alone. Not only is this upstart text the most egregious instance of a general compulsion 'to read every book that fashion renders prevalent in conversation'. It also threatens to consolidate a new age of permanently dumbed-down taste, and 'when no longer upheld by the short-lived breath of fashion . . . this ridiculous compound will be the cause of many more productions, witless and humourless, perhaps, but indecent and absurd'.[1]

Elsewhere, Richardson's praise of the pious citizens of Manchester 'for the Example they set in such a *Shandy*-Age as this' uses Sterne's text as pejorative shorthand, a metonym of degraded modernity, and similar implications are at work when he recommends to his friend Lady Bradshaigh a new didactic novel, *The Histories of Some of the Penitents in the Magdalen*

---

[1] *Selected Letters of Samuel Richardson*, ed. John Carroll (Oxford: Clarendon Press, 1964), 341 (to Mark Hildesley, Feb.–Mar. 1761).

House, on the grounds that it has 'no *Shandying* in it'.[2] Formally undis-
rupted and morally unimpeachable, this novel was indeed free of flippant
Shandying; but by the same token it had proved almost unmarketable in
the Shandy age that now prevailed, and had only limped into print thanks
to Richardson's influence in the trade. Its refusal to be formally playful or
teasingly bawdy was a refusal, beyond these things, to be novel, modish,
and modern—qualities that made *Tristram Shandy* the defining cultural
product of its day, and one (as Lady Bradshaigh replied with ill-disguised
relish) that is 're'd by all the world'.[3]

Sterne had gone to great lengths to make his opening volumes look fashionably in the swim. In *A Political Romance* (a satire on diocesan politics in
York, structured in imitation of *A Tale of a Tub*), he had looked inward for
his subject matter and backward for his mode of addressing it, thereby
consigning the work to provincial oblivion even before its suppression.
Tristram Shandy, by contrast, was a campaign for nationwide fame and
fortune, in which elements of Sterne's earlier style (a parochial setting
'of four *English* miles diameter' (1.7.10); ongoing Scriblerian echoes and
tricks) now coexisted with elements astutely geared to modern metropolitan taste, including satirical play on the latest novelistic conventions and
knowing allusions to current bestsellers such as Voltaire's *Candide*. Less
ostentatious invocations of other works first published in 1759 (from
Adam Smith's *The Theory of Moral Sentiments* to Thomas Sheridan's *A
Discourse . . . Introductory to His Course of Lectures on Elocution*)[4] suggest
that Sterne was strategically devouring and reworking the most prominent new publications, and he gives out a similar message in the material
form of his writing. By initially specifying that *Tristram Shandy* be mod-
elled in appearance on Jane Collier's *Art of Ingeniously Tormenting* (1753)
and printed on the same paper and type as Johnson's *Rasselas* (1759),
Sterne used the very format of his text to flag the modernity of its literary
identity and frame of reference. To his many detractors, the gambit was all
too successful. Richardson was far from alone (though his vantage point
was special) in seeing *Tristram Shandy* as a farrago of eye-catching gestures
and opportunist allusions, a work that exaggerated the debilitating trends
of a marketplace for print in which surprise was all that mattered. Sterne

---

[2] In his revision of Daniel Defoe, *A Tour thro' the Whole Island of Great Britain*, 6th edn., 4
vols. (1761), 3: 249; letter to Lady Bradshaigh of June 1760, Victoria and Albert Museum,
Forster MSS, xi, fo. 269.

[3] To Richardson, 23 Aug. 1760, Forster MSS, xi, fo. 274.

[4] See *TS Notes*, 355–6, 184–5; also, on Smith, scholia to the Florida annotations in
Scriblerian, 31/1 (Autumn 1998), 133 and *Scriblerian*, 32/2 (Spring 2000), 402.

had cleverly perceived that traditional literary values were now in abeyance, and by addressing more frivolous and fleeting tastes had become 'the only model of fine, easy, modish writing', which 'engrosses all the literary attention of the age'. In so doing, he had reinforced the trends he exploited, expelling the outmoded aesthetics of reason and order to the point where 'one would imagine the crazed inhabitants of Moorfields . . . guided the taste of the public, and poured forth their incoherent rhapsodies, for the entertainment of the good people of England, once reputed so sensible and judicious'.[5]

As the decade wore on, the flagrant modernity for which Sterne's writing became a byword seemed to pervade not just fiction but every branch of literary production, from satirical verse to theological prose. Churchill's *The Ghost* was 'this Shandy in Hudibrastics', Warburton's two-volume *Doctrine of Grace* 'these little Shandean Volumes'.[6] *Tristram Shandy* became (to adapt a well-known formulation) the most typical work of 1760s literature, all the more so because its voguish textual manœuvres geared it thematically as well as practically to an age preoccupied as never before by the irresistible mechanisms of fashion, and by the consequences for literature. (As Churchill put it at the height of Sterne's fame, 'The love of Novelty and Fashion' was now the only stable thing, for 'Fashion so directs, and Moderns raise, | On Fashion's mould'ring base, their transient praise'.[7]) A few months after Sterne's death, the centrality of his writing in the culture of the decade, informed by and informing the contemporaneous successes with which it jostled and interacted, was flamboyantly illustrated by John Hamilton Mortimer in the etching reproduced as Fig. 5 of this study. Commissioned to illustrate Evan Lloyd's satire of modern authorship, *The Powers of the Pen*, the etching depicts the ritual condemnation of new writing by ghoulish periodical reviewers. In the latest batch of publications, *A Sentimental Journey* arrives for review with *The Powers of the Pen*, while pasted to the wall of the reviewers' cave are the title pages of other prominent victims from the Shandy age. *Tristram Shandy* itself is there, cheek by jowl with Edward Thompson's *The Meretriciad* and Churchill's *The Ghost*; *The Sermons of Mr. Yorick* are sandwiched between Lloyd's *The Methodist* and Wilkes's *North Briton*.[8]

---

[5] *CH* 95 (*Grand Magazine*, June 1760), 146 (*Critical Review*, June 1762). Moorfields was the site of Bedlam and a newer madhouse, St Luke's.

[6] *Monthly Review*, 29 (Nov. 1763), 397; 27 (Nov. 1762), 370.

[7] *The Poetical Works of Charles Churchill*, ed. Douglas Grant (Oxford: Clarendon Press, 1956), 74 (*The Ghost*, bk. 1, l. 352), 22 (*The Rosciad*, ll. 679–80).

[8] For fuller discussion, see below, Ch. 5 and Fig. 5.

This widespread contemporary sense of *Tristram Shandy* as the defining
work of its immediate day, tied intimately into the writing of a culture it
both reflects and influences, is rarely registered in modern criticism. Two
competing traditions continue to dominate the field, and both (though
they meet in little else) present the work as essentially an anachronism,
with much more natural and extensive affiliations to earlier or later
modes. I use the term 'work' advisedly at this point, since the question of
generic identity—should we call *Tristram Shandy* 'novel' or 'satire'?—is
central to the debate. One tradition, inaugurated by the classic formalist
analysis of Viktor Shklovsky and perpetuated in recent studies like John M.
Warner's *Joyce's Grandfathers*,[9] approaches Sterne as generically a novelist
and temperamentally an honorary modern. Unlike the efforts of his more
or less primitive contemporaries, with their serene confidence in the capacity of language and narrative to deliver represented worlds, coherent
selves, and uncontested meanings to the reader, the deconstructive sophistication of Sterne's writing looks centuries ahead. By defining him instead
as a writer of proto-modernist or proto-postmodern fiction (the identikit
yoking of 'modernist' and 'postmodern' endemic in this approach says
much about its broad-brush manner), criticism can restore him to his
proper place as our own contemporary. In the keynote essay to *Laurence
Sterne in Modernism and Postmodernism* (the proceedings of a conference
held in York in 1993), Carol Watts is intelligently aware of the need
to explain 'why such a complex narrative form should have arisen at the
mid-eighteenth-century', and recognizes that to call *Tristram Shandy*
'postmodernist in every sense except the moment in which it was written'
may amount to little more than 'narcissistic misrecognition'. Having
voiced these caveats, however, Watts is more interested in rationalizing the
misrecognition than exploring its oversights, and concludes that the ludic
and sceptical emphases of *Tristram Shandy*—on parody and pastiche, on
referentiality as problematic, on identity as provisional, on time and history as constructs—do indeed lift it clear of the culture in which it was
written. 'An aesthetic anachronism . . . to Sterne's contemporaries', it remains—as though by inevitable conclusion from this dubious assertion—
'a modernist or postmodernist text *avant la lettre*'.[10]

[9] Viktor Shklovsky, 'The Novel as Parody: Sterne's *Tristram Shandy*', in Shklovsky, *Theory of Prose* (Elmwood Park, Ill.: Dalkey Archive Press, 1991), 147–70; John M. Warner, *Joyce's Grandfathers: Myth and History in Defoe, Smollett, Sterne, and Joyce* (Athens, Ga.: University of Georgia Press, 1993), 89–120.
[10] Carol Watts, 'The Modernity of Sterne', in David Pierce and Peter de Voogd (eds.), *Laurence Sterne in Modernism and Postmodernism* (Amsterdam: Rodopi, 1996), 19–38 (at 26, 19).

The alternative approach, influentially outlined in D. W. Jefferson's much-reprinted essay on '*Tristram Shandy* and the Tradition of Learned Wit'[11] and richly elaborated in the collaborative notes to the Florida edition, involves an equal and opposite explanation. Though *Tristram Shandy* may indeed anticipate and enable gestures we now associate with the postmodern, the effect arises not from some prescient experimental spirit on Sterne's part, but on the contrary from literary allegiances that were outmoded even by his own time, let alone by the modernist era. A belated exponent of a tradition of learned-wit satire that reaches back to Erasmus and finds its final flourish in Swift and Pope, Sterne roots himself creatively in a period when the novel genre (as conventionally understood) was barely a twinkle in its progenitors' eyes. It is with the satirical tradition that *Tristram Shandy* belongs, and in this context Sterne's apparent parody of the realist novel appears for what it is, the chance by-product of a formally disrupted mode of writing that is pre- and non-novelistic. Resuming Jefferson's theme, Donald R. Wehrs notes that '*Tristram Shandy* has proved suspiciously congenial to . . . modernist, metafictional, existential, deconstructive, and Lacanian readings',[12] and insists that the textual features on which these readings depend, far from implying sceptical modernity, are functionally very conservative, and use sceptical forms for fideist ends on the model of Renaissance satire. By this account, Sterne remains an anachronism in the mid-eighteenth century, but one of a thoroughly different kind: not a stranded modern but a wilful Renaissance throwback, or (as Melvyn New has recently put it) a 'reluctant participant in the late Renaissance movement Kant identified as Enlightenment'.[13]

In *Laurence Sterne as Satirist*, the Florida edition of *Tristram Shandy*, and his polemical contributions to the *New Casebooks* and *Twayne Masterworks* series, New's critically adroit and massively substantiated account of *Tristram Shandy*'s Renaissance/Scriblerian inheritance is a weighty counter-argument to constructions of a postmodern Sterne. Reprinting Jefferson and Wehrs in the casebook, New celebrates the fact that at last 'a new Sterne is emerging, separated from novel-centred discussions . . . and, most importantly perhaps, free from the need to see him as "one of us", as a secular sceptic or existentialist'.[14] The Florida annotations are his

[11] Originally published in *Essays in Criticism*, 1 (1951), 225–48.

[12] Donald R. Wehrs, 'Sterne, Cervantes, Montaigne: Fideistic Skepticism and the Rhetoric of Desire', *Comparative Literature Studies*, 25 (1988), 127–51 (at 127).

[13] Melvyn New, 'Three Sentimental Journeys: Sterne, Shklovsky, Svevo', *Shandean*, 11 (1999–2000), 126–34 (at 127).

[14] Melvyn New, *Tristram Shandy: Contemporary Critical Essays* (New York: St Martin's Press, 1992), 7–8.

trump card here, unanswerably reclaiming some of *Tristram Shandy*'s most celebrated encounters with linguistic indeterminacy or representational impasse as features of a satirical tradition in which established norms are reinforced through parody of trends that disrupt them. Even Tristram's famous declaration that 'we live amongst riddles and mysteries' (4.17.350) turns out to be lifted verbatim from a seventeenth-century sermon.[15] Not only do the Florida annotations thus overturn casual assumptions about Sterne's essential modernity. In their sheer bulk, as New insists, they relocate him generically by highlighting 'an essential difference between novels, the narrative emphasis of which limits the amount of annotation required to elucidate them, and satires, which have always required extensive annotation because of the satirist's reliance upon parody and burlesque, upon contemporary targets and issues, and upon the valorizing effects of cross-reference, allusion, and recognizable imitation'. In practice, this demonstration of satirical identity is one in which contemporary issues turn out to be greatly outweighed by literary allusions, and by allusions in particular to much earlier sources. Among the most frequent points of reference are Rabelais, Montaigne, Cervantes, and Burton, the result being to pull Sterne back not only from his postmodern identity, but also from his own contemporaneity: 'within the history of literature, Sterne's interests seem uniformly directed toward the past rather than toward what was happening in his own day'.[16]

In these contexts, the goal of the present study will seem doubly perverse. Whether one finds in the text a disruptive sophistication that looks forward to postmodern fiction or a tissue of learned-wit recoveries that harks back to Renaissance satire, *Tristram Shandy* can all too easily seem to escape its time. The former option is critically compelling, the latter a scholarly given. Yet to slip from either of these perceptions into an assumption that *Tristram Shandy* is purely proleptic or simply belated is to miss the equally important features I aim to foreground here. These include a close engagement with the novel genre in the crucial period of its formation (which is to say in the two decades immediately prior to *Tristram Shandy*'s launch); an ongoing responsiveness, through the mechanisms of serialization, to key texts, trends, and events as they developed in

---

[15] See Melvyn New, 'The Odd Couple: Laurence Sterne and John Norris of Bemerton', *Philological Quarterly*, 75 (1996), 376–7; also *Sermons*, n. to 19.182, where the relevant passage (from Norris's *Practical Discourses* of 1691) is quoted in full.

[16] Melvyn New, *Tristram Shandy: A Book for Free Spirits* (New York: Twayne, 1994), 21, 6.

the ensuing decade; the subtextual presence (already quietly registered in parts of the Florida edition and amplified thoughout this study) of specific contemporaneous intertexts, some of them very pervasive; an element of topical, and indeed political, satirical innuendo that is not incidental but systematic and central (though also, of course, non-committal). Above all, my purpose is to reinsert Sterne's writing into its rich and heterogeneous cultural moment, and to do so in ways that, by adjusting rather than denying the critical traditions outlined above, open up a telling area of potential convergence between them. Although I dispute identifications of *Tristram Shandy* as a solitary postmodern anticipation or a Renaissance/Scriblerian throwback, I do indeed see it as heavily conditioned by satirical traditions that culminate with Swift, and I also see it as a self-conscious exercise in metafiction. More strenuous and targeted attempts to historicize both these critical perceptions, satire-centred and novel-centred, can move them closer together, specifically by demonstrating how *Tristram Shandy* not only absorbs but also updates the learned-wit tradition, redeploying its satirical arsenal on a literary culture that had undergone radical transformation since *A Tale of a Tub*.

Central to this new culture is the novel genre, and it is here that a satirical inheritance derived from Swift and a strain of parody that targets narrative convention most clearly meet. If *Tristram Shandy* is a satire, I argue, it is above all a satire on the novel, and in this respect it cleverly capitalizes on a potentiality that *A Tale of a Tub* had intimated but been unable to fulfil. As a book about market-led modern authorship, exuberantly immersed in the culture it mocks, Swift's satire is often seen as groping towards the novel as its proper subject. As J. Paul Hunter writes, '*A Tale of a Tub* is not exactly a parody of the novel—it is hard to parody something that has as yet no concrete form, tradition, or definitive example—but it is an exposure of the cast of mind and set of values that ultimately produced novels'.[17] By the time of *Tristram Shandy* fifty years later, the situation had utterly changed. Now the novel was securely established as the chosen medium of Swift's 'freshest moderns', the crowning achievement of the energies they represent, the quintessential mode—subjective, circumstantial, digressive, transgressive—of commercialized modern

[17] J. Paul Hunter, *Before Novels: The Cultural Contexts of Eighteenth-Century English Fiction* (New York: Norton, 1990), 108; see also Brean Hammond's suggestion (*Professional Imaginative Writing in England, 1670–1740* (Oxford: Clarendon Press, 1997), 159) that Swift's hack persona may partly derive from the example of John Dunton, whose *Voyage round the World* was republished in the 1760s for its proto-Shandean qualities.

writing. In the intervening years, glancing applications of Swift's satirical model to the novel had been ventured in passing, notably in the walk-on part given to Eliza Haywood in works by Pope and Fielding (the *Dunciad*'s scandalously productive 'Eliza'; 'Mrs. Novel' in *The Author's Farce*). But it is only with *Tristram Shandy* in the 1760s, when mid-century novelists including Fielding himself had lifted the novel to generic prominence and even prestige, that Swift's hack could be fully reinvented as a narrator whose writing evokes, exaggerates, and subverts the ambitions and techniques of modern fiction. Here the Swiftian mindset and mode of Sterne's text bump up against phenomena that Swift could barely have foreseen, and in this respect it becomes possible to think of *Tristram Shandy* not only as satirical and novelistic in an integrated sense, but also as profoundly of its time.

This novelistic aspect of *Tristram Shandy* was instantly recognizable to early readers, and in Chapter 1 I explore the features that made it so, including the parodic intensification of narrative techniques that had already become standard, and a sophisticated engagement with formal and rhetorical questions thrown up by Richardson and Fielding. My analysis demonstrates Sterne's application of his satirical resources to contemporaneous modes and texts, while also historicizing the novel-centred approach—an approach that, though critically persuasive, has never been grounded with specific reference to mid-eighteenth-century conventions and tropes. For all its undoubted anticipation of later trends, Sterne's complicated play on narrative representation, linguistic indeterminacy, and reader response turn out to be firmly rooted in these prior conventions, to which *Tristram Shandy* responds with witty parody, intricate elaboration, and occasional outright theft. But it was not only the headline novels of Richardson and Fielding that Sterne used as grist to his mill, and Chapter 2 reads *Tristram Shandy* as intervening in a more localized debate within and about the novel in the later 1750s, when the genre was widely perceived as technically and commercially in the doldrums, or even in terminal decline. Emphasis is placed here on the material as well as literary gestures that Sterne used to make his mark in this debate (some of them heralded in experimental novels that *Tristram Shandy* permanently eclipsed), and specifically on his innovative use of print technology to satirize narrative conventions and interrogate their points of impasse. Throughout this analysis, I stress the sophistication with which the forms and techniques encountered in *Tristram Shandy* had already been developed, and the knowingness with which they were often practised. Though Sterne's posture towards the genre he entered was always satirical in charge, it misrepresents his complex relationship to the fiction of the day to make crude distinctions between lofty sophistication in *Tristram Shandy* and blundering naivety all around. Sterne is always a step ahead, adding a showy new twist or flourish, rendering an implicit perception explicit, or systematizing metafictional gestures left latent or scattered in earlier novels. Sometimes, however, the lead is relatively short.

Sterne's engagement with new and innovative writing was not confined to the novel genre. By serializing *Tristram Shandy* over seven years, he not only dramatized the work's preoccupation with the insufficiencies of representation, staging for his readers a prolonged performance of digressive writing and progressive disease in which Tristram fails to record his life in the past while watching it fade in the present. He also equipped himself with a vehicle flexible and capacious enough to respond to new writing as it emerged in the intervals of serialization, improvising the details of his text in a state of rolling openness to external pressure. One effect of improvisatory serialization in *Tristram Shandy* is that Sterne was able to keep pace with ongoing innovations and developments in the novel, and the process is nicely observable in the case of contemporaneous serial fiction by Smollett and others, which interacts with *Tristram Shandy* in an ongoing tangle of reciprocal allusions. With the publication in the early to mid-1760s of successful works by Frances Sheridan, Sarah Scott, Frances Brooke, and Henry Brooke, the rise of sentimental fiction was probably the most important development in the novel genre in the years of *Tristram Shandy*'s serialization, and I have dealt elsewhere with Sterne's complex response to this process in later instalments of *Tristram Shandy* and *A Sentimental Journey*.[18] But many other modes of writing are registered in *Tristram Shandy*, not least the Shandean vogue itself, in that later instalments of Sterne's serial could respond, as they did in a variety of explicit and implicit ways, to the public reception of their precursors. The result is that *Tristram Shandy* becomes (among its many other qualities) a uniquely sensitive optic through which to read the complex and shifting trends of its cultural moment—a moment often seen in literary history as peculiarly unstable, transitionally 'post-Augustan' or 'pre-Romantic', and characterized more by its varieties of innovation, experimentation, and

---

[18] Thomas Keymer, 'Sentimental Fiction: Ethics, Social Critique, and Philanthropy', in John Richetti (ed.), *The Cambridge History of English Literature, 1660–1780* (Cambridge: Cambridge University Press, in press). It is in this context that the most successful readings of Sterne through his contemporaneous literary culture have been attempted: see especially John Mullan's fine account in *Sentiment and Sociability: The Language of Feeling in the Eighteenth Century* (Oxford: Clarendon Press, 1988), 147–200.

redefinition of traditional forms than by any strong collective identity or literary consensus.[19]

Having analysed the practical mechanisms, interpretative implications, and intertextual consequences of serialization, I devote my final chapters to the relationship between *Tristram Shandy* and specific poetic intertexts, all of which had vogues of their own in the period of serialization and retain an ambient presence in the resulting text. By re-emerging at irregular intervals on the literary culture of the decade, absorbing or addressing its new products, Sterne could make available to himself an inexhaustible repertoire of intertextual possibilities on which to play, and so subject his own fashionability to perpetual refreshment and renewal. Sometimes there is an adversarial edge to the process, an appearance of satirical challenge; but it is also clear that new writing (or, in one important case, newly revived writing) could have a positive, enabling effect as Sterne worked to develop his largest emphases and themes. In particular, the poetic intertexts I analyse here played a key role in unlocking and developing, in the middle and later instalments of *Tristram Shandy*, the melancholy possibilities always inherent in the work's fixation on incommunicable and irremediable pasts. Sterne alludes to this jocoserious or tragicomic dimension at the very outset, presenting the work to William Pitt as written against 'the infirmities . . . and other evils of life' (*TS* 1, dedication) and to the Marquis of Rockingham as 'wrote in affliction; & under a constant uneasiness of mind' (*LY* 360). But it is especially in later instalments, marked as they are by specific contemporary intertexts, that this gloomy undertow moves close to the surface. Chapter 5 explores the process in relation to James Macpherson's immensely popular Ossianic prose poems of the early 1760s, focused as they are on plangent evocations of loss, and to the contemporaneous 'Nonsense Club' satire of Churchill and his imitators, in which Ossian is aggressively debunked. Chapter 6 explores the intricate relationship between the Toby 'under-plot' and the Civil War poetry of Andrew Marvell (specifically Marvell's great poem about gardens and war, *Upon Appleton House*), which was enjoying a major revival in political circles to which Sterne seems to have gained entry. This last example also opens up an important sense in which *Tristram Shandy* engages, albeit with wry obliqueness, in urgent topical concerns. In Sterne's ingenious reworking of Marvell's distinctive topos, literary intertext and political context converge on the vexed debate surrounding (in a formulation Sterne

---

[19] See Marshall Brown, *Preromanticism* (Stanford, Calif.: Stanford University Press, 1990), 1–21.

uses elsewhere) the 'devastation, bloodshed, and expence' of global war (*Sermons*, 32.309).

In the last major research monograph to have been published about *Tristram Shandy*, Jonathan Lamb exhibits marked defensiveness about the relationship between his study and the Florida edition. By positioning *Tristram Shandy* 'in a grid of borrowings, quotations and allusions that considerably restricts the freedom to read beyond the annotated pale', the annotations steal interpretative initiatives from readers, and leave Lamb himself (in pursuing his own alternative associations) to talk about 'authors not as influences, I hasten to add, but as possibilities of reading'.[20] Yet it is hard to see anything very coercive about the specification of intertextual webs, which—intricately spun and playfully tweaked as they are in Sterne's writing—will always extend or complicate our interpretative options, never close them down. The existence in the *Scriblerian* of a standing column of 'scholia' to the Florida annotations constitutes in effect an expanded second edition-in-progress, and is a positive stimulus to ongoing reading beyond the pale. Nor is there any need, in presenting the case for new intertextual patterns, to don the poststructuralist armour Lamb calls on at this point, in which intertextuality is an infinite field of potential relations from which readers, unconfined by authorial intention or editorial fiat, select at will. Some intertextual modes are more susceptible of annotation than others, and the more concrete and localized allusions identified in the following chapters will no doubt enter future editions.[21] Others are more generally ambient than locally pronounced, however, and at several points I draw on the work of Gérard Genette and other theoreticians of intertextuality to clarify their place in a middle ground between positivist claims about 'influence' and free-floating 'possibilities of reading'. A quotative local allusion will always seem to have a more determinate status (and will always in practice be easier to note) than a subtextual presence that, however large in structural impact or pervasive in thematic significance, may never disclose itself with the solidity of verbal echo. Sometimes, as in the case of Sterne's engagement with the novel genre and its prevailing conventions, the 'source' in question is a discursive pattern so widely diffused that specific attributions of derivation would be misleading. In reading beyond the pale as it currently stands, I do not relinquish the claim that the connections I explore are inherent in Sterne's text, even

---

[20] Jonathan Lamb, *Sterne's Fiction and the Double Principle* (Cambridge: Cambridge University Press, 1989), 2, 5.

[21] The process has already begun in the case of Sterne's Marvell reworkings: see *SJ* 368; also *A Sentimental Journey*, ed. Paul Goring (London: Penguin, 2002), 134.

when it is hard to see exactly where or how they might enter traditional line-by-line annotation. But the larger consequences of this study are for the act of interpretation, and for our overall sense of the generic and cultural place of Sterne's writing, its involvement with the novel and the modern. Neither Renaissance satire nor postmodern metafiction, it draws on one to herald the other, in ways enabled and informed by the contemporaneous literary hinterland outlined below.

PART ONE

Narrative Discourse and Print Culture from *Pamela* to *Tristram Shandy*

1

Sterne and the 'New Species of Writing'

Of the plurality of discourses and traditions that bump up against one another in *Tristram Shandy*, two have dominated critical attempts to make generic (and hence interpretative) sense of Sterne's richly heteroglot text. One strain of criticism reads *Tristram Shandy* as a belated exercise in Renaissance learned wit; the other as a parody (or, if the implications of its parodic gestures are pursued, a deconstruction) of representational conventions in the modern novel. Each identity, all too often, is presented as exclusive of the other, and the critical dichotomy persists not least because its most evident point of stress—the overtly Cervantic aspect of *Tristram Shandy*—has been obscured by readings that present Cervantes himself as primarily an exponent of Erasmian satire, or of fideistic scepticism in the vein of Montaigne, rather than in his alternative guise as a proto-novelist.[1] The difficulty of grounding the novel-centred approach to Sterne in features equivalent to the close and direct allusiveness of his learned-wit set pieces, moreover, has often left it stranded in anachronism or generality, so fuelling the counterclaim that *Tristram Shandy*'s subversiveness of novelistic convention is nothing more than accidental or proleptic, or even a mere illusion. At best, in this view, the metafictional element in Sterne's writing is a chance by-product of his co-option, within a mock-autobiographical framework, of Scriblerian techniques of fragmentation and disruption, and lacks any solid connection to a genre in which he took little or no provable interest.

Yet it is not necessary for the novel-centred approach to *Tristram Shandy* to take refuge in classic poststructuralist theory, with its rationale for cutting relational meanings loose from inconvenient circumstances of

---

[1] On Cervantes and humanist satire, see Donald R. Wehrs, 'Sterne, Cervantes, Montaigne: Fideistic Skepticism and the Rhetoric of Desire', *Comparative Literature Studies*, 25 (1988), 127–51; also J. T. Parnell, 'Swift, Sterne, and the Skeptical Tradition', *Studies in Eighteenth-Century Culture*, 23 (1994), 220–42.

chronology or intention. To acknowledge the prominence of the learned-wit tradition in Sterne's writing need not be to deny the deliberacy of its engagement with newer forms. Instead we may find within it a cornucopia of textual relations in which Menippean satire and metafictional self-consciousness coexist and unfold themselves in different intertextual modes, and display, as they do so, a hybridization of traditions and genres that in itself is typically novelistic. Here the satirical mode is characteristically determinate, involving necessary connections with specific precursors named, quoted, or otherwise verbally indicated in the text, and this applies even where (as in the instances of determinate intertextuality that fill the standing *Scriblerian* column of 'scholia' to the Florida annotations) the verbal indications are so subtle, or the indicated sources so recondite, that they pass undetected for centuries. The novelistic mode, by contrast, is characteristically aleatory, gesturing towards a plurality of potential intertexts through its play on terms, tropes, or conventions that all of them hold in common, but necessarily specifying no single one.[2]

Although Sterne's engagement with the novel genre, I argue below, can occasionally be pinned down to concrete allusion, this fuzzier kind of intertextuality is its usual and appropriate mode for several reasons. The expectations inevitably generated by *Tristram Shandy*'s title and fictional content, coupled with the fashionable prominence of the 'new species of writing' over the previous twenty years, made it unnecessary for Sterne to flag his entanglement with the genre with anything like the specificity needed to evoke historically more distant imbrications—imbrications that, as a result, have dominated the work of source-hunters since the time of John Ferriar's *Illustrations of Sterne* (1798). Sterne's primary interest, moreover, is with large questions about the novel and its mechanisms, not with the uniqueness of particular novels. Where a specific instantiation of the genre does help to clarify these larger generic conditions, the towering contemporary stature of certain key works—by Richardson and Fielding above all—acts as a natural check on the randomness of association otherwise generated by aleatory intertextuality, so that only the faintest of allusive touches can serve to bring to mind a specific reference point.

---

[2] On the distinction between determinate and aleatory intertextuality (first formulated by Riffaterre), see Graham Allen, *Intertextuality* (London: Routledge, 2000), 130–1, 140. I use the term 'aleatory' here in a strictly limited sense, to denote textual features that call to mind a genre in general but specify no single example, so that different readers, according to the contingencies of their individual reading experiences, will sense different particular hypotexts (i.e. earlier novels) beneath the hypertext of *Tristram Shandy*.

The coexistence with Sterne's noisy displays of learned wit of this quiet but no less pervasive engagement with the novel genre—an engagement that also seems, if we listen to the evidence of reception, to have been immediately accessible to early readers—takes several forms, and marks not only the 'novelistic-sentimental' final volumes of *Tristram Shandy* but also its 'satirical-Scriblerian' opening. *Tristram Shandy* absorbs and resumes the most vexed topics of experimentation and debate in novels such as *Clarissa* and *Tom Jones*, notably the mimetic efficacy (or otherwise) of narrative language, the dynamics of communication between narrator and reader, and the openness of narrative meaning to plural construction. Several years intervened, however, between the well-publicized retirements of Richardson and Fielding and the inaugural instalment of *Tristram Shandy*, and in the interim novelists had made further innovatory gestures while explicitly registering the new (and in some respects newly adverse) conditions of authorship and publication in the later 1750s. In this respect, forgotten experimental novels of this decade such as John Kidgell's *The Card*, the anonymous *Life and Memoirs of Mr. Ephraim Tristram Bates*, Thomas Amory's *The Life of John Buncle, Esq.*, William Toldervy's *The History of Two Orphans*, and Edward Kimber's *The Juvenile Adventures of David Ranger, Esq.*, constitute an equally significant body of precursor texts. Sterne not only adopts the episodic repertoire and formal reflexiveness of the subgenre represented by these novels, ostentatiously trumping their prior deployment of both with elaborate displays of narrative involution and excess. He also digests and reworks the most innovative feature they share, which is their tendency to push a literary self-consciousness inherited from Fielding into a more directly practical self-consciousness about the mechanisms and institutions of print culture: specifically, about the relationship between authorial production and its materialization as a printed object, and about the overdetermination of both by the forces of literary commodification, consumer fashion, and regulatory reviewing. Sterne's systematic exploitation of this incompletely realized potentiality in the novels of the 1750s, like his parodies of circumstantial realism in Richardson or his Fieldingesque tropes of narrative as conversation or travel, is too capricious and ironic to be assimilated to a consistent thesis about the emerging genre. *Tristram Shandy* recurrently indicates, however, an explosive scepticism about the referential and rhetorical pretensions of novelistic discourse, specifically as these were developed and interrogated in the twenty years preceding its opening volumes of December 1759.

TRISTRAM SHANDY, SATIRE, AND THE NOVEL

The competing traditions of *Tristram Shandy* criticism reach back to the earliest reviews. At one extreme is a fatuous puff in the *London Magazine* for February 1760, which finds *Tristram Shandy* 'rare' and 'unaccountable', and asks: 'what shall we call there?—Rabelais, Cervantes, What?' (*CH* 52). The point is carried no further, but clearly heralds that modern approach to Sterne that finds its *locus classicus* in Jefferson's influential essay on '*Tristram Shandy* and the Tradition of Learned Wit', and its amplest expression in the rich intertextual annotations of the Florida edition: the idea that *Tristram Shandy*, inexplicable by the literary norms and conventions of its own day, can be understood only by analogy with Renaissance satire (and only then with reference to some idiosyncratic further element in the brew, an indefinable 'What'). Here the *London* obligingly picks up a message that Sterne had carefully embedded in his opening volumes, and that his fashionable promoters were spreading about town. It is in the second instalment that Sterne most pointedly stakes his claim (with Tristram's oath 'by the ashes of my dear *Rabelais*, and dearer *Cervantes*' (3.19.225)) to be the true heir to these long-dead masters, a latterday phoenix sprung from their embers; but the claim is hinted well enough in the opening volumes, with their pervasive Rabelaisian echoes and several overt allusions to *Don Quixote*. It gained resonance from the pontifications of Bishop Warburton, who, having previously published two genealogical accounts of the modern novel (one culminating with Richardson, the other with Fielding), presented Sterne as a case apart. Here was 'the English Rabelais', Warburton was telling anyone who would listen, who had written '*an original composition, and in the true Cervantic vein*'[3]—praise that (with nice economy of contradiction) makes plain the advantage Sterne reaped by flagging such distant forebears as his primary models. At a time when Richardson's status as the very type of originality had been sealed by the dedication to him of Young's *Conjectures on Original Composition* (1759), and similar claims had been made for Fielding in commentaries like *An Essay on the New Species of Writing Founded by Mr. Fielding* (1751),

---

[3] *CH* 56: Warburton's widely repeated words are reported here by Horace Walpole, who notes the contradiction inherent in making *Tristram Shandy* 'the only copy that ever was an original'. For Warburton on the novel genre, see his preface to the first edition of *Clarissa* (1747–8), 3: iii, which he later adapted (shifting the compliment from Richardson to Fielding) as an extended note to Pope's *Epistle to Augustus* (*The Works of Alexander Pope*, 9 vols. (1751), 4: 166–9). Warburton had earlier contributed an essay on romance (as 'A Supplement to the Translator's Preface') to Charles Jarvis's translation of *Don Quixote* (1742).

it is as though the noise Sterne makes about Rabelais and Cervantes could pre-empt allegations of indebtedness to his immediate contemporaries, and so assist his standing, paradoxically, as an original himself.

A yet earlier reviewer, however, had been willing enough to accept the originality of *Tristram Shandy* while unhesitatingly associating it with the modern novel. Writing in the *Monthly Review*, which had been complaining for years about the staleness of the fiction churned out since the retirement of Richardson and Fielding ('those loads of trash, which are thrown in upon us under the denomination of *Lives, Adventures, Memoirs, Histories*, & c.'[4]), William Kenrick praised Sterne's work for reconfiguring the hackneyed outlines of the genre. Sterne's title implied the whole process. 'Of Lives and *Adventures* the public have had enough, and, perhaps, more than enough, long ago,' Kenrick writes, with all the weariness of a jobbing reviewer: 'A consideration that probably induced the droll Mr. Tristram Shandy to entitle the performance . . . his Life and *Opinions*.' *Life and Adventures* had indeed been a standard formula since the days of *Robinson Crusoe*, and Kenrick was right to imply that there had been no previous *Life and Opinions*. (Unsurprisingly, the collocation crops up *within* works of fiction as far back as John Dunton's *Voyage round the World* (1691), and Sterne may have had in mind a passage from *Rasselas* that heralds his hobby-horsical theme: 'In time some particular train of ideas fixes the attention . . . false opinions fasten upon the mind, and life passes in dreams'.[5] By creatively recasting the usual formula, and playing on its terms in the text itself, Sterne advertises his self-conscious preoccupation with discourse over story (or opinion over transaction, as Tristram would have it), and thereby flags his ironic relationship to the genre as a whole. Kenrick seems to understand as much when recommending him, in conclusion, 'as a writer infinitely more ingenious and entertaining than any other of the present race of novelists' (*CH* 47–8). In this usage it is the modern sense of 'novelist' that clearly applies, though Kenrick's larger

---

[4] *Monthly Review*, 11 (Dec. 1754), 470.

[5] Samuel Johnson, *Rasselas*, ed. J. P. Hardy (Oxford: Oxford University Press, 1988), 105; see also John Dunton, *A Voyage round the World*, 3 vols. (1691), where the narrator claims that his 'design of making a Man's self the Subject of his Writing' is as excusable in his obscure case as 'in *Rare-and-Famous-Men* . . . whose Life and Opinions may serve for Example' (3: 19). In 1762 Dunton's work was republished in a two-volume abridgement, with commentary, as evidence that 'shandeism . . . (or something very like it) had an existence in this kingdom long before a late well-known publication' (*The Life, Travels, and Adventures of Christopher Wagstaff, Gentleman, Grandfather to Tristram Shandy*, 2 vols. (1762), 1: vii; see also, for full discussion of the Dunton–Wagstaff connection, René Bosch, *Labyrinth of Digressions: Tristram Shandy in Engeland in de Achttiende Eeuw* (Utrecht: Gottman & Fainsilber Katz, 1999), 79–98).

point is that Sterne himself is also a 'novelist' in what then was the primary sense.[6] He is a novelist among novelists, an innovator among writers of fiction—a judgement that gains real weight from Kenrick's extensive recent experience of where the genre now stood. As a new recruit to the *Monthly*, he seems to have been allocated a disproportionate share of novels, and had reviewed at least twelve in the previous year—several of which, as he confesses in the case of William Guthrie's *The Mother; or, The Happy Distress*, were 'so very little interesting, that we could not bear to read through them at all'.[7]

Kenrick was not alone in his view of *Tristram Shandy*'s opening instalment as essentially (though also eccentrically) novelistic. His diagnosis of the work as pointedly disrupting the norms of the genre was echoed by Horace Walpole, who wrote of it as 'a kind of novel . . . the great humour of which consists in the whole narration always going backwards'—as though we might find in *Tristram Shandy* a precursor of much more recent narrative experiments like Martin Amis's novel in rewind, *Time's Arrow* (1991).[8] From here it is a simple step to that alternative line of interpretation advanced by modern commentators who (like Kenrick before them) approach *Tristram Shandy* via a specific professional interest in the novel as a genre: the view that this is not a belated exercise in learned-wit satire but a modern novel about novel-writing, which self-consciously stages (as Everett Zimmerman succinctly puts it) 'a complex parody of conventional narrative procedures'.[9]

But whose narrative procedures, and which ones? There is a telling evasiveness in Zimmerman's phrasing here, and specifically in 'conventional', which haunts this whole approach. Sterne writes at a time when the con-

---

[6] 'Innovator; assertor of novelty' (Johnson, *A Dictionary of the English Language* (1755), s.v. 'Novelist'). Johnson's secondary sense, 'A writer of novels', had been current since the 1720s, though Johnson gives no illustration.

[7] *Monthly Review*, 21 (Apr. 1759), 380. Kenrick joined the *Monthly* in February 1759, by which time novels were normally relegated to short notices in the 'monthly catalogue' appendix (*Rasselas* and *Tristram Shandy* being the only works of fiction to win main-review billing in 1759). These notices are listed by number alone in Benjamin Christie Nangle, *The Monthly Review, First Series, 1749–1789: Indexes of Contributors and Articles* (Oxford: Clarendon Press, 1934), 231–4: they correspond to entries about Sarah Fielding's *The Countess of Dellwyn*, Voltaire's *Candide*, and minor novels such as *The Campaign: A True Story*, *Abassai: An Eastern Novel*, and *The Auction: A Modern Novel*.

[8] Walpole was writing in April 1760 (*CH* 55), and of course later instalments of *Tristram Shandy*, in their narrative loops and involutions, are far less straightforward (or straight-backward) than his comment suggests: see Samuel L. Macey, 'The Linear and Circular Time Schemes in Sterne's *Tristram Shandy*', *Notes and Queries*, 36 (1989), 477–9.

[9] Everett Zimmerman, *The Boundaries of Fiction: History and the Eighteenth-Century British Novel* (Ithaca, NY: Cornell University Press, 1996), 203.

ventions of fictional representation, such as they were, remained fluid, ill-defined, and keenly contested: witness the Richardson–Fielding dispute of the 1740s, which was as much about competing narrative strategies as it was about religion and ethics, or ideologies of gender and class. Do we assume that *Tristram Shandy* is sending up the minute and massive particularizations of Richardsonian narrative, the magisterial manipulations of Fielding's, something else entirely—or all three at once? Or do we assume no relationship at all to any specific precursor, and read the anti-novelistic element of *Tristram Shandy* as essentially fortuitous—a deconstructive potential inherent in the text, which illuminates, through strictly synchronic analysis and without any corresponding diachronic claim, the assumptions and mechanics of narrative realism in its classic (that is, later) phase? Michael McKeon elegantly conflates the diachronic and synchronic versions of this approach to Sterne when writing that the formal breakthroughs achieved by novelists of the 1740s were 'pursued with such feverish intensity over the next two decades that after *Tristram Shandy*, it may be said, the young genre settles down to a more deliberate and studied recapitulation of the same ground, this time for the next two centuries'.[10] Equations as deft as these have a powerful appeal, but they also reveal the extent to which a strictly formalist case about Sterne's affinity with postmodern narrative (McKeon's 'next two centuries' take us, of course, to the 1960s) can slip, almost by default and without demonstration, into a historical assertion about his posture towards Richardson, Fielding, and the novelists who wrote in their wake. An implied analogy with writers of experimental metafiction like Barth, Burroughs, or B. S. Johnson, or with the French *nouveau roman* (a critique, overtly theorized as such by exponents like Robbe-Grillet, of nineteenth-century realism), is being used to support a proposition about Sterne's relationship towards his own precursors. This proposition is otherwise unsubstantiated—and has never, indeed, been argued through.

To review the rise of *Tristram Shandy*'s reputation as a work that counts Richardson and Fielding (as much as Warburton, say, or Locke) among its satirical butts—as a work in which the groaning conventions of mid-eighteenth-century fiction meet their parodic waterloo—is to see this slippage in action. The classic pre-war readings of *Tristram Shandy* as parodic anti novel or sophisticated meta novel are unabashedly ahistorical, and largely sidestep the question of Sterne's posture towards experiments with

---

[10] Michael McKeon, *The Origins of the English Novel, 1600–1740* (Baltimore: Johns Hopkins University Press, 1987), 419.

narrative, and debates about it, in the decades before he wrote. It is hardly surprising (given the resources available to him in 1920s Russia) that Vik-tor Shklovsky's celebration of Sterne as 'a radical revolutionary as far as form is concerned' is based on little acquaintance with earlier novels, and Shklovsky's claim, though brilliantly substantiated through formal analy-sis, has no historical weight. Foils for his argument about the antithetical relationship 'between the conventional novel and that of Sterne' are re-peatedly found in the repertoire of the century to follow, and, although generalizations about prior conventions are occasionally ventured—'Sterne was writing against a background of the adventure novel with its extremely rigorous forms that demanded . . . that a novel end with a wed-ding' (which hardly touches the most prominent background novels, such as *Amelia* or *Clarissa*)—the overall case is synchronic.[11] In much the same period, though of course independently, Virginia Woolf remarked of Sterne that 'no young writer could have dared to take such liberties with . . . the long-standing tradition of how a novel should be written', but did little to develop this instinctive sense of *Tristram Shandy*'s iconoclastic stance towards earlier fiction. Instead Woolf was mainly concerned with an ulterior motive in the present: that of co-opting Sterne for her ongoing campaign against the bricks-and-mortar realism typified by Galsworthy and Bennett. Her deft reading of *A Sentimental Journey* converts it into a stream-of-consciousness novel *avant la lettre*, laudably indifferent to its material environment, and alert to the fluidity of perception: 'no writing seems to flow more exactly into the very folds and creases of the individual mind, to express its changing moods, to answer its lightest whim and impulse.'[12]

From influential analyses such as these—which finely adumbrate Sterne's proleptic unravelling of high-realist conventions, but fail to ground it in any demonstrable response to eighteenth-century fiction—flows the more or less unexamined assumption, in more recent criticism, that the narrative conventions unpicked by Sterne are specifically those of his immediate precursors: the novelists who, like Richardson and Fielding, self-consciously saw themselves as giving shape (or shapes) to 'a New

---

[11] Viktor Shklovsky, *Theory of Prose* (Elmwood Park, Ill.: Dalkey Archive Press, 1991), 147, 156.

[12] Virginia Woolf, *The Common Reader, Second Series*, ed. Andrew McNeillie (London: Hogarth Press, 1986), 78, 79. Woolf's piece first appeared in 1928 (as an introduction to the World's Classics *Sentimental Journey*), four years after her famous essay on 'Mr. Bennett and Mrs. Brown', on which its valorization of disorder and fragmentation as truer to conscious-ness appears to draw.

Species of Writing'.[13] Literary historians of the post-war years made more targeted attempts to seal the connection, but even the most distinguished, Ian Watt, found his proposition that Sterne turns irony 'against many of the narrative methods which the new genre had so lately developed' hard to substantiate in practice. Sometimes Watt simply flannels, as in his strained analogy with Defoe (whose 'brilliant economy of suggestion' Sterne is held to absorb) or in his odd claim that 'Fielding's criticism of Richardson is implicit in the way that Sterne's masculine embodiment of sexual virtue is pitted against the Widow Wadman's villainous Lovelace'.[14] And, whereas other aspects of Watt's thesis have been valuably developed or contested by a second wave of rise-of-the-novel studies in the 1980s and 1990s, this particular part has stayed much where it is. McKeon's excellent *Origins of the English Novel* typifies the tendency of revisionist studies to cut out in mid-century, thereby confining Sterne's relationship to the tradition to passing reference (the sentence cited above being McKeon's only mention of *Tristram Shandy*). The most authoritative recent overview of the century as such, by John Richetti, guardedly sidesteps the issue by restating the Renaissance-satirical inheritance of *Tristram Shandy* and stressing its identity as 'almost *sui generis*', 'not a novel in the customary sense'. By confining Sterne to his chapter on sensibility, Richetti focuses his analysis instead on ethical rather than narratological aspects of *Tristram Shandy*'s contemporary resonance, and specifically its equivocal status as 'a proleptic parody of the novel of sentimental education'.[15]

One possible response at this point would be to say that Sterne's status as a witty parodist (and/or a sophisticated deconstructor) of the 'new species of writing' and its underlying conventions is so self-evident that demonstration would be pointless. Watt has made the general point that 'Sterne's narrative mode gives very careful attention to all the aspects of formal realism: to the particularisation of time, place and person; to a natural and lifelike sequence of action; and to the creation of a literary style which gives the most exact verbal and rhythmical equivalent possible of the object'.[16] Add to this Watt's recognition that this attention is typically

---

[13] For Richardson's use of this term, see *Selected Letters of Samuel Richardson*, ed. John Corroll (Oxford: Clarendon Press, 1964), 78 (26 Jan. 1747); for Fielding's, see *Joseph Andrews and Shamela*, ed. Douglas Brooks-Davies, rev. and intr. Thomas Keymer (Oxford: Oxford University Press, 1999) (hereafter *JA*), 8 (preface).

[14] Ian Watt, *The Rise of the Novel: Studies in Defoe, Richardson, and Fielding* (London: Chatto & Windus, 1957), 291, 294.

[15] John Richetti, *The English Novel in History, 1700–1780* (London: Routledge, 1999), 271.

[16] Watt, *Rise of the Novel*, 291.

parodic in cast, and chapter-and-verse specification seems otiose. More recently, however, formidable questions have been posed that demand a direct answer. Why, in this most allusive of works (to say nothing of every other published or manuscript source from Sterne's pen), does Sterne never refer explicitly to Richardson or Fielding, and why has no modern editor of *Tristram Shandy* (including Watt himself, in the Riverside edition of 1965) caught Sterne reworking any specific passage from their fiction? As the Florida edition so richly documents, the embeddedness of *Tristram Shandy* in a learned-wit tradition from Rabelais and Montaigne to Swift and the Scriblerians is not only close but also overt. Locke, Sterne's philosophical source-cum-stooge, is cited by name on fully seven occasions. Intertextual allusiveness is *Tristram Shandy*'s stock in trade, and from volume 1, which will be 'no less read than the *Pilgrim's Progress* itself' (*TS* 1.4.5), to volume 9, which will 'swim down the gutter of Time' with Warburton's *Divine Legation* and *A Tale of a Tub* (*TS* 9.8.754), Sterne's strategy is to highlight its operation (though his total silence about Robert Burton, incontestably a major source for *Tristram Shandy*, should make us pause before assuming that 'Sterne's system of imitation', in Jonathan Lamb's phrase, always proclaims its own workings[17]).

One explanation—Melvyn New's—is that this absence should not surprise us: Sterne fails to cite the novelists for the simple reason that he takes no interest in them. The assumption that he has any such interest derives not from the text itself, but from an inherent bias in our institutional and pedagogic arrangements, in which casual juxtapositions slide inexorably into causal conclusions. As New puts it, 'what might appear to us as innocent, neutral, or inevitable—the inclusion of *Tristram Shandy* in the eighteenth-century novels course, immediately following Fielding and Richardson—is in fact an interpretative act, one that preconceives the genre—and hence our expectations—of the work'. Our sense of Sterne's responsiveness to the representational practices of *Clarissa* or *Tom Jones* is simply 'the result of teleologically structured novels courses and the critical writing they generate', not of any concrete connection to works that (as New insists elsewhere) Sterne 'gives no sign anywhere of having read'.[18] From this point of view, those features that seem to offer mileage for reading *Tristram Shandy* as directly responsive to earlier novels are better ex-

---

[17] See Jonathan Lamb, 'Sterne's System of Imitation', *Modern Language Review*, 76 (1981), 794–810.

[18] Melvyn New, 'Swift as Ogre, Richardson as Dolt: Rescuing Sterne from the Eighteenth Century', *Shandean*, 3 (1991), 49–60 (at 50, 55); Melvyn New, *Tristram Shandy: A Book for Free Spirits* (New York: Twayne, 1994), 103 (and see also pp. 17–18).

plained as accidental by-products of the learned-wit tradition, solidly attributable to the disrupted forms and self-conscious literariness of genuine precursor texts like *The Anatomy of Melancholy* or *A Tale of a Tub*. Pursuing these same objections, J. T. Parnell identifies the formal techniques of Swift and Sterne as a satirical inheritance from Erasmus, Montaigne, Rabelais, and other writers of a fideistic-sceptical tradition, which both inheritors could redeploy in mockery of Enlightenment system-building. The resulting effect of structural havoc and communicative impasse may retrospectively look like parody of novelistic discourse, but is something entirely other. 'Some well-worn commonplaces of Sterne criticism may have to be put to rest,' Parnell concludes: we must now accept 'that he may never have read the "novelists," let alone contemplated a devastating critique of the shortcomings of the emerging genre'.[19]

My argument in this chapter is that Sterne did indeed contemplate a critique of the emerging genre, and also that he achieved it. I do not mean, however, to deny the centrality of the Rabelaisian–Cervantic inheritance detected by some of *Tristram Shandy*'s earliest readers and emphasized in the formidable line of scholarship that culminates with New and Parnell. It is vital, moreover, to retain one telling part of New's objection to the novel-centred approach, which is that (in so far as it works at any such level of detail at all) the reading of *Tristram Shandy* as a sophisticated dismantling of mid-eighteenth-century narrative practices almost invariably works by caricaturing these practices as lumbering and epistemologically naive—'by turning Fielding and Richardson into dolts', as New robustly puts it.[20] Rather than seeing Sterne as engaged in mockery alone, I see him as alert and responsive to problems that Richardson and Fielding were themselves intelligently exploring, and as following up these explorations in a mode of exaggeration or *reductio ad absurdum* that, though certainly often parodic, is not necessarily dismissive. Sterne was indebted to both the Rabelaisian–Cervantic tradition and to the modern novel, and wholly rejected neither; and in this respect the very plenitude of *Tristram Shandy*'s discursive entanglements intensifies its allegiances to the modern novel, this being the medium *par excellence* of generic hybridization and polyglossia.[21]

---

[19] Parnell, 'Swift, Sterne', 239.

[20] New, 'Swift as Ogre', 50.

[21] Jack Lynch puts it nicely in his account of the book as 'made up of the "shreds and clippings" of other discourses', such that 'the eminently Erasmian *Tristram Shandy* is Bakhtinian heteroglossia writ large' ('The Relicks of Learning: Sterne among the Renaissance Encyclopedists', *Eighteenth-Century Fiction*, 13 (2000), 1–17 (at 16)).

For this sense of creative coexistence between learned wit and novelism, as opposed to either/or competition between them, one may look back again to _Tristram Shandy's_ earliest reception, and specifically to a third review, which appeared in the _Critical Review_ immediately between the notices of the _Monthly_ and the _London._ Like Kenrick's in the _Monthly_, it is a review that gains authority from its provenance in a periodical that, since its foundation in 1756, had extensively covered developments in the novel genre. Having voiced its uncertainties about the literary identity of this new work, the _Critical_ moves implicitly towards a composite identity by calling Toby, Trim, and Slop 'excellent imitations of certain characters in a modern truly Cervantic performance, which we avoid naming' (_CH_ 52). Alan B. Howes has convincingly identified this unnamed work as _Peregrine Pickle_ (written, of course, by the editor of the _Critical_, Tobias Smollett, who was also _Don Quixote's_ most recent translator); and by invoking this simultaneously modern yet Cervantic performance the _Critical_ adroitly registers _Tristram Shandy's_ double face. Backward looking yet up to date, Sterne's work absorbs from Cervantes his sophisticated debunking of romance conventions (the aspect of _Don Quixote_ that dominated the views of mid-eighteenth-century readers who, like Smollett, thought it written 'with a view to ridicule and discredit' heroic romance[22]) but redirects this metafictional concern towards the species of fiction now generally held, as in Charlotte Lennox's recent _The Female Quixote_, to have rendered romance obsolete. In later reviews the _Critical_ pulled markedly away from the analogy with _Don Quixote_: Sterne's imitation was so botched as to leave 'no more resemblance between his manner and that of Cervantes, than there is between the solemnity of a Foppington and the grimace of a Jack Pudding'. But even as it did so the _Critical_ continued to indicate the overlap between learned wit and novelism, stressing now the Rabelaisian inheritance of _Tristram Shandy_ as seen in 'the same sort of apostrophes to the reader, breaking in upon the narrative . . . the same whimsical digressions; and the same parade of learning'.[23] In the broadest terms, _Tristram Shandy_ draws from the learned-wit tradition of which both Rabelais and

---

[22] Miguel de Cervantes, trans. Tobias Smollett, _The History and Adventures of the Renowned Don Quixote_, 2 vols. (1755), 1: x.

[23] _CH_ 126. James G. Basker attributes this second review to Smollett himself (_Tobias Smollett: Critic and Journalist_ (Newark, Del.: University of Delaware Press, 1988), 260), a supposition lent weight by Smollett's fondness for the proverbial 'Jack Pudding' allusion (as in Tobias Smollett, _Peregrine Pickle_, ed. James L. Clifford, rev. Paul-Gabriel Boucé (Oxford: Oxford University Press, 1983), 387: 'the grimaces of a jack-pudding'). Foppington is also proverbial, from Cibber's celebrated creation of the role in Vanbrugh's _The Relapse_ (1696) and his own _The Careless Husband_ (1704).

Cervantes were part, up to and including *A Tale of a Tub*, an overall preoccupation with textuality, indeterminacy, and fragmentation of form, adding, once again, the new move of focusing this preoccupation on the novel—which by now had become the preferred genre, of course, of Swift's 'freshest moderns'. This redeployment on to new objects of traditional satirical moves is characterized, moreover, by the same ambivalence that had marked Swift's response to Grub Street half a century beforehand (an ambivalence also discernible, it might be added, in the increasingly complex attitude to romance that develops as *Don Quixote* progresses). Sophisticated aloofness mingles throughout with intense imaginative absorption, and for all its interludes of ridicule and hostility *Tristram Shandy* is better seen as wittily developing the rigorous self-consciousness of earlier novelists, rather than as magisterially revealing to these writers narratological cruxes that they had been pondering all along.

IMAGINING DR SLOP

One way of establishing the groundedness of *Tristram Shandy* in mid-eighteenth-century fiction, yet also the resistance of this feature to single-source annotation, is through localized close reading. Consider a well-known passage from volume 2, in which, having self-consciously 'prepared the reader's imagination for the enterance of Dr. *Slop* upon the stage' (2.8.120), Tristram introduces the physician and man-midwife in chapter 9. Then follows Slop's farcical unseating, in which, continuing his play in the novel with ill-matched durations of action and narration, Sterne brilliantly inverts the familiar comic technique of burlesque acceleration (the effect that predominates in Fielding's *Shamela*, for example, with its high-speed parodic rerun of *Pamela*'s plot). An entire chapter lingers here on the events of a few seconds, slowing down the frames of its narrative to particularize how the overweight Slop 'left his pony to its destiny, tumbling off it diagonally, something in the stile and manner of a pack of wool' (2.9.122–3). Two chapters later, Tristram goes on to theorize about his own narrative practice, in ways prompted by his depiction of Slop.

The episode is famous not least because Sterne cites it himself as an instance of his comic technique. He specifies, indeed, the technique's source. Addressing a reader who had criticized the pre-publication version for its overload of ornamentation, he is ready, he says, to 'reconsider Slops fall & my too Minute Account of it—but in general I am perswaded that the happiness of the Cervantic humour arises from this very thing—of describing silly and trifling Events, with the Circumstantial Pomp of great Ones' (*Letters*, 77; see also 79). Minutely particularized, and with a mock solemnity that lurches into comic bathos (the fussy redundancy of 'stile and manner'; the crashingly inelegant—though also oddly evocative— 'pack of wool'), the passage brings back to life the satirical repertoire of *Don Quixote*. It is as though the pompous elaboration is there to assert, purely at the level of style, the claim that Sterne was more explicitly making in other private and public identifications of *Tristram Shandy* as a work of 'Cervantic Satyr' (*Letters*, 120)—as a work of ostentatiously literary mock-heroic, in other words, which in its seventeenth-century origins has little to do with more recent, trashier fiction.

Critics anxious to stress the Cervantic inheritance of *Tristram Shandy* have seized on this passage and Sterne's commentary to press their case, and this same sense of a text drenched in the traditions of Renaissance satire is richly substantiated by the Florida notes, which associate Slop's fall with similar equestrian mishaps in Montaigne and Scarron. One might even press further down this route, and invoke other, non-satirical sources to locate Sterne's playfulness with material little different in kind from the diet of satirists such as Burton a century beforehand. In the relentless domino effect of Dr Slop's losses—first his whip, then his stirrup, then his seat, 'and in the multitude of all these losses . . . the unfortunate Doctor lost his presence of mind' (2.9.122)—Sterne pirouettes around a proverbial sequence first imported from France in seventeenth-century collections such as George Herbert's *Outlandish Proverbs* (1640), and recently revived by Benjamin Franklin: 'For want of a nail the shoe is lost; for want of a shoe the horse is lost; for want of a horse the rider is lost.'[24] Two chapters later, a reference back to 'Dr. *Slop*'s sad overthrow' (2.11.126) is another mock-heroic touch, jokily enlisting the physician among the rebel angels who, in *Paradise Lost*, 'rue the dire event, | That with sad overthrow and foul defeat | Hath lost us heaven'.[25] Not only does Sterne's text spring a practical joke here on the critic who tries to locate it, luring him within range of its own satire on the scholarly equivalent of over-circumstantial narrative (or 'writing like a Dutch commentator', as Tristram puts it elsewhere (9.13.763)). It also seems to disclose, as the outcome of any such commentary, a picture of provincial isolation in which the literary materi-

---

[24] *Oxford Dictionary of English Proverbs*, 3rd edn. (Oxford: Clarendon Press, 1970), 865. Another of Herbert's imports from France is a version of Maria's '*God tempers the wind* . . . *to the shorn lamb*' (*Oxford Dictionary of Proverbs*, 312–13; see *SJ* 369).

[25] Milton, *Paradise Lost*, ed. Alastair Fowler (London: Longman, 1971), bk. I, ll. 134–6.

als Sterne plays on are those of the minster library or the local great house, and not of the fashionable modern marketplace for new fiction.

But not exclusively so. The Florida annotations also record, at the very outset of the chapter, a striking parallel with Le Sage's picaresque novel, *Gil Blas*, specifically in Smollett's 1748 translation. 'Imagine to yourself a little, squat, uncourtly figure of a Doctor *Slop*, of about four feet and a half perpendicular height,' Tristram begins, setting up an intermittently anaphoric sequence of imperatives ('imagine . . . imagine . . . imagine') that culminates in his much-quoted resolution, two chapters later, to halve meanings with the reader and 'leave him something to imagine . . . as well as yourself' (2.11.125). As the Florida editors note, the instruction bears comparison with Smollett's wording ('Figure to yourself a little fellow, three feet and a half high, as fat as you can conceive . . .'), and it is possible that Sterne was elaborating its specific gestures. The more important general point, however, is that the 'imagine to yourself' / 'figure to yourself' formula was a standard trope in the fictional repertoire of the day, used in particular to herald set-piece exercises in the grotesque. 'Imagine to yourself, a man rather past threescore, short and ill made, with a yellow cadaverous hue, great goggling eyes, that stared as if he was strangled,' as Cleland introduces one of his heroine's less appetizing clients in *Memoirs of a Woman of Pleasure* (1748–9).[26] Specific suggestions about derivation become unnecessary here, and perhaps even misleading. By adopting what had become a cliché of modern novelistic discourse, and using it to build towards the famous writing-as-conversation passage, Sterne does much more than echo Smollett, Cleland, or any other source. He prepares his readers to understand this passage as addressing, in general, the stock rhetoric of fictional representation as practised in the past two decades.

In the sentence following this 'imagine to yourself' formula, Tristram's allusion to Hogarth's *Analysis of Beauty* adds to the effect in ways again partly registered by the Florida editors. Citing a set of instances from Fielding and Smollett (as first collated by William V. Holtz in his account of *Tristram Shandy*'s engagement with contemporary aesthetic theory), they identify 'Sterne's evocation of Hogarth in relation to character-drawing' as a commonplace of the day.[27] It might be added that the reference here to Hogarth on how a figure may be 'caracatur'd, and convey'd to the mind' (2.9.121) points, more directly than any of Holtz's four examples,

[26] John Cleland, *Memoirs of a Woman of Pleasure*, ed. Peter Sabor (Oxford: Oxford University Press, 1985), 15.

[27] *TS Notes*, 153, citing William V. Holtz, *Image and Immortality: A Study of Tristram Shandy* (Providence, RI: Brown University Press, 1970), 43.

to the Hogarth-centred discussion of character and caricature in the preface to *Joseph Andrews* (which Hogarth himself had prominently cited in
his print of 1743, *Characters and Caricaturas*, 'for a Farthar Explanation of
this Difference').[28] Even in its opening sentences, Sterne's chapter is keying
itself very firmly to the mimetic codes and conventions developed in
fiction since the *Pamela* controversy, and specifically to the novel's self-
consciousness about them.

And this is merely the tip of the iceberg. Episodic precedents for Slop's
sad overthrow are easily as frequent in fiction of the 1740s and 1750s as in
Montaigne or Scarron, and often much closer in detail. Banana skins were
thin on the ground in eighteenth-century England, but of the alternative
hazards to which comic novels of the period expose their characters,
falling off a horse must be the surest. A conspicuous victim is Parson
Adams, who nearly manages it twice in a single chapter, and then only 'by
good Luck, rather than by good Riding' (*JA* 4.16.300). Closer to Slop's case
is that of Dr Zachary Heartley, a physician and man-midwife in William
Toldervy's *The History of Two Orphans* (1756), who early in the narrative
rides out into the country, having been 'summoned to attend a woman in
labour, four miles distant from the town where he lived'. Like Sterne, this
minor novelist derives the humour of his scene from a comic dispropor-
tion between action and narration. The difference is that, where Sterne
lavishes too much detail on Slop's fall, Toldervy's offhand abruptness
involves too little. Heartley rides full speed to his destination without
mishap, and safely delivers the baby; 'but, returning homewards on a gentle trot, the legs of his horse flew up, and the doctor pitching upon his head,
died on the spot'. The inevitable instruction ensues: 'our readers may more
easily figure to themselves the deplorable situation of Mrs. *Heartley*, on her
receiving this terrible account, than we can describe.'[29]

The likelihood that Sterne knew Toldervy's novel (which is prominently
advertised in another he must surely have known, the anonymous *Life and
Memoirs of Mr. Ephraim Tristram Bates*) is strengthened by other situa-
tional parallels, including the obsessive reminiscences of a half-pay soldier
whose companions 'can't take a nap after pudding' (as one of them complains) 'but must be disturbed with your curs'd expeditions to *Flanders*'.[30]
Whether or not he saw himself as stealthily reworking Toldervy's text,
however, hardly matters. As with the 'figure to yourself' instance from *Gil
Blas*, the significant thing about Heartley's 'sad catastrophe' (as Toldervy

[28] See Martin C. Battestin with Ruthe R. Battestin, *Henry Fielding: A Life* (London:
Routledge, 1989), 366 and plate 35.
[29] William Toldervy, *The History of Two Orphans*, 4 vols. (1756), 1: 25.
[30] Ibid. 1: 80.

calls it in his chapter title) is that it typifies the repertoire of the genre. Whatever Sterne's relationship to any individual case, the underlying point is that he is playing ostentatiously here with some of the most hackneyed formulae, both verbal and episodic, of the modern novel in general. By calling to mind the standard clichés of the genre, he clearly identifies this genre as the subject of his theoretical and satirical play on representation and reading in the chapters to come, while displaying his virtuosity as a writer able to take its stalest gestures and render them fresh.

As the display goes on, Sterne continues to lift his ideas from the genre, even as he trumps it. His 'Circumstantial Pomp' of narration may very loosely be thought of as Cervantic, but its particular distinguishing feature—pompous scientism—has a more immediate ancestry that the emphasis on Cervantes obscures. With its incongruous technical vocabulary, the mock-scientific account of Obadiah's speeding horse ('a phænomenon, with such a vortex of mud and water moving along with it, round its axis . . . to say nothing of the NUCLEUS . . . the MOMENTUM of the coachhorse') is less original than it might seem in applying the lexical resources of Newtonian physics to slapstick collisions and falls. (All these terms, of course, would originally have suggested a much more specialized register than they do today, a fact pointed up by Tristram's etymologically fussy spelling of 'phenomenon' and the typographical emphasis of 'nucleus' and 'momentum'.) In *Peregrine Pickle* (1751)—the novel identified by the *Critical Review* on other grounds as a proximate source for *Tristram Shandy*—Smollett exaggerates his distinctive effect of random violence and brutality by framing it, with amused detachment, in the language of scientific observation. Here too a speeding horse terrifies 'a waggoner who . . . saw this phenomenon fly over his carriage'; a food-fight is observed by a witness 'secure without the vortex of this tumult'; an assailant twists his victim's nose 'with the momentum of a screw or peritrochium'.[31] Anna Seward may or may not have been right to judge that Slop's fall, 'so happily told, outweighs . . . all the writings of Smollett', but she was certainly right to sense the connection.[32] The difference is that Sterne distils and concentrates into a single chapter a comic resource that Smollett leaves scattered and latent.

This well-known episode of Slop's fall makes clear the groundedness of

---

[31] Smollett, *Peregrine Pickle*, 39, 239, 665.

[32] *CH* 270 (letter to George Gregory, 5 Dec. 1787). Seward takes a similar view of Sterne's debt to, and transcendence of, Smollett's characterization: 'You observe that Toby Shandy is the Commodore Trunnion of Smollett. It is long since I read *Peregrine Pickle*, and it made so little impression, that I have no remembrance of the Commodore. It is impossible that I should ever, even after the slightest perusal, have forgotten . . . Toby Shandy.'

Tristram Shandy in modern fiction. Though identifying the passage as distinctively 'Cervantic' in its mock-heroic elaboration of trivial matter, Sterne pursues this goal by reworking one of the most familiar plot devices in the mid-eighteenth-century repertoire, and doing so in terms that pick up and exaggerate verbal formulae and narrative tropes from identifiable recent novels. Nor should this convergence of Renaissance satire and modern fiction surprise us, given the extent to which Sterne's neo-Cervantic pose was anticipated by many eighteenth-century writers who saw Cervantes as first and foremost a novelist himself—as the pioneer, indeed, who 'introduced novel writing', or founded a 'Species of Fiction . . . of *Spanish* invention'.[33] Ronald Paulson has documented the role of *Don Quixote* (with *Paradise Lost*) as 'one of two books that profoundly shaped English writing of the eighteenth century',[34] and here Sterne's identification with Cervantes binds him more rather than less closely with recent developments in the novel, the genre in which this shaping was most actively felt. Fielding had already won for himself the designation of 'our *English Cervantes*',[35] and the title-page claim of *Joseph Andrews* to be 'Written in Imitation of the *Manner* of CERVANTES' is reminder enough that, in harking back to *Don Quixote*, Sterne was not bypassing the work of recent novelists, but drawing on a stock that Fielding had made common to them all. The intensive Cervantic gestures of *Roderick Random* and *Peregrine Pickle* were among the more prominent results, and by the 1750s minor writers were queueing up to associate their novels with this tradition. *The Juvenile Adventures of David Ranger* (in which Edward Kimber asks the 'inspirer of the inimitable *Cervantes*, of the facetious *Scarron*, of the thrice renowned *Sage* . . . to shed thy influence on thy humble votary') typifies the trend, while also indicating the impossibility of disentangling it, now, from the mediating influence of Fielding and Smollett: more directly overshadowing his text, Kimber acknowledges, are 'the multiloquacious *Henry F———*, or that poetical, critical, physical, political novelist Dr. ———'.[36] Clearly enough, to be Cervantic by now was to be in the mainstream of novelistic production, in which responsiveness to *Don Quixote* (even via conduits such as the Motteux–Ozell translation of 1700–3, which

---

[33] 'A Short Discourse on Novel Writing', in *Constantia: or, A True Picture of Human Life*, 2 vols. (1751), 1: x; William Warburton, preface to *Clarissa* (1747–8), 3: iii.

[34] Ronald Paulson, *Don Quixote in England: The Aesthetics of Laughter* (Baltimore: Johns Hopkins University Press, 1998), p. ix; on Sterne, see pp. 150–8.

[35] Francis Coventry (?), *An Essay on the New Species of Writing Founded by Mr. Fielding*, ed. Alan D. McKillop, Augustan Reprint Society Publication No. 95 (Los Angeles: Clark Library, 1962), 46 (see also p. 33).

[36] Edward Kimber, *The Juvenile Adventures of David Ranger, Esq.*, 2 vols. (1756), 1: 1.

Sterne appears to have used) could no longer fail to be coloured by the modern novels that now defined and diffused the influence of Cervantes's text.

Nor is it any easier to disentangle from this strictly modern hinterland to *Tristram Shandy* the other Renaissance satirical sources that Sterne most clearly flags, who like Cervantes are standard points of reference, too, in Fielding, Smollett, and their school. Even the punctilious Pamela is a reader of Rabelais (though only when decently married in Richardson's sequel), and Smollett's scathing remarks about readers 'who eagerly explore the jakes of Rabelais' while primly castigating contemporary fiction make clear his currency in a period when sanitizing translation and learned annotation had brought Rabelaisian bawdry within the pale of politeness (or almost so).[37] The reference to Lucian, Rabelais, and Cervantes in *Tristram Shandy* (3.19.225) has an obvious precedent in *Tom Jones*'s invocation of 'thy *Lucian*, thy *Cervantes*, thy *Rabelais*', and this or similar invocations of tradition were regularly imitated in between, in works ranging in distinction from *Ferdinand Count Fathom* (which throws in Scarron, Le Sage, and Swift for good measure) to Adolphus Bannac's *The Life and Surprizing Adventures of Crusoe Richard Davis* (which made the *Critical Review* scoff at its claim to be following '*Lucian*, *Rabelais* and *Swift*').[38] Fielding gets in first, too, when adopting from 'the celebrated *Montagne*, who promises you one thing and gives you another' (*JA* 2.1.77), the quintessentially Shandean idea—or so one might have thought it—of a chapter that fails to get round to its advertised content.[39]

To say all this, of course, is not to revive the tedious old scandal of Sterne the plagiarist, or to intensify it by alleging that in the very act of imitating Renaissance satire Sterne was also imitating the imitations of more recent novelists. By juxtaposing explicit references to Cervantes and others with implicit invocations of modern fiction, Sterne could present *Tristram Shandy* as doing to the 'new species of writing' what *Don Quixote* had done to romance, which was to test, explore, and satirize its working

[37] Tobias Smollett, *Ferdinand Count Fathom*, ed. Damian Grant (Oxford: Oxford University Press, 1971), 8; see also Shaun Regan, 'Translating Rabelais: Sterne, Motteux, and the Culture of Politeness', *Translation and Literature*, 10 (2001), 174–99.

[38] Henry Fielding, *Tom Jones*, ed. Martin C. Battestin and Fredson Bowers (Oxford: Clarendon Press, 1975) (hereafter *TJ*), 13.1. 686; Smollett, *Ferdinand Count Fathom*, 7–8; *Critical Review*, 2 (Nov. 1756), 357.

[39] On Montaigne's currency in the period, see Claude Rawson, *God, Gulliver, and Genocide: Barbarism and the European Imagination, 1492–1945* (Oxford: Oxford University Press, 2001), 69–70; also Fred Parker, *Sceptical Thinking in Eighteenth-Century Literature: Studies of Pope, Hume, Sterne, and Johnson* (Oxford: Oxford University Press, forthcoming).

assumptions. Though one of the defining features of the 'new species' in general was its formal self-consciousness, *Tristram Shandy* brings new sophistication to bear on a primary area of narrative experimentation and narratological debate at the time: the question of how the novelist, addressing the unknown mass readership of the modern literary market, can simultaneously stimulate and control the responses of the distant, diversified audience that consumes his writing. It does so as intensively as anywhere else in the 'Cervantic' passage concerning Slop's fall, above all as elaborated in the chapters that follow.

Varying a remark about drama that he will shortly attribute to Walter ('there is something in that way of writing, when skilfully managed, which catches the attention' (2.17.165)), Tristram similarly finds in oral media a recipe for circumventing the distancing effects of print. Writing, 'when properly managed', should resemble conversation (2.11.125). Absence, in this now celebrated analogy, will turn into presence, and print become talk—not mere unstructured chat (conversation being an art), but a regulated transaction with interlocutors who will be given a reciprocal role. Fielding offers a relevant sense of the required balance between rules and ease in an essay that defines as synonymous '*Good Breeding . . .* or the *Art of pleasing in Conversation*', and finds that art most pleasurable when practised in egalitarian spirit: conversation works best, he writes, 'in the Society of Persons whose Understanding is pretty near on an Equality with our own', and must arise 'from every one's being admitted to his Share in the Discourse'.[40] This is very much the spirit in which Tristram applies the conversation trope to his own narrative practice:

As no one, who knows what he is about in good company, would venture to talk all;—so no author, who understands the just boundaries of decorum and good breeding, would presume to think all: The truest respect which you can pay to the reader's understanding, is to halve this matter amicably, and leave him something to imagine, in his turn, as well as yourself. (2.11.125)

The anonymity of print is dispelled, and perfect communication prevails.

Or that is Tristram's theory. But in a novel where perfect or even adequate communication is conspicuous by its absence, and conversation as practised by its characters the least auspicious way of making it happen, a whiff of contextual irony is hard to dispel. Nor is there any sense at this point (though the experience of serialization would later provide it) that

---

[40] Henry Fielding, 'An Essay on Conversation', in *Miscellanies I*, ed. Henry Knight Miller (Oxford: Clarendon Press, 1972), 124, 142, 146. See also Sterne's *Sermons*, 5.194: 'Conversation is a traffick.'

conversation in any genuinely interactive sense is within the novel's reach. Tristram will talk to his readers, and they will imaginatively respond; but there the conversational flow of response and counter-response must come to a halt. Thereafter only Tristram's manic construction of imaginary inscribed readers, including—notoriously in recent feminist criticism—the prurient, imperceptive 'Madam', can simulate a way round the impasse. At this point there is not even a hypostasized reader of the 'Madam' kind on show, and in the absence of any audibly responsive voice it is not long before Tristram is forced to contravene his own theory, in a welter of bossy imperatives. ' 'Tis his turn now', he magnanimously tells his reader; but then, far from bestowing on this reader the creative or proactive role implied by the conversation model, he becomes increasingly directive.

Let the reader imagine then, that Dr. *Slop* has told his tale;——and in what words, and with what aggravations his fancy chooses:——Let him suppose that *Obadiah* has told his tale also, and with such rueful looks of affected concern, as he thinks will best contrast the two figures as they stand by each other: Let him imagine that my father has stepp'd up stairs to see my mother:—And, to conclude this work of imagination,—let him imagine the Doctor wash'd,——rubb'd down,—condoled with,—felicitated,—got into a pair of *Obadiah's* pumps . . .' (2.11.126)

In the first flush of reader-response theory, commentators turned a blind eye to the fussy overdetermination of response at this point. But it is now a familiar observation that Tristram's mutualist narrative aesthetic has unceremoniously been dumped. Within a few sentences, the relaxed convenor of collaborative meanings has mutated into a control freak. Already we are on the way to an answering passage from volume 5, in which, with condescending mock solicitude, Tristram explicitly retracts the collaborative model. 'It is in vain to leave this to the Reader's imagination,' he now writes. The task is beyond his audience, whose brains should not be tortured: ' 'Tis my own affair: I'll explain it myself' (5.18.450).

These instructions on how to view Dr Slop brilliantly complete (and collapse) the discursive sequence that begins with Tristram making ready 'the reader's imagination' for this character's appearance in chapter 8—a sequence we must recognize not only as a memorably vivid exercise in farce, but also as a sophisticated exploration of the dynamics of narrative communication. As such, it has become an almost compulsory reference point for the novel-centred approach to Sterne, whether in readings that take at face value Tristram's aesthetic of reader participation and equate it with Sterne's own, or in those that detect ironic space between these positions.[41] The advantage of this second option is that it lets us see the extent to which Sterne is playing sceptically not just with a narratological issue in the abstract, but with an urgent and explicit area of debate in the fiction of the previous two decades.

REPRESENTATION AND READING IN RICHARDSON AND FIELDING

How does a novelist stimulate the imagination, and so facilitate the transmission of meaning, without giving imagination such autonomy that transmission is disrupted or subverted? Richardson's novels were drafted and first revised within a community of like-minded readers (reminiscent in its operation of pre-commercial practices of coterie production and scribal publication) on whom their effects could be tested before entering the uncontrolled environment of speculatively published print. They contain within themselves, moreover, models of interpretative consensus, albeit ones that take time to establish. Yet in the basic matters of motive and cause, right and wrong, *Pamela* and *Clarissa* are much more open to divergent reading then anything written by Sterne, and in each case the divergent readings are articulated within the text itself, above all in the competing analyses of the heroine's conduct that are intermittently voiced by Pamela's antagonists (Mr B, Mrs Jewkes, Lady Davers) and much more exhaustively documented by Clarissa's (the Harlowes, Lovelace). Each novel closes by staging agreement about its major ethical cruxes—an agreement that is complete and explicit in Pamela's case, and nearly so with the Harlowes' repentances, Lovelace's self-accusing madness, and the discursive dominance of the reforming Belford at the end of *Clarissa*. The problem was that readings in the wider world remained obstinately unreconciled. Fielding's *Shamela* gleefully exposes the possibility of reading all of *Pamela* according to Mr B's early view of its heroine as a devious 'Mistress' of 'romantic Invention', and as 'an artful young Baggage' on the make. His *Jacobite's Journal* notice of *Clarissa* makes much the same point when recording (and this time sympathetically deploring) the contradictory views of its early readers; and this compliment was expanded by

---

[41] Notably, in the first category, Wolfgang Iser, *Laurence Sterne: Tristram Shandy* (Cambridge: Cambridge University Press, 1988), 60–71; in the second, Elizabeth W. Harries, *The Unfinished Manner: Essays on the Fragment in the Later Eighteenth Century* (Charlottesville, Va.: University Press of Virginia, 1994), 41–55; Helen Ostovich, 'Reader as Hobby-Horse in *Tristram Shandy*', *Philological Quarterly*, 68 (1989), 325–42.

Sarah Fielding in *Remarks on Clarissa* (1749): Clarissa was 'an undutiful Daughter—too strict in her Principles of Obedience to such Parents—too fond of a Rake and a Libertine—her Heart was as impenitrable and unsusceptible of Affection, as the hardest Marble'.[42]

Richardson's response to this renewed experience of semantic openness and interpretative chaos was interestingly divided. On the one hand, he began to voice increasingly phlegmatic, even enthusiastic, attitudes towards interpretative diversity, writing in terms one might call Shandean were they not so firmly *pre*-Shandean. His fiction 'abounds, and was intended to abound, with situations that should give occasion for debate, or different ways of thinking', he says in one letter. Another adds that by making readers 'differ in Opinion as to the Capital Articles' he has devolved his own interpretative authority on them—or has done enough, at least, to 'make them all, if not Authors, Carvers', who must choose meanings for themselves.[43] On the other hand, Richardson also sought to rein in the most hobby-horsical excesses of early readers (pro-Lovelacean interpretation, in particular) by assuming a stricter distinction between authorized reading and deviant misreading, and by insinuating into the revised text a quasi-authorial controlling presence. Typographical emphasis, and specifically italicization, would be used 'to obviate as I went along, tho' covertly, such Objections as I had heard';[44] hectoring footnotes could be appended at the key interpretative junctures to rebuke 'inattentive' readers and send them back to reread.

In Richardson's final novel, *Sir Charles Grandison*, enormous effort goes into authenticating the reliability of key narrators, thereby reducing the scope for interpretative scepticism and resistance. It is here that Richardson's techniques of minute circumstantial realism achieve their most exhaustive, self-conscious form. 'You will be glad of every minute particular', as one character puts it before launching on a crushingly prolix report. 'How does this narrative letter-writing, if one is to enter into minute and characteristic descriptions and conversations, draw one on!' confesses another.[45] Notoriously, a concealed stenographer—'one of the

---

[42] Samuel Richardson, *Pamela*, ed. Thomas Keymer and Alice Wakely (Oxford: Oxford University Press, 2001), 93, 28; Henry Fielding, *The Jacobite's Journal and Related Writings*, ed. W. B. Coley (Oxford: Oxford University Press, 1975), 120 (no. 5, 2 Jan. 1748); Sarah Fielding, *Remarks on Clarissa*, intr. Peter Sabor, Augustan Reprint Society Publication Nos. 231–2 (Los Angeles: Clark Library, 1985), 13.

[43] *Selected Letters of Richardson*, 311 (21 Aug. 1754), 296 (25 Feb. 1754).

[44] Ibid. 125 (12 July 1749).

[45] Samuel Richardson, *Sir Charles Grandison*, ed. Jocelyn Harris, 3 vols. (Oxford: Oxford University Press, 1972) (hereafter *SCG*), 1: 131, 1: 60.

swiftest short-hand writers of the age' (*SCG* 1: 267)—is enlisted to take un-
ambiguous minutes of a crucial showdown, and every narrator becomes
expert in the elaborate transcription of attitude and gesture. Sometimes—
as when Everard Grandison 'sat down, threw one leg over the knee of the
other, hemm'd three or four times, took out his snuff-box, tapped it, let the
snuff drop thro' his fingers, then broke the lumps, then shut it, and twirled
it round with the fore-finger of his right-hand, as he held it between the
thumb and fore-finger of the other' (*SCG* 1: 293)—the effect tips into
teasing comedy. But more often the goal of Richardson's narrators seems
serious: a rigorous and self-authenticating hyperrealism, in which the
troubling gap between lived experience and narrative transcription falls
away, so conferring on the text an authoritative transparency. When
Charlotte plays with her ring, 'sometimes pulling it off, and putting it on;
sometimes putting the tip of her finger in it, as it lay upon the table, and
turning it round and round, swifter or slower, and stopping thro' downcast
vexation, or earnest attention, as she found herself more or less affected'
(*SCG* 1: 397), the readerly imagination is directed in the smallest details of
visualization, and also in the assessment of mood. More generally, interpretative licence is restricted through Richardson's near-elimination of
the rich scope offered in *Pamela* and *Clarissa* for suspecting partiality—
either bias or omission—in the narrative mediation of events. The cost of
all this is huge in terms of the novel's material bulk and glacial narrative
pace (prompting the reviewer of one rather more action-packed novel of
the 1750s to reflect that, 'had the writer of *Sir Charles Grandison* been to
have worked on his materials, he would easily have swelled them into
twenty folio volumes'[46]). For all its unrelenting exhaustiveness and lan-
guor, however, *Sir Charles Grandison* also achieves an immediacy of representation that was to become an enduring technical benchmark. It is a
feature that lends special weight to Ralph Griffiths's claim, in the *Monthly
Review* for February 1765, that 'the delicate, the circumstantial RICHARD-
SON himself, never produced any thing equal to the amours of Uncle Toby
and the Widow Wadman' (*CH* 166–7).

Fielding's solutions were very different, though in *Amelia* he moves in
discernibly Richardsonian directions by highlighting the need for narrative to specify the 'minute Causes' from which large events spring, and by
distributing swathes of this narrative (in the form of embedded memoirs
or hypodiegetic reports) to narrators who confess their weakness for 'run-

---

[46] *Critical Review*, 1 (Apr. 1756), 261 (reviewing *The Supposed Daughter: or, Innocent
Impostor*).

ning into too minute Particulars'.[47] Having exposed and intensified the hermeneutic free-for-all surrounding *Pamela*, and having later lamented the effect in *Clarissa*, he develops in *Tom Jones* a sophisticated awareness of readerly autonomy and unruliness, along with equally sophisticated mechanisms for turning the problem to advantage.

Joseph Andrews makes early moves in this direction, not least in its playful awareness of the heterogeneous and stratified nature of its readership, the preface's well-known distinction between 'the Classical Reader' and his 'mere *English*' counterpart (*JA* preface, 3–4) being only the first of this kind. Inscribed readers of *Joseph Andrews* come, indeed, in every shape: they are 'swift' or 'impatient', in contrast to the 'slower and more accurate Reader' (*JA* 2.1.76–8); there are 'Female Readers' as well as 'our Males' (2.10.126), the latter including the 'Reader of . . . Speculation, or Experience, though not married himself' (1.18.75); there are readers 'of an amorous Hue' who should abstain from one paragraph, and 'Prudes' who should skip another (2.12.132–5); and all these readers may by turns be sensible, good-natured, judicious, or (especially) sagacious in more or less ironic senses. Throughout, Fielding plays ingeniously—and with a recurrent air of teasing condescension—to all these varied constituencies, and in so doing he reflects self-consciously on both the narrative mediation of fictional worlds and the likely diversity of response. But in prominent passages of metanarrative commentary, such as the chapter upon chapters that kicks off his second book, he also suggests how *Joseph Andrews* might unite its motley readership in a single movement, sociable and progressive, towards shared understanding. The process is made manifest in the material organization of the text. The 'little Spaces between our Chapters' become points of rest and reflection, while the 'vacant Pages' between books 'are to be regarded as those Stages, where, in long Journeys, the Traveller stays some time to repose himself, and consider of what he hath seen in the Parts he hath already past through' (*JA* 2.1.76).[48] Freedom of movement remains, and readers may even skip unpromising chapters. But the novel-as-stagecoach trope also implies a carefully structured and phased course laid out for the reader's imagination, oscillating productively between illustration and reflection, with a common terminus for all.

This stagecoach model survives in *Tom Jones*, but with a new definition of the journey as strictly a discursive event. Now the narrative becomes a

---

[47] Henry Fielding, *Amelia*, ed. Martin C. Battestin (Oxford: Clarendon Press, 1983), 1.1.17, 2.8.93; see also 1.9.55 ('running into too minute Descriptions').

[48] For reasons outlined below, I do not accept the Florida editors' suggestion (*TS Notes*, 308) that 'Sterne does not seem to have been influenced by Fielding's chapter'.

protracted 'Conversation' between author and readers, who are likened, in the bickerings, animosities, and raillery that define their relationship, to 'Fellow-Travellers in a Stage-Coach'—fellow travellers, moreover, of shifting and uncertain identity, for it is only at the end of the novel that 'whatever Characters any of the Passengers have for the Jest-sake personated on the Road, are now thrown off, and the Conversation is usually plain and serious' (*TJ* 18.1.913). Audience input, it would seem, has become more independent and assertive; and, just as the reader's role now involves conversing as well as observing, so the status of the 'little Spaces' and 'vacant Pages' of the novel's volumes is whimsically changed. An implicit sideswipe is directed towards the Richardsonian method of 'writing to the moment', with its steady parity of duration between narrative and story, when Fielding's narrator announces that he will not resemble a newspaper-writer who fills a uniform quantity of paper regardless of the quantity of news, or 'a Stage-Coach, which performs constantly the same Course, empty as well as full'. Chasms or 'Blanks in the grand Lottery of Time' will be left unreported (*TJ* 2.1.76), and the lottery figure gains further resonance when Fielding later solicits the filling of these blanks by arbitrary whim and chance. The childhood years in which Tristram's narrative stalls will in Tom's case be bypassed in the blank space between two volumes, thereby leaving the reader 'an Opportunity of employing that wonderful Sagacity, of which he is Master, by filling up these vacant Spaces of Time with his own Conjectures' (*TJ* 3.1.116). It is hardly a serious invitation, though Fielding then elaborates on it by considering how readers of varying competence might set to the task; and that idea of the varying predispositions and abilities of the nameless readers who together constitute the interpretative community of *Tom Jones* becomes the novel's keynote. Later Fielding writes of the constructive roles of readers in now familiar terms (and again, we might suppose, with a critical glance at Richardsonian authorial absence). He will guide at points of interpretative difficulty, 'as we do not, like some others, expect thee to use the Arts of Divination to discover our Meaning', but at other points the reader's own 'Attention' and 'Sagacity' must come independently into play (*TJ* 11.9.614).

This passage neglects, however, the practical problem: that as soon as interpretative resolution is left to readers, we enter a dynamic in which meaning is not neutrally discovered by wilfully created. 'Reader, it is impossible we should know what Sort of Person thou wilt be,' as Fielding has already announced (*TJ* 10.1.523). Yet on that identity depends resolution of the many matters of interpretation and judgement in *Tom Jones* where authorial (or pseudo-authorial) assistance is ambiguous or absent. In yet another of his many models of reader response, Fielding categorizes varying audience judgments of Black George's theft of Tom's pocketbook in terms of social class (their positions in a playhouse, and thus the cost of their tickets), and this is only one among several ambiguously circumstanced misdemeanours about which, as the narrator acknowledges in another case, 'our Readers will probably be divided in their Opinions' (*TJ* 12.14.680–1). If the narrative transaction may indeed be figured as conversation, as Fielding's final book suggests, it is conversation of a peculiarly unfamiliar kind, in which the interlocutors are unknown to one another, and unable to agree.

The fiction written by Richardson and Fielding in the two decades prior to *Tristram Shandy* displays, in short, a much more sophisticated and anxious attentiveness to the dynamics of reception and interpretation than is attributed to it in even the best modern treatments of Sterne's relationship to the 'new species of writing'. If Richardson ever made the claim attributed to him by Donald Wehrs, 'that mimetic, plausible narrative could secure inductively certain interpretation', it is a claim he rapidly relinquished. His career as a novelist is better represented as a series of encounters with the problem, complex and deliberate in their adumbration of narratological and hermeneutic issues, and intelligently aware of— though often concerned to minimize—the fractures and interruptions that interfere between meanings intended and received. Nor does Wehrs's view of Fielding as 'persistently drawn to the possibility that mimesis, managed rightly, could naturalize interpretation' adequately register Fielding's persistence—sometimes playfully insouciant, sometimes genuinely troubled—in recognizing that in practice this will never happen. All the features that Wehrs attributes by contrast to Sterne—the rejection and subversion of naturalized interpretation by offering 'multiple inductive possibilities, proliferating connotations, and thus dramatizing the reader's role . . . in manufacturing a form of coherence'—are at the very least incipiently there in Richardson and Fielding.[49] Most are problems with which they explicitly and recurrently engage, in modes that range across the body of their works from strenuous damage-limitation to nonchalant play. Of the rich possibilities their novels supply, all the illustrations highlighted above have been cited not only for the clarity with which they anticipate the kind of narrative dilemma we tend to think of as distinctively Shandean, but also because they inform the particular terms and tropes that Tristram employs. Although Sterne's recognition that reading

[49] Wehrs, 'Sterne, Cervantes, Montaigne', 129.

is arbitrary and subjective looks uniquely modern—as he told John Eustace in 1768, a reader's 'own ideas are only call'd forth by what he reads, and . . . 'tis like reading *himself* and not the *book*' (*Letters*, 411)—this recognition is already substantially formed in Richardson and Fielding. Without the intelligent openness with which Richardson and Fielding relinquish the ideal of a unified, like-minded readership when confronting the real-world audiences of *Clarissa* or *Tom Jones*, moreover, it is hard to see how Sterne could have capped this troubled insight in his own distinctive way, by dramatizing the motley crew of individual inscribed readers whom Tristram struggles to keep together throughout his narration. To say as much is not to deny the extent of Sterne's originality. But it is to say that we must read him as responding directly to these predecessors, to the issues they had defined and explored, and to the distinctive terminology in which they had done so.

Sterne cannot, of course, have known the sophistication of Richardson's thinking about reader response as set out in letters that were then unpublished, and he does indeed seem to have read *Clarissa* and *Grandison* as unavailing exercises in hyperrealistic narration and interpretative ultimatum. Although the terminology of 'minute particulars' was now becoming diffused in the novel genre (and later entered biography in the massively circumstantial shape of Boswell's *Life of Johnson*), Richardson is its primary source, and when Sterne appropriates this language in *Tristram Shandy* the Richardsonian resonance is unmistakable. In this respect Tristram's repeated failure to make the technique work implies a comic interrogation of its efficiency, as a way either of advancing a story or of transmitting an imagined world. In *Clarissa* the heroine notes that her addressee 'will always have me give you minute descriptions', so gaining full imaginative grasp of her friend's situation, and Richardson reinforces the underlying theory in his defiant conclusion, at the close of this massive text, 'that there was frequently a necessity to be very circumstantial and minute, in order . . . to represent real Life'.[50] For Richardson's characters, the sense of reality thus achieved is strong enough to be felt as a burden, as when a weary Sir Charles asks why his cousin would 'oppress me with so circumstantial an account of the heavy evil that has befallen him' (*SCG* 2: 512). Tristram's mistake, by contrast, is to misapply the technique to barely relevant trivia such as 'the midwife's licence, of which you have had so circumstantial an account' (1.10.17–18), the result being that his text threatens

[50] Samuel Richardson, *Clarissa*, intr. Florian Stuber (New York: AMS Press, 1990), 1: 7; 8: 297.

to swell into Grandisonian dimensions while making even less progress with its story. A mock-Richardsonian defensiveness about the resulting bulk of his text modulates into irritable defiance as Tristram complains that, if the reader cannot visualize Toby's bowling green, 'the fault is not in me,—but in his imagination;—for I am sure I gave him so minute a description, I was almost ashamed of it' (6.21.534).

Sometimes the relationship between Tristram's displays of circumstantial realism and the looming model of *Grandison* seems little more than derivative, as when the kind of comic pantomime arising with Everard's snuffbox is only slightly intensified. One might think here of Walter 'surveying [his pipe] transversely as he held it betwixt his finger and his thumb,—then foreright,—then this way, and then that, in all its possible directions and foreshortenings' (3.40.281), or alternatively that earlier moment when he 'gave a loud *Hem!*—rubb'd the side of his nose leisurely with the flat part of his fore finger,——inserted his hand cautiously betwixt his head and the cawl of his wig', and so on (3.33.260). Elsewhere Richardsonian replays of this kind take on a more critical edge, in ways that seem to challenge the pretensions of circumstantial realism to disclose inward psychological truth as well as outward material fact (a key plank in a theory of fiction claiming to reveal—as Warburton, for one, had said of it—'the recesses of the Human Mind').[51] The fine discriminations of mood read into Charlotte's fiddling with her ring ('downcast vexation, or earnest attention') tip into bathos as Tristram attempts a similar move from elaborately detailed gesture to interpretation. Having described his mother as 'conjugally swinging with her left arm twisted under [Walter's] right, in such wise, that the inside of her hand rested upon the back of his—she raised her fingers, and let them fall', Tristram abandons his effort to pinpoint the meaning of this gesture with an excuse: ''twould have puzzled a casuist to say, whether 'twas a tap of remonstrance, or a tap of confession' (9.1.735–6). Incapable of Richardson's psychological (or indeed casuistical) discriminations, he fritters away his pages, even in this desperate last volume of his work, on particularizations of gesture that fail to bring him any closer to his characters' inward lives than, engrossed within their hobby horses, they get to one another's.

But it is in relation to the interpretative footnotes of *Clarissa* that Sterne's parodic stance looks clearest (and also, given the notoriety of these footnotes in modern criticism, most prescient). Much has been written about the disputatious relationship between Tristram and the particular

---

[51] In his preface to volumes 3 and 4 of *Clarissa*'s first edition, p. v.

inscribed reader—careless, frivolous, and only dubiously chaste—he addresses as 'Madam' or 'my fair reader' (1.18.56). As Barbara M. Benedict has argued, 'Madam' becomes the target for a neo-Scriblerian cultural politics in *Tristram Shandy*, standing for a prurience of taste and degeneration of understanding that are held to typify the modern, and increasingly female, literary consumer.[52] What has been neglected is the directness with which *Tristram Shandy* here picks up a gendering of reading already articulated in *Clarissa*, and specifically in the paratextual instructions appended to its third edition. To recover this context is to see how much the 'Madam' apostrophes work at Tristram's own expense, to the point where the laugh is not so much on the female reader as on the blustering efforts of the male author to regulate her reading. The passage in which Tristram rebukes 'Madam' for being 'so inattentive in reading the last chapter' (1.20.64) and insists that she reread a previous chapter—Sterne pushes the effect to absurdity by having Tristram continue his narration in her absence—wittily apes Richardson's interventions, which were at the most intemperate in cases where he saw susceptible female readers as having been rhetorically seduced by Lovelace. Sometimes Richardson's formula is indirect: 'the attentive Reader need not be referred back . . .', or 'it is easy for such of the Readers as have been attentive to Mr. Lovelace's manner of working, to suppose . . .' (*Clarissa*, 6: 177; 2: 305). Elsewhere he shifts into accusation, regretting that 'several of our Readers (thro' want of due attention) have attributed to Mr. Lovelace . . . a greater merit than was due to him' (2: 158), or referring back to an earlier passage critics of Clarissa's conduct who 'have not paid a due attention to the Story' (3: 14). Often these readers are specifically women. Where Clarissa has been censured 'even by some of her own Sex' (4: 106–7), the censurers are given a checklist of passages from the previous volume to reread and absorb, while other footnotes lament the misreadings of 'many of the Sex [We mention it with regret]' (3: 77) and request 'the particular attention of such of the Fair Sex as are more apt to read for the sake of amusement, than instruction' (3: 79).

The echoings of this unusual practice on Richardson's part—one that derives, as Janine Barchas has shown, from his experience of debating the novel with one particular reader, Lady Bradshaigh[53]—remain audible in the mock-Richardsonian condescension with which Tristram greets and interrogates his 'fair Lady' on her return. The echoes persist when he

[52] Barbara M. Benedict, 'Rhetoric, Cultural Politics and the Female Reader in Sterne's *Tristram Shandy*', *Studies in Philology*, 89 (1992), 485–98.

[53] Janine Barchas, with Gordon Fulton (ed.), *The Annotations in Lady Bradshaigh's Copy of Clarissa*, ELS Monograph Series No. 76 (Victoria, BC: University of Victoria, 1998), 20–1.

pompously voices his intention 'to rebuke a vicious taste . . . of reading straight forwards, more in quest of the adventures, than of the deep erudition and knowledge which a book of this cast, if read over as it should be, would infallibly impart' (1.20.65). Here the target, with teasing elaborations, is Richardson's final complaint that, amid the 'general depravity' of taste at the time, he has had limited success in reminding *Clarissa*'s readers 'that the Story . . . was to be principally looked upon as the Vehicle to the Instruction' (8: 279; 8: 297). Inherent in the whole episode is Sterne's implication that, in the real world of reading and reception, when the hypothetical reader gives way to living readers with their own desires and wills (wittily embodied in the gaggle of Madams, Sirs, Critics, and Your Worships whom Tristram addresses), any such ideal transmission is forever disrupted.

The parodic stance that Sterne adopted towards Richardson's realism of minute particulars and his attempts at interpretative policing leaves out of account many countervailing features of Richardson's narrative practice, and may indeed suggest that *Tristram Shandy* was primarily concerned to debunk. With Fielding, however, the picture is less clear-cut, if only because so wittily self-conscious a novelist might seem immune to parody. In Fielding's case too one can point to passages that subject his fiction to witty exaggeration, but here the effect is more to draw out latent implications than to suggest a critique from without. A clear example comes with *Joseph Andrews*'s definition of the material gaps between chapters and books as spaces for rest and reflection by the reader on 'the Parts he hath already past thro''. Already Sterne has set his narrative close to Fielding's on this issue, the early chapter on author and reader as fellow travellers who grow in familiarity while the former 'put[s] on a fool's cap' or 'trifle[s] upon the road' (*TS* 1.6.9) being only a slight elaboration of *Tom Jones*'s closing model of fellow passengers jesting and personating in the stagecoach. Later Tristram's insistence 'that chapters relieve the mind' (*TS* 4.10.337) shifts the focus back to *Joseph Andrews*, where chapter breaks provide the reader with a 'Resting-Place', while volume breaks offer 'repose'. In this context *A Sentimental Journey* might plausibly be read as enacting the stage-coach trope on a large scale, the work being structured and its chapters divided so that the geographical stages of Yorick's journey coincide (in chapters headed 'Calais', 'Montreuil', 'Amiens', and so on) with the metaphorical stages of the reader's own. But the echo of Fielding is more locally and literally present at the opening of volume 6 of *Tristram Shandy*, where Sterne brilliantly trumps the *Joseph Andrews* conceit, adding a side-joke about the materiality of his novel that derives from the unusually

small format (about five inches in height) of the original volumes: 'We'll
not stop two moments, my dear Sir,—only, as we have got thro' these five
volumes, (do, Sir, sit down upon a set——they are better than nothing) let
us just look back upon the country we have pass'd through' (*TS* 6.1.491).
The effect is vertiginous, and not only for the reader balanced *a posteriori*.
Now the novel is simultaneously, and incompatibly, a metaphorical journey through a landscape, and a material object within this landscape to
be sat on when the horses stop. As well as exaggerating and complicating
Fielding's model, Sterne then represents it, in Tristram's hands, as breaking
down. At the comparable point in *Joseph Andrews* Fielding goes on to aver
that 'a volume without any such Places of Rest resembles the Opening of
Wilds or Seas', and cites as evidence of his orderly fictional landscape the
rigorous labelling of his chapters: it is here that he expresses his anxiety
to avoid 'imitating the celebrated *Montagne*, who promises you one thing
and gives you another'. By contrast, Tristram finds his own narrative landscape 'a wilderness', and by now has strewn it with endless unkept promises (though the 'chapter upon chapters, which I promised to write' (*TS*
4.10.337) has at least a vestigial presence).

One further area of lost control is in the forward planning that Fielding
makes so ostentatious a feature of his narrative form. Sometimes he writes
that he will immediately 'proceed to lay before the Reader' some previously
withheld knowledge (*TJ* 5.1.212). At other times the withholding playfully
goes on, as when he promises that 'we shall inform the Reader in due Time'
of one fact (*Amelia*, 8.9.346), or delays another 'which the Reader . . . will
know in due Time' (*TJ* 4.5.168). Sterne was not the only writer to take up
this formula, which rapidly became a cliché of narrative discourse in the
1750s, and was imitated by many novelists from Smollett onwards.[54] But he
is the only one to work creatively with it, building on its foundation the
structure of endless, chaotic deferral of text that is one of his central jokes.
The explanation of Tristram's crushed nose, which (as he writes in the
opening volume) 'shall be laid before the reader all in due time', is delayed
by two volumes, and the 'train of vexatious disappointments' proceeding
from the event is never fully disclosed (1.15.47). Here is only one of Tristram's many other promises of future matter—'many other book-debts',
as he later puts it, 'all of which I shall discharge in due time' (5.8.434)—to
remain undelivered; and the same goes for the spin-off volumes he speculatively proposes to publish from the family archives, 'all, or most of which
will be printed in due time' (5.12.440 n.). The rigour of Fieldingesque or-

---

[54] See e.g. Smollett, *Ferdinand Count Fathom*, 231, 322.

ganization, in Tristram's hands, falls chaotically apart, and on more than one occasion, of course, this falling-apart is a material fact. Less prominent than the famous 'chasm' in volume 4 of the work (when Tristram's removal from his book of an unwanted chapter leads to a gap of several pages, and then a disorienting resumption of page numbering that switches odd numbers to verso pages and even numbers to recto)[55] is Sterne's anticipation of this joke in the closing words of volume 1. In a gesture that brilliantly fuses Fielding's alertness to the 'vacant Pages' between his books, his idea of a reader filling these 'vacant Spaces . . . with his own Conjectures', and his strategy of maintaining suspense until 'due Time', Tristram not only refuses to deliver his material all at once, but even appears to take some of it back. Following his remark 'that if I thought you was able to form the least judgment or probable conjecture to yourself, of what was to come in the next page,—I would tear it out of my book' (1.25.89), the volume abruptly ends, setting up a joke that, like that of volume 4's chasm, is available only to the reader of *Tristram Shandy* in its original nine-volume format, for whom only vacant endpapers now follow.

Much of *Tristram Shandy* can be explained as a creative exaggeration of jokes already inherent in Fielding. In a case like this, satirical models such as *A Tale of a Tub* (with its ostentatious lacunae and fragmentation of the material text into discontinuous units) are also in play, but Tristram's language here is much more closely keyed to Fielding's than to Swift's. The effect becomes most clear if we return to the famous writing-as-conversation chapter, which can now be seen, like the earlier passage about jesting on the road, as resuming the model of stagecoach conversation from the ending of *Tom Jones*. Here, by talking of the respect he wishes to pay 'the reader's understanding' by leaving him something to imagine, Tristram presents himself as a careful observer of Fielding's method, which is to avoid over-explicit description for just this reason. As Fielding puts it on one such occasion, 'it is a Kind of tacit Affront to our Reader's Understanding, and may rob him of that Pleasure which he will receive in forming his own Judgment' (*TJ* 4.2.157). The difference is that, whereas Fielding repeatedly offers his reader's imagination a generous but circumscribed field over which to roam, Tristram oscillates wildly between garrulous domination of his conversation with the reader and baffling intractable silence. On this occasion his hectoring imperatives attempt

---

[55] On this device (4.25.372), see Peter de Voogd, '*Tristram Shandy* as Aesthetic Object', *Word & Image*, 4 (1988), 383–92 (at 385). It indicates the ongoing subversiveness of this joke to book-trade professionals that no modern publisher will apply it: where Sterne's first edition skips nine pages (omitting 147–55), modern editions skip ten.

complete direction of the reader's imaginative realization, thus departing markedly from Fielding's more genuinely participatory gestures, which typically call for help ('If the Reader's Imagination doth not assist me, I shall never be able to describe the Situation . . .' (*TJ* 15.5.798)) or offer freedom ('What Sophia said, or did, or thought . . . shall all be left to our Reader's Imagination' (*TJ* 16.3.844)). The famous blank page in which Tristram leaves it to the reader not only to imagine but actually to ink in the 'concupiscible' Widow Wadman (*TS* 6.37.565) swings to the other extreme, as though literally enacting Fielding's jokey suggestions that imaginative portraiture might compensate for the absences and silences of his text. Announcing that he will refrain from 'attempting to describe [Sophia] from Despair of Success', Fielding comments that his readers will imagine it themselves well enough, 'and the few who cannot, would not understand the Picture . . . if ever so well drawn' (*TJ* 4.14.208). Later he refrains from describing Lady Bellaston in a compromising position, 'which we despair of rendring agreeable to the Reader; unless he is one whose Devotion to the Fair Sex, like that of the Papists to their Saints, wants to be raised by the Help of Pictures' (*TJ* 13.9.722).

By allowing readers to produce the picture of their own choice, whether chaste or profane, Sterne literalizes a favourite Fielding joke in such a way as to highlight the sheer impossibility of collaboration with the reader as a mechanism for generating determinate meaning. This impossibility, however, was one that Fielding himself had often exposed and exploited. The blank page tells us nothing new about narrative and its discontents, though it adds a showy crowning twist to the novels from which it derives. As such, it bears quiet witness to the close involvement of Sterne's writing with the novel genre as practised by his leading precursors—and reminds us, too, that the relationship needs to be seen in more nuanced terms than simply those of sophisticated parodic hypertext (*Tristram Shandy*) to naive parodied hypotexts (*Grandison, Amelia*, and earlier novels).

2

Novels, Print, and Meaning

NOVELS OF THE 1750S

So far I might seem to have described a traditionally Bloomian kind of *agon*: a contest for supremacy, strenuously Oedipal beneath its parodic surface, in which Sterne forges a mode of his own by creatively misreading the dominant novelists of the previous generation. And this would be a sustainable position. The category difference that now divides Richardson and Fielding from their contemporaries is not a modern invention but a critical consensus cemented in the period itself. It was also a commercial fact that would not have escaped a writer ambitious (in terms Sterne borrowed from Colley Cibber, the very type of Grub-Street thriving) to be famous as well as fed.[1] By the measure of sales, both Richardson and Fielding had reached peaks that even *Tristram Shandy* would struggle to hit: seven editions of *Pamela* in its first two years, one alone of which (the third) is know to have run to 3,000 copies and sold out in two months; 10,000 copies of *Tom Jones* within nine months, and a spectacular (though, as it turned out, overambitious) print run for *Amelia*'s first edition of 5,000 sets.[2] The evident reworking in *Tristram Shandy* of key terms and tropes from Richardsonian fiction, or from the metanarrative chapters of *Tom Jones*, gives firm textual evidence of such a struggle, and indicates the vulnerability of Tristram's claim that his work is *sui generis*, 'a species by itself' (*TS* 1.22.80–1). The very wording of this claim, which inevitably recalls the terminology in which both main pioneers of the 'new species of

---

[1] See *Letters*, 90, 92 n.; also *TS* 5.16.446.
[2] See introductions to *Pamela*, p. xxxv; *TJ*, p. liii; *Amelia*, p. xlix. Sterne was well placed to observe the high commercial stakes that *Pamela* generated when, at the height of Sterne's journalistic career in 1741, Richardson's fierce quarrel in the London press with, among others, Caesar Ward (co-publisher of the spurious *Pamela's Conduct in High Life*, and later the printer of *A Political Romance*) spilled into the pages of Ward's *York Courant* and Jaques Sterne's *York Gazetteer*. First-edition print runs for *Tristram Shandy* seem to have been set at 4,000 copies, reduced to 3,500 for volume 9 (*LY* 94), and the most successful instalment (the first) did not reach its sixth edition for seven years (*TS*, app. 5).

writing' described the genre they were shaping, discredits it from within.
Here, no less than in the celebrated denial of plagiarism that Tristram pla-
giarizes from Burton's partial plagiarism of earlier sources, is one of
Sterne's performed puns of the kind to which Jonathan Lamb applies the
term 'pleonasm', the implicit meaning subverting the explicit proposition.[3] *Tristram Shandy* is not a species by itself; it belongs, for all its
aberrancies, to the new species.

But intertextual relations are rarely as straightforward as the Bloomian
paradigm would suggest, least of all in the swarm of echoes, retrievals, and
recastings that constitutes the text of *Tristram Shandy*. To identify the engagement with Richardson and Fielding is to excavate only the most recent
of the novel's multiple (and fissured) intertextual layers—and perhaps not
even the most recent. Several years separate *Amelia* and *Grandison* on one
hand from *Tristram Shandy* on the other, years that—marked as they also
are by Smollett's suspension of novel-writing between *Ferdinand Count
Fathom* (1753) and *Sir Launcelot Greaves* (1760–1), and by Eliza Haywood's
death in 1756—are often thought to mark a hiatus for the genre. The output of fiction was going on, however, and there is good evidence that
Sterne was monitoring it in the later 1750s. Perhaps he did so most closely
in the final year of the decade, as he searched for the ingredient he needed
to convert the unmarketable parochial satire he was then producing (*A
Political Romance*, the 'Rabelaisian Fragment') into the fashionable metropolitan triumph of *Tristram Shandy*. It is hard to find another explanation
for the radical metamorphosis undergone by the published work from its
earliest drafts (so far as these can be reconstructed), in which Shandy Hall
was apparently to have been the venue for an extended satire on polemical
divinity and the Book of Job. Here, as Arthur Cash persuasively puts it, 'the
mode was that of Menippean satire, not the novel', with the interwoven Job
allegory echoing *A Tale of a Tub*, and 'the threading of satirical episodes
upon a fanciful story of the birth and education of a child suggest[ing]
Martinus Scriblerus' (*EMY* 280).

The best-known instance of this novelizing process comes with *The Life
and Memoirs of Mr. Ephraim Tristram Bates* (1756), a work confidently
identified by Hester Thrale, when she stumbled across it in a Derby
bookshop in 1774, as 'the very novel from which Sterne took his first idea'.[4]

---

[3] Jonathan Lamb, *Sterne's Fiction and the Double Principle* (Cambridge: Cambridge
University Press, 1989), 48; see also, on the Burton example, my discussion below, pp. 153–4.

[4] Hester Thrale, *Autobiography, Letters, and Literary Remains of Mrs. Piozzi (Thrale)*, ed. A.
Hayward (1861), 1: 325–6, quoted by Helen Sard Hughes, 'A Precursor of *Tristram Shandy*',
JEGP 17 (1918), 227–51 (at 227–8).

The rich discursive entanglements of *Tristram Shandy* cannot be so simply explained, least of all with reference to such a workaday model; but comparison with *Ephraim Tristram Bates* reveals more than just some general set of methods and procedures that Sterne could take and transform. Two points of contact are selected for inclusion in the Florida annotations (*TS Notes*, 76, 144–5), but many more exist, beginning with an opening sentence in which the hero's mother attributes his gloomy disposition and misfortunes in life 'to the many Shocks the Fortunes of her Family met with the very Year she bore him'.[5] The problem begins with a farcical sequence of events surrounding the hero's birth, which fatefully blight his future. Partly his trouble stems from the 'two very particular Names' he takes from his two godfathers (*ETB* 8), which seem to pre-empt achievement and make him wish (in a passage that contains the germ of *TS* 1.19.57–64) that 'his Godfathers had been Officers, and that his Christian Name had been *Eugene, Saxe, Cumberland*, or any other great General' (*ETB* 131). Partly the trouble stems from an inauspicious mock baptism performed on him by the family servant, Betsey, who, having sprinkled him from a half-full chamber pot, panics like Susannah at the window sash, and promptly 'quitted the Country' (*ETB* 14). This leaves the hero's mother to insist, to the end of the novel, 'that *Betsey's wicked Scheme* ruined her Son' (*ETB* 238). Thereafter Tristram—'for we shall sometimes call him by one *Sponsor's* Name, and sometimes by another', the narrator resolves (*ETB* 22)—turns into rather more of a Toby. Obsessed by military tactics, he spends his childhood 'exercising Soldiers, raising Banks, and sinking Trenches'; talks endlessly 'of Doubts, Ride-outs, Ravelins, Javelins, Half-moons, Whole-moons, Carps, Counter-carps, and the Lord knows what' (*ETB* 18); and practises drill in a 'Bowling-green . . . so surrounded with Hedge-row that no one suspected any People there' (*ETB* 35). He later develops a sentimental bond with a fellow soldier so strong that homosexuality is suspected ('for base Minds have no Idea of a benevolent Heart' (*ETB* 53)), but these suspicions are then dispelled with passing reference to his courtship of women. 'His Amours may well be the Subject of future Books', the narrator temptingly adds (*ETB* 48). No such books were ever to materialize—unless, that is, we see *Tristram Shandy* itself as attempting to supply them. If so, we should perhaps think of Sterne as responding to the *Critical Review*'s concluding verdict on 'this motley production', which is that it had at least identified 'a subject which wou'd appear to admirable advantage handled by a man of abilities'.[6]

---

[5] *The Life and Memoirs of Mr. Ephraim Tristram Bates* (1756) (hereafter *ETB*), 7.
[6] *Critical Review*, 2 (Sept. 1756), 139, 143.

Resemblances between *Ephraim Tristram Bates* and *Tristram Shandy* are formal as well as episodic, the work being typical of its period in the leaden gestures of narrative sophistication and reflexiveness it often makes. The opening chapters are representative in their unfulfilled promises of future explanation—'I will tell you why, or leave you to guess, in a succeeding Chapter' (*ETB* 15)—and in their calculations about structure: 'What followed would make this Chapter too long; and, with a small Addition, is enough for the next' (*ETB* 25). There are also gratuitous gestures of literary fragmentation and incoherence, which were pronounced enough to make the *Critical Review* think the novel, 'if not the production of a fellow of the college of St *Luke*'s Moorfields, at least the work of a correspondent of that respectable body'. The text is ostentatiously allusive, often with an ironic edge that is typified by its playfulness with Shakespeare: '*Oh*, Hamlet, *What a falling off was there!*' as the narrator exclaims when a shelf of books collapses. Closer to *Tristram Shandy* is the lament elicited from passengers who stop to look at the hero's tomb:

The Stone Mason . . . tells me, he can scarce go on in his Work, on account of the numberless Questions ask'd him; and scarce an Hour in the Day passes, but Strangers enquire for his Tomb; and, striking their Breasts, Cry!

Alas! poor Bates. ~   (*ETB* 238)

Other features apart, this whimsical concluding passage alone makes it hard to believe that Sterne did not know *Ephraim Tristram Bates*, which, though obscure enough, was reissued in 1759. At the very least, it represents a repertoire to which he had ample alternative access.

Helen Sard Hughes's conclusion that our sense of Sterne's uniqueness has survived 'only because of our limited knowledge of the minor fiction that preceded him' remains as apt today as when she disinterred *Ephraim Tristram Bates* in 1918. Few other unread novels of the 1750s will offer such striking analogies, but the episodic parallels already noted from another novel of the same publisher and year (Toldervy's *History of Two Orphans*; see above, p. 30) suggests that Sterne was reading widely in the fiction of the day, and indeed that *Tristram Shandy* may turn out to be as thoroughly grounded in this kind of material as the *Dunciad* and *Peri Bathous* are in hack verse of the 1720s. It is possible that Sterne even selected the output of specialist publishers, with the same eye that later made him move *Tristram Shandy* from a general publisher whose interest in novels was dwindling (the Dodsley brothers) to the largest and most fashionably specialized fiction publisher of the 1760s: 'a brand name for new fiction', as James Raven calls the partnership of Becket and Dehondt.[7] William Owen had carved out a similar niche, though smaller, in the 1750s, when his oddly diversified business combined publishing fiction with importing that equally voguish and frothy commodity, Seltzer spa water.[8] In devoting the final leaf of *Ephraim Tristram Bates* to advertising *The History of Two Orphans* ('In the Press, and speedily will be published . . .'), Owen used his usual technique of marketing each new novel to readers of the last (*ETB* 239).[9] His list, however, is now forgotten, and with it almost every other novel written between *Grandison* and *Tristram Shandy*. Recent feminist scholarship has brought individual works by women writers back to notice, especially fiction from the early part of the decade like Haywood's *Betsy Thoughtless* (1751), Lennox's *The Female Quixote* (1752), and Sarah Fielding's conclusion to *David Simple* (1753). The follow-up novels by all these women are still neglected, however, and once-popular male novelists like Edward Kimber and Charles Johnstone remain almost unknown.[10] No deep trawl of the kind so illuminatingly performed by Jerry C. Beasley on the output of fiction between *Pamela* and *Tom Jones* has been undertaken for the 1750s.[11]

Yet this is a crucial decade in the history of the novel, and one that poses an interesting challenge to our assumptions about the genre. It is clear in the first place that, if the breakthrough novels of the 1740s generated an anxiety of influence in the next generation, the anxiety was not Sterne's alone. In preface after preface the shadows of Richardson and Fielding loom large, and essentially the same picture recurs. The years since *Clarissa* and *Tom Jones* have seen a quantitative rise in the output of fiction, but at the same time a qualitative fall; the present novel deserves to be ranked with these eminent precursors, but is different and original for rea-

[7] James Raven, *British Fiction, 1750–1770: A Chronological Check-List* (Newark, Del.: University of Delaware Press, 1987), 3. Raven's statistics on the relative share of publishers in the market for fiction are on pp. 34–5 (figs. 2–3).

[8] On Owen's significance as a publisher of fiction, see Raven, *British Fiction*, 36; for Owen's tradecard, advertising books, and spa water, see John Brewer, *The Pleasures of the Imagination: English Culture in the Eighteenth Century* (London: HarperCollins, 1997), 175.

[9] William Toldervy's *The History of Two Orphans* was published in late October 1756 (*Daily Advertiser*, 26 Oct.), a few weeks after *Ephraim Tristram Bates*, which was first reviewed in the *Critical Review* for September.

[10] From numbers of editions published, Raven (*British Fiction*, 14) calculates the most popular native novelists of the period 1750–69 to have been (after Sterne, Fielding, Haywood, Smollett, Defoe, and Richardson) Edward Kimber (who ties on 17 editions with Mme Riccoboni), Charles Johnstone (16 editions), and Sarah Fielding (15 editions discounting one false attribution in Raven's list).

[11] Jerry C. Beasley, *Novels of the 1740s* (Athens, Ga.: University of Georgia Press, 1982).

sons then pleaded or urged. Writing in the immediate wake of *Grandison*, the author of *The Friends: A Sentimental History* (1754) acknowledges an 'unavoidable Similarity of Sentiment' with Richardson's towering model, both being true depictions of the same human nature, but optimistically adds that 'all that a Writer has to do, is to endeavour to vary his Manner, so as to make it *his own*, and to preserve the Reader from being affected by a tiresome *Sameness* with what he has read, of a like Nature, in other Authors'. The unknown author of *The Adventures of a Valet* (1752) laments 'that in an Age in which there is so uncommon, so unequalled a Multiplicity of Writers in this Way, there should be only two worthy of Exception'; but he himself, though above 'the common Herd of Adventure-makers', will not stoop to imitate even such masterpieces as *Clarissa* or *Tom Jones*, and 'would take more Pride in being but an indifferent Original, than the best Copier in the World'.[12]

In comparison with their predecessors of the 1740s and earlier, all these novelists were writing under newly intensified pressure to assert their own distinctiveness, not only because of the growing importance of originality as an evaluative criterion, but also because the foundation of the *Monthly Review* in 1749 had created a regulatory institution that (all the more when reinforced by the *Critical* in 1756) was crushingly comparative in its habits of judgement.[13] The *Critical* was especially free in invoking the precedent of Richardson or Fielding to damn a new production. In 1756 Christopher Anstey's *Memoirs of the Noted Buckhorse* was proof that Fielding had done in fiction 'what *Pope* attributes to Lord *Burlington* in architecture, | Fill'd half the world with imitating fools', and in 1759 the author of *The Campaign*, having properly paid 'homage to . . . Mr. Fielding, as the father of novel-writing in England', had then done nothing more than 'pillage' this father's work. An adjacent review of another work displaying 'all the machinery of a modern novel' added, in equally familiar complaint, that, 'as the *Campaign* is attempted in the manner of Fielding, so the *Brothers* [by Susan Smythies] may be termed an humble imitation of the author of *Clarissa*, and *Sir Charles Grandison*'.[14] One result of all this carping appears to have been to place a new premium on self-conscious rejections of prior convention, especially in terms of form, thereby intensifying a dynamic

[12] William Guthrie, *The Friends: A Sentimental History*, 2 vols. (1754), 1: A2ᵛ; anon., *The Adventures of a Valet*, 2 vols. (1752), 1: iv–vi.

[13] See Joseph F. Bartolomeo, *A New Species of Criticism: Eighteenth-Century Discourse on the Novel* (Newark, Del.: University of Delaware Press, 1994), 112–60; Frank Donoghue, *The Fame Machine: Book Reviewing and Eighteenth-Century Literary Careers* (Stanford, Calif.: Stanford University Press, 1996), 1–55.

[14] *Critical Review*, 2 (Oct. 1756), 276; 7 (Jan. 1759), 78, 79.

powerfully present in Richardson and Fielding themselves, and leading all but the period's dullest novelists to cast around for unorthodox turns and techniques. While demanding originality, however, the reviewers were typically scathing about the kinds of formal experimentation and disruption produced in response: '*any thing for a surprize*, as the author of the treatise on the Bathos has it', commented the *Monthly*, scathingly, on the limited innovatory gestures of *The Unfortunate Beauty* (1757).[15]

Predisposed by our knowledge of the generic pre-eminence to come, and by the stories we tell about the historical inevitability of the novel's emergence, we tend to think of the mid-eighteenth-century novel as firmly on the 'rise'. Yet this may be a teleological error, and intriguing evidence survives to indicate, by contrast, that in the run-up to *Tristram Shandy* the genre was quite widely held to be past its peak, or even burning itself out. This was certainly the reviewers' refrain, as though the impossibility of endlessly renewing the defining quality of the genre—the sheer impossibility of being forever novel—meant that the 'new species of writing' contained within itself the seeds of its own destruction. 'Even novels themselves no longer charm us with their novelty', the *Monthly* declared in March 1752. Both journals regularly wrote of the genre as having sunk into formulaic mass production or cynical commodification, savaging 'the innumerable pieces of the novel manufacture which have proceeded from the warehouse of Mr. *Noble*', or again 'that endless train of Memoirs, Adventures, and Histories, of which the teeming presses of our modern Curls have been so extremely fruitful'. The *Critical* wrote in 1759 that 'novels at present bear so strong a resemblance to each other, that a person might be often tempted to think them the production only of one writer, did not their multiplicity exceed the abilities of an hundred', and well into the next decade the *Monthly* was continuing to predict that the 'common machinery' and 'general sameness' now shared by all novels will 'render them at length tiresome'. More explicit notices of the genre's moribund condition begin much earlier, and in 1756 only the conspicuous eccentricity of *Ephraim Tristram Bates* could persuade the *Monthly* to conclude that 'the chapter of Novels is not yet quite exhausted'.[16]

That exactly this note was still being sounded as *Tristram Shandy* appeared (Kenrick begins his review by announcing that the public had long ago had 'enough, and, perhaps, more than enough' of conventional

---

[15] *Monthly Review*, 16 (May 1757), 452.

[16] *Monthly Review*, 6 (Mar. 1752), 231; *Critical Review*, 2 (Nov. 1756), 351; *Monthly Review*, 19 (Dec. 1758), 581; *Critical Review* 7 (May 1759), 460; *Monthly Review*, 39 (July 1768), 84; *Monthly Review*, 15 (Oct. 1756), 426.

novels) might indicate that the genre was more resilient than is registered by the reviewers, who tended to make novels the primary scapegoat for their neo-Scriblerian hostility to middlebrow print. But there is hard statistical evidence that the output of fiction did indeed suffer a significant dip in the later 1750s, and that novels were becoming hard for their authors to place. Raven describes the 1750s and 1760s as 'a period of marked if sometimes halting growth' in the publication of new fiction,[17] but it is only in the 1770s that expansion really takes off, and only by extrapolation back from that time that the growth looks to outweigh the halts. A peak in the number of new novels published in 1741 was not reached again until after Sterne's death, and, if any coherent trend is discernible between the *Pamela* craze and *Tristram Shandy*, its curve is gently downward. The five years following *Grandison* saw a steady, year-on-year decline in the total number of novels published from fifty-one in 1754 to twenty-three in 1758, and the modest rally staged at the end of the decade is largely attributable to a sudden leap (from five in 1758 to twenty-three in 1759) in the number of reprinted titles. Reading the statistics this way, one might almost sense a dark Ossianic prediction in the reviewers' habit of referring to the 'present race' of novels and novelists: this race might soon be extinct.

At just this time, several experienced novelists found themselves having to publish new works at their own risk or by private subscription. The subscription publication of Sarah Fielding's quasi-novel *The Lives of Cleopatra and Octavia* (1757) was probably a positive choice, but when Susan Smythies used this method for her third novel, *The Brothers* (1758), it was evidently the only option (one urged on her by Richardson) following her failure to find a publisher. In 1759 *The Mother*, William Guthrie's follow-up to *The Friends*, was among at least four new novels to identify themselves as 'Printed for the Author', and others (including, of course, the York edition of *Tristram Shandy*) were less openly published on this basis.[18] Robert Dodsley's initial rejection of Sterne's work as too uncertain a proposition, in mid-1759, makes much more sense when we remember the difficulties experienced a few months beforehand by Richardson, for all his influence in the trade, in securing a publisher for *The Histories of Some of the Penitents in the Magdalen House* (by Lady Barbara Montagu or

[17] Raven, *British Fiction*, 7. I base my following remarks on a rereading, contrary to Raven's own, of the valuable statistical evidence he presents on pp. 8–9.
[18] T. C. Duncan Eaves and Ben D. Kimpel, *Samuel Richardson: A Biography* (Oxford: Clarendon Press, 1971), 464; for the 1759 novels, see Raven, *British Fiction*, 148–55 (items 462, 470, 473, 493). Packaging novels with magazine material, as Smollett and Lennox independently began to do in 1760, seems to have been another response to this market slump: see below, pp. 129–30.

an unknown friend, which after much negotiation was published in a small edition of 750 copies at Lady Barbara's risk). Andrew Millar was among the booksellers to have rejected this work, and in explaining Millar's view of the state of the market Richardson adds his own gentle endorsement. 'He says, that the Demand for that Species of Writing is over, or nearly so', Richardson told Lady Barbara: 'Other Booksellers have declared the same thing. There was a Time, when every Man of that Trade published a Novel, 'till the Public (in this Mr. Millar says true) became tired of them.' Robert Dodsley had also rejected this work (using the same excuse he was to give Sterne, which is that he was turning his business over to his brother, and would not bequeath risk), and Richardson adds that Dodsley too was 'one of those Booksellers, who think the Day of Novels is over'.[19]

J. Paul Hunter identifies one quite successful example of the exploratory stance into which many novelists seem to have felt pushed, a formally innovative dialogue novel by Sarah Fielding and Jane Collier, when he writes in passing that, 'like most novels of the early 1750s, *The Cry* is consciously experimental in the powerful definitional wake of *Clarissa* and *Tom Jones*'.[20] More often, however, the air of novelty went no further than decorative gesture, and rather than establish new structures and techniques most novelists of the 1750s did nothing more than fiddle at the margins with the old. Wayne Booth's classic essay 'The Self-Conscious Narrator in Comic Fiction before *Tristram Shandy*' remains the most useful map of the decade's output in this regard. Part of Booth's essay pays close attention to the foregrounding of narrative form and rhetoric in seventeenth-century fiction from Cervantes to Congreve, but Booth also notes how, after Marivaux and Fielding, self-conscious disruptions of narrative order become endemic. 'The very devices Sterne uses to emphasize his ostensible chaos, and thus to "explode the novel", were merely extensions of what everyone was borrowing from Fielding', Booth reports, and his survey of forgotten trash fiction from the 1750s finds anticipations of almost every category of intrusive or disruptive gesture deployed in *Tristram Shandy*

---

[19] To Lady Barbara Montagu, 17 Feb. 1759, cited by Eaves and Kimpel, *Samuel Richardson*, 434–4; see also William M. Sale, *Samuel Richardson: Master Printer* (Ithaca, NY: Cornell University Press, 1950), 119. Markman Ellis assumes Lady Barbara Montagu's authorship of the novel in *The Politics of Sensibility: Race, Gender and Commerce in the Sentimental Novel* (Cambridge: Cambridge University Press, 1996), 179, while Peter Sabor notes, but does not endorse, the speculations of Catherine Talbot and Elizabeth Montagu that at least part of the work was by Sarah Fielding (in his edition of Sarah Fielding's *The Adventures of David Simple* (Lexington, Ken.: University Press of Kentucky, 1998), pp. xxi–xxii).

[20] J. Paul Hunter, 'Novels and History and Northrop Frye', *Eighteenth-Century Studies*, 24 (1990–1), 225–41 (at 234).

(except—a point I return to below—typographical disruption). The difference is that, where proto-Shandean narratives of this kind play on their own conventions in ways that are always random, incidental, and undigested, Sterne's achievement 'is in taking forces which had become more and more disruptive in comic fiction, and synthesizing them, with the help of older models, into a new kind of fictional whole'.[21]

For all the formalist bias of Booth's judgement (his valorization, in particular, of unified content and form), the basic distinction he makes is hard to contest. His evidence allows us to account for *Tristram Shandy* in light not only of the acknowledged masterpieces of 1740s fiction, but also of the way their techniques and insights may have been transmitted to Sterne by intermediary sources. If Tristram's debates with his cast of inscribed readers develop Fielding's acknowledgements of audience diversity and unruliness, while also sending up Richardson's fire-fighting annotations to *Clarissa*, they can now be seen to do so in ways heralded in the interim by minor novels like *The History of Charlotte Summers* (1750). This work moves beyond Fielding in several ways, intercalating its narrative with imaginary scenes of its own reception at the hands of 'pretty Triflers' like Miss Pert or Beau Thoughtless, defending its own integrity in apostrophes to Miss Censorious, and curtailing one of its chapters when yet another inscribed reader, Miss Arabella Dimple (whose maid is reading it aloud to her), falls asleep. Again, if Tristram's appeal to the reader to sit on volumes 1 to 5 of *Tristram Shandy* and 'look back upon the country we have pass'd through' picks up Fielding's recommendation to the reader to rest in *Joseph Andrews*'s blank pages and consider 'the Parts he hath already passed through', it may also do so by way of imitations such as William Goodall's *Adventures of Captain Greenland* (1752). Here the stages of a reader's journey through the novel are similarly marked by material features of the text: 'the Number of our Pages may serve for Mile-stones, and when he is weary, and has travelled his Day, at the end of our Chapter he may put up his Horse.'[22]

Far from representing some radically original scrutiny of novelistic convention, self-referential gestures of this kind had become just another part of the convention. John Shebbeare ('a low Imitator of all Novel Writers', as Lady Bradshaigh described him to Richardson) suggests as much when coming up with yet another Fieldingesque analogy for novel-writing, in this case an analogy between 'Authoring' and 'Tayloring', which, like

---

[21] Wayne Booth, 'The Self-Conscious Narrator in Comic Fiction before *Tristram Shandy*', *PMLA* 67 (1952), 163–85 (at 176, 185).

[22] Ibid. 181–2, 184.

Goodall's pages-as-milestones and Sterne's volumes-as-travelling-stool, originates in the same fruitful chapter of *Joseph Andrews*. As he confesses, 'the many Comparisons which Authors have already drawn of themselves, one would imagine, should have utterly exhausted all Similies on that Subject'.[23] In this context, Sterne's originality was clearly not in foregrounding and interrogating conventions on which everyone, post-Fielding, was playing, but in shifting the balance between fictional and metafictional elements in such a way as to make the latter his primary mode. No doubt he did so with reference to *A Tale of a Tub* (in which story is similarly usurped in the hands of a bumptious but incompetent narrator whose text sprawls out of control), thereby applying to the post-Scriblerian genre of the novel a Scriblerian satirical resource. But it may also be that what impels the brilliance of *Tristram Shandy*'s metafiction is the existence of so much immediate competition, which, as in the similarly hackneyed raw material of Slop's fall, he could simultaneously plunder and ingeniously outdo.

The case for viewing Sterne as a voracious reader of new fiction gains further support from the sale catalogue of his library, which includes several of the novels mentioned by Booth, including Marivaux's *Pharsamond* in its English translation of 1750 and Edward Kimber's *The Juvenile Adventures of David Ranger* (a novel presenting itself, to the derision of the reviewers, as a *roman à clef* about Garrick).[24] Several other self-conscious novels of the 1750s are present, including Cleland's *Memoirs of a Coxcomb* (1751; lot 1590), the anonymous *Constantia: or, A True Picture of Human Life* (1751; lot 1488), Fielding's *Amelia* (1751; lot 1528), the anonymous *Cleora: or, The Fair Inconstant* (1752; lot 1489), and Shebbeare's *Lydia: or, Filial Piety* (1755; item 1580). Also in the catalogue are incomplete sets or odd volumes of Lennox's *Harriot Stuart* (1750; lot 2481); Smollett's *Peregrine Pickle* (1751; lot 2502); *The Adventures of a Valet* (1752; lot 2490); Richardson's *Sir Charles Grandison* (1753; lot 2486); an anticipatory imitation of *Grandison* (similar in kind to the spurious volume 3 of *Tristram Shandy*) entitled *Memoirs of Sir Charles Goodville* (1753; lot 2493); William Dodd's *The Sisters* (1754; lot 2488); Haywood's *Invisible Spy* (1754; lot 2466); Sarah Scott's *A Journey Through Every Stage of Life* (1754; lot 2469); the anonymous *History of My Own Life* (1756; lot 2477); and William Guthrie's *The*

---

[23] John Shebbeare, *Lydia: or, Filial Piety*, 4 vols. (1755), 2: 3; 2: 1. Richardson quotes Lady Bradshaigh's comment back to her in a letter of 29 May 1756, Forster MSS, xi, fo. 180.

[24] The catalogue of the books, as sold in York in August 1768, is reproduced in *Sale Catalogues of Libraries of Eminent Persons*, ed. A. N. L. Munby, vol. 5. (London: Mansell, 1972), 257–356. Both *Pharsamond* (lot 2487) and *David Ranger* (lot 2467) were published in two volumes, only the first of which is listed in the sale catalogue. On *David Ranger* and Garrick, see *Critical Review*, 2 (Nov. 1756), 379; *Monthly Review*, 15 (Dec. 1756), 655–6.

Mother (1759; lot 2479). Although the sale catalogue notoriously adds to Sterne's 'Entire Library' a number of books from other sources, without specifying which are which, all of the above titles occur in parts of the list that, in Nicolas Barker's persuasive analysis of the structure of the list, seem to relate to Sterne.[25] Even if some of these items were indeed from other collections, it hardly weakens the underlying point, which is the relevance to *Tristram Shandy* not of particular obscure novels but of a widely diffused set of practices and conventions in the fiction of the period—a fiction demonstrably present in bulk not only in the metropolis but also in the bookshops, circulating libraries, and private houses of York and Yorkshire. It is worth adding that, although we know Sterne to have been a bulk buyer of books (all the more enthusiastically when they came from the bargain basement), he no doubt borrowed many more from wealthy friends such as Hall-Stevenson, or from sources such as the circulating library that his York printer Caesar Ward had been operating since the 1730s, in ways that are now untraceable.[26] The only sure record of his book-borrowing is in the register of York Minster Library, the contents of which, while documenting the scholarly and conservative aspects of Sterne's literary tastes, inevitably fail to register his appetite for the voguish or trashy.[27] Subscription lists reveal something of his access to contemporary verse, and he appears, for example, on the lists for Francis Fawkes's *Original Poems and Translations* (1761), Robert Lloyd's *Poems* (1762), and Christopher Smart's *Translation of the Psalms of David* (1765). But subscription publication was rare in the case of fiction, and he subscribed to neither of the exceptional cases noted above, *The Lives of Cleopatra and Octavia* and *The Brothers* (though Garrick, Warburton, and Wilkes were subscribers to both).

Other traces of Sterne's novel-reading habits are fleeting, but also telling, such as John Croft's report (in the context of a short paragraph on 'the Books that he studied and drew from most') that he was 'a great Admirer' of novels by Prévost and Marivaux.[28] One of the few books to

---

[25] Nicolas Barker, 'The Library Catalogue of Laurence Sterne', *Shandean*, 1 (1989), 9–24 (at 14).

[26] 'I have bought seven hundred books at a purchase dog cheap', Sterne gloated from Coxwold on 28 July 1761 (*Letters*, 142). On Ward's circulating library, see Alan D. McKillop, 'English Circulating Libraries, 1725–50', *Library*, 14 (1933–4), 477–85 (at 478–9).

[27] C. B. L. Barr and W. G. Day, 'Sterne and York Minster Library', *Shandean*, 2 (1990), 9–21.

[28] John Croft, 'Anecdotes of Sterne vulgarly Tristram Shandy', in *Whitefoord Papers*, ed. W. A. S. Hewins (Oxford: Oxford University Press, 1898), 225–32 (at 230). This passage, with several other items of evidence highlighted in this chapter, has recently been noted by Ian Campbell Ross, *Laurence Sterne: A Life* (Oxford: Oxford University Press, 2001), 114–15. Ross's account of Sterne's reading is a significant advance on Cash's, though he continues to assert that 'of any familiarity on Sterne's part with the great outpouring of prose fiction in England in the 1740s and 1750s there is scarcely a trace' (p. 115).

survive with his ownership inscription is an odd volume of Rousseau's novel of education, *Emile*, and in *A Sentimental Journey* he refers by title to Crébillon's *Les Egarements du cœur et de l'esprit* (as he also does, more obliquely, in a letter of 1760).[29] His careful monitoring of the most recent French fiction, and of its commercial impact, is evident from *Tristram Shandy*'s early apostrophe to the Moon, who 'has most power to set my book a-going, and make the world run made after it', but who may at present be 'too busy with CANDID and Miss CUNEGUND's affairs' (1.9.16–17). At least six editions of *Candide* had appeared in English, in three rival translations, since publication of Voltaire's French original in January 1759, and the reference does more than reveal how closely Sterne kept his finger on the pulse of the literary market. It openly announces *Tristram Shandy*'s self-consciousness as encompassing not only the technical procedures of the novel genre but also its commercial status—a topic less euphorically resumed when Tristram's early anxiety about strictly literary difficulties gives way to panic about the 'ten cart-loads' of his work that are still unsold (8.6.663).

The other conspicuously successful work of fiction in the months before *Tristram Shandy* began to appear was Johnson's *Rasselas*, and there is evident significance in Sterne desire for *Tristram Shandy* to resemble Johnson's work in material form: 'two small volumes, of the size of Rasselas, and on the same paper and type' (*Letters*, 80). His reasoning must be guessed at, however. The earliest advertisements specify that *Tristram Shandy* will be 'Printed on a superfine Writing Paper, and a new letter',[30] and Sterne may simply have had a connoisseurly interest in textual formats, and a desire to establish *Tristram Shandy* in its very fabric as an upmarket product. Alternatively, his intention may have been to make his text look longer than it was, and so command a higher price. The consummately professional Johnson appears to have intended as much himself (*Rasselas* would 'make about two volumes like the little Pompadour that is about one middling volume',[31] he had told William Strahan), and *Tristram Shandy* soon became a byword for the deceptive packaging of slender matter. Reviewing volumes 3 and 4 of *Tristram Shandy*, Owen Ruffhead looked back on their predecessors as 'two pigmy octavos, which scarce contained the substance of a twelve-penny pamphlet' (*CH* 122), and the same format

[29] Kenneth Monkman, 'Books Sterne Owned?', *Shandean*, 2 (1990), 215–25 (at p. 215, referring to a volume in the Beinecke Library); *SJ* 87; *Letters*, 88.

[30] Anne Bandry, 'Early Advertisements', *Shandean*, 4 (1992), 244–5 (quoting *London Chronicle*, 20 Dec. 1759).

[31] *The Letters of Samuel Johnson*, ed. Bruce Redford, 5 vols. (Oxford: Clarendon Press, 1992), 1: 178 (20 Jan. 1759). The reference is apparently to *The History of the Marchioness of Pompadour* (1758).

was retained in the later volumes. The 'expansive type' of another Becket and Dehondt novel of 1765, John Langhorne's *Correspondence of Theodosius and Constantia*, was criticized by Ralph Griffiths as showing 'the difference between our modern *Shandy-like* pages, and the ample Half-crown's-worth's afforded us in the days of honest Jacob Tonson'. Addison and Steele knew everything about writing books, Griffiths adds, but nothing about 'the art of *vending* them', and where they gained five pieces by their lucubrations, 'a Sterne . . . would have pocketed *fifty!*'[32]

But Sterne was also keenly aware of the semantics of typography and layout, even at this early stage (and in the case of *A Political Romance* had made this awareness clear by including within the text (*PR* 49–51) his instructions to the printer for its presentation). To make *Tristram Shandy* look like *Rasselas* may also have been to signal materially the less tangible ways in which, in its overall structure, Sterne's work ludicrously enacts some of the implications of *Rasselas* that Johnson had left undeveloped: the idea of 'opinions' obsessing the mind while 'life' passes, for example, or the idea of a conclusion in which nothing is concluded.[33] More generally, the *Rasselas*-style format could only have worked to signal a basic generic affinity, much as Sterne would also have signalled this affinity through his earlier idea of presenting *Tristram Shandy* in the same size, 'allowing the same Type & Margin', as a Richardson-printed volume of 1753, a partly fictionalized satirical conduct book by Jane Collier, co-author of *The Cry* (*Letters*, 74). In its very format, *Tristram Shandy* would look broadly similar to fiction of the time, but also—by virtue of its 'new letter'—innovative on close inspection. It thus set a minor fashion for flagging formal oddity or unorthodox content by strictly typographical means. Not only were direct imitations like *The Life and Amours of Hafen Slawkenbergius* (1761) and 'Jeremiah Kunastrokius's' *Explanatory Remarks upon . . . Tristram Shandy* (1761) advertised as printed in 'the size and manner' or 'the same letter and size' of *Tristram Shandy*.[34] Reviewers identified a similar trend in other genres, describing Warburton's digressive and intermittently irreverent *Doctrine of Grace* (1762) as 'these little Shandean volumes', and Churchill's serialized poem *The Ghost* (1762–3) as 'a kind of *Tristram Shandy* in *verse*' or again 'this Shandy in Hudibrastics'.[35]

[32] *Monthly Review*, 32 (Jan. 1765), 20.

[33] On these *Rasselas* connections, see above, p. 19, and below, p. 142.

[34] Anne Bandry, 'Imitations of *Tristram Shandy*', in Melvyn New (ed.), *Critical Essays on Laurence Sterne* (New York: G. K. Hall, 1998), 39–52 (at 45, 41).

[35] All three instances (from the *Monthly Review*, 27 (Nov. 1762), 370; 27 (Oct. 1762), 316; 29 (Nov. 1763), 397) are noted in Alan B. Howes, *Yorick and the Critics: Sterne's Reputation in England 1760–1868* (New Haven: Yale University Press, 1958), 17 n., 3.

Samuel Paterson described his own *Another Traveller!* (1768) as 'a couple of *Shandean* duodecimos'.[36]

LITERARY COMMODITIES AND PRINTED ARTEFACTS

Typographical play (or, more generally, play on the physicality or 'book-ness' of the literary text) is a feature of *Tristram Shandy's* reflexiveness neglected by Booth's more strictly narratological focus on authorial intrusion and reader response. Booth says little, too, about other features of Sterne's practice that have come to be emphasized since publication of his essay: the problematization of subjectivity inherent in Tristram's unavailing efforts to stabilize and communicate a self in literary form, for example, or the self-conscious positioning of *Tristram Shandy* as a commercial venture that attempts to manipulate, while also being subject to, an audience of reviewers and consumers. Yet here too *Tristram Shandy* is the dazzling culmination of a decade-long trend, not some solitary post-modern anticipation or Rabelaisian–Cervantic throwback. The 'necessary and unavoidable Deficienc[y]' that *The Adventures of a Valet* begins by confessing—the impossibility for the narrator of satisfactorily 'acquaint-ing the Reader who I am'—announces identity as just what it becomes in *Tristram Shandy* and *A Sentimental Journey*: a 'puzzle' (*TS* 7.33.633) or 'perplexing affair' (*SJ* 112). Titles like *The History of My Own Life* express increasingly widespread self-consciousness about the novelistic construc-tion of first-person subjects, amplified in this case by the commentary of an editorial persona who meditates on 'the Oddity of the Title' or again 'the Unmeaningness of it'.[37] Thomas Amory's *The Life of John Buncle, Esq.* (1756–66) is a more extended and eccentric exploration of this issue, organized by an associationist logic deriving from the narrator's comic preoccupation with Locke's *Essay Concerning Human Understanding*. (Or perhaps *dis*organized: this was, the *Critical Review* observed in parody of its mock-learned style, 'the most *doleful* jumble of *miscellany thoughts, replications,* and *haring, scaring diabolism* that was ever *posited* in the *sen-sory* of a man's *head*'.[38]) From Locke Amory's narrator draws (having read the work three times) both 'a thorough acquaintance with my own under-standing' and a sense of 'how greatly true knowledge depended on a right

[36] Samuel Paterson, *Another Traveller!*, 2 vols. (1768), 1: viii.
[37] *The Adventures of a Valet*, 1: 1; *The History of My Own Life*, 2nd edn., 2 vols. (1756), 1: A3ᵛ; 1: A5.
[38] *Critical Review*, 2 (Oct. 1756), 227.

meaning of words'; but in terms of narrative coherence the result is disaster. Compendious and pedantic, his attempt 'to write a true history of my life and notions' disintegrates beneath his efforts to record everything he thinks as well as everything he does.[39] As Katie Trumpener has noted, 'Amory's narrators move between narrative locales, between landscape description, antiquarian annotation and philosophical digressions, creating epistemological uncertainty in the narrative', and she may be right to infer that 'Sterne's explorations of the discursive construction of time build on Amory's work on the discursive construction of place'.[40] Time itself is a preoccupation here. Anxious, like Tristram, to record transaction and opinion in equal measure, and to disseminate them for the good of mankind, Buncle stages his attempt with a pressing sense of fading pasts and approaching extinction. The Shandean combination of mock pomposity and desperate obsessiveness that marks his writing was sensed by the publisher who, a century and a half later, enterprisingly renamed the work *The Life and Opinions of John Buncle, Esquire*:

That the Transactions of my Life, and the observations and reflections I have made on men and things . . . might not be buried in oblivion, and by length of time, be blotted out of the Memory of Men, it has been my wont . . . to write down *Memorandums* of every thing I thought worth noticing, as men and matters, books and circumstances, came in my way; and in hopes they may be of some service to my fellow-mortals I publish them.[41]

Autobiographical or mock-autobiographical works staging the collapse of life-writing into narrative disorder were not, of course, an invention of the 1750s, though they do appear to have had a special appeal to contemporary tastes. While recognizing the mutual interaction of *John Buncle* and *Tristram Shandy* (mutual in that Amory's work, in its 1766 sequel, gained a new lease of life from Sterne's success), one might also note the distant ancestry of both in Restoration ramble fiction. The sprawling narrative republished in 1762 for its Shandean anticipations, Dunton's *Voyage round the World*, is only one example of this obscure subgenre. Another is Francis Kirkman's *The Unlucky Citizen* (1673), a vigorous farrago of tales and digressions, which the narrator interrupts at one point to excuse 'these my *Sallies* and Freedom, for I confine my self to no order in my Writing,

---

[39] Thomas Amory, *The Life of John Buncle, Esq.*, 4 vols. (1756–66), 1: 6; 1: v.

[40] Katie Trumpener, *Bardic Nationalism: The Romantic Novel and the British Empire* (Princeton: Princeton University Press, 1997), 167–8.

[41] Amory, *John Buncle*, 1: 1. Amory's work was republished as *The Life and Opinions of John Buncle, Esquire*, with an introduction by Ernest A. Baker, in Routledge's 'Library of Early Novelists' (1904).

but as I think convenient, so I manage my Story; but still keeping to the *Thread* of it: I know I have left it at present, and shall do so for a while'.[42] Works of this kind use autobiographical form as a convenient receptacle for miscellaneous matter, however, rather than being directly concerned with subjectivity itself. They lack the central irony arising in Amory and Sterne, of a frustrated quest to stabilize personal identity by inscribing it in a material text that, in its elliptical, fragmentary, unresolved state, then becomes unstable itself.

Other emphases were more genuinely exclusive to the period, and the conditions for one—anticipating Tristram's debate with the jackass-critics whose monthly surveillance was now transforming the conditions of authorship and publication—had only just arisen. Short-lived reviewing monthlies had come and gone (such as the *History of the Works of the Learned* (1737–43), which reviewed *Pamela*), but Frank Donoghue is right to highlight the sea change that divides *Tom Jones*'s high-handed warnings to the critics, on the eve of the *Monthly*'s launch, and *Tristram Shandy*'s much more complicated negotiations in the 1760s, by which time the *Monthly* and the *Critical* were powerful organs.[43] Where Donoghue's argument is more questionable is in his assumption that the influence of this new institutional force in the reception of fiction took Sterne by surprise. *Evelina* (whose dedication of 1778 'To the Authors of the Monthly and Critical Reviews' Donoghue cites) was not the first novel to recognize in this way that the old conditions of patronage were now radically altered. *John Buncle* begins with a dedicatory preface 'To the Criticks', ironically fawning in tone, in which the narrator begs the favour of 'such great and impartial judges', and concludes with the hope (in mocking allusion to their sacerdotal pretensions) 'that your heads may lack no ointment, and your garments be always white and odoriferous'.[44]

Many other novels of the period joke about their new vulnerability to the monthly press. In the final chapter of *David Ranger*, Kimber moves on from addressing the 'gentle reader' to a now more important group, representing the proto-Shandean games with time played within his narrative as challenges to the magazine reviewers:

And now, ye tremendous criticks, with whom our times are so replete, nothing remains, but to say a word or two to your worships, before I lay down my pen, and recur to my former obscurity. To exercise your talents, you will find in these

---

[42] Francis Kirkman, *The Unlucky Citizen* (1673), 261 (ch. 14).

[43] Donoghue, *Fame Machine*, 16–17; see also, on Sterne, pp. 56–85.

[44] Amory, *John Buncle*, 1: iv; 1: ix.

memoirs abundance of *Anachronism,* and *Parachronism* too: And, as I have written in a gay, disengaged manner, you will also find abundant matter to object against my stile and language in many instances. Some notions here and there advances, are new-fangled ones, which will employ a great deal of your skill to refute; and many quotations are made, with the loose and careless air of a gentleman, tho' not with the precision that your grave censorships, perhaps, will insist upon as necessary. That I might also leave free scope for your humour to vent itself, you will, here and there, also find some *polite Latin,* and also some *Greek* phrases *Anglicised,* all which, tho' I do not at all fear it, will pass the censure of your awful and damning tribunal.[45]

From here it is a short step to Tristram's appeal for a '*day-tall* [i.e. daily-paid or freelance] critick' (4.13.340) to get Walter and Toby off the stairs, or to his mock-deferential habit of apostrophizing the critic as 'your worship' (1.13.40). Other novels draw self-referential attention to the influence of market-sensitive publishers, as *Ephraim Tristram Bates* does in several scenes of negotiation between the hero and booksellers who insist on meeting a present demand in the trade for '*Bawdy* and *Treason,* or at least something very *Anti-ministerial*' (which the novel partly does by attacking the war policy of the Newcastle ministry) (*ETB* 181–2). In the final chapter of *Lydia,* John Shebbeare lays emphasis not directly on reviewers or booksellers, but on the way an author might circumvent their power by using subscription publication. Here a high-born group of inscribed readers voice their objections to the novel, and the Duchess of ****** proposes a more scandalous subject that would make her 'subscribe for twenty Sets, and procure a List of hundreds more'. The narrator then expresses his regret that her suggestion 'comes too late to alter what is past', but closes by floating another idea, proposals for printing which 'will be left, and Subscriptions taken in, at *Arthur's*'.[46]

These examples extend to an area neglected by Booth—*Tristram Shandy's* play on its own commodification in a marketplace regulated by reviewers—the overall pattern he detects. Features of Sterne's practice that we think of as distinctively Shandean turn out to be quite extensively anticipated in forgotten novels of the 1750s, the difference being that what other novelists confine to the paratextual margins (dedications and prefaces, typically, or concluding chapters) become structurally and rhetorically central in *Tristram Shandy*. Much the same picture recurs as we move from the commodification of literary texts to the related issue of their materiality, and specifically to the readiness of novelists to explore

[45] Edward Kimber, *The Juvenile Adventures of David Ranger, Esq.,* 2 vols. (1756), 2: 286–7.
[46] Shebbeare, *Lydia,* 4: 257–60.

the impact of print technology and publishing format on literary meaning and the reading experience. J. Paul Hunter aligns *Tristram Shandy* with the variorum *Dunciad* of 1729 in its innovative use of its own printedness, or in the extent to which it makes this printedness a part of its own subject, and a recent essay by Christopher Flint restates the Scriblerian connection with reference to lacunae in *A Tale of A Tub*. The more immediate context for *Tristram Shandy*'s typographical experiments is novelistic, however, as Hunter indicates with passing reference to 'the special issues involved in reading printer-writers such as Richardson and John Dunton' and Flint in his more sustained account of Richardson's use of character-specific ornaments or florets to distinguish, visually, *Clarissa*'s various narrators.[47] *Clarissa* pioneered a range of techniques for the expressive use of typography, which, whether intended or not to foster the mimetic illusion, tended in practice to accentuate the literariness of the work. These include the printed fold-out of music that accompanies Clarissa's 'Ode to Wisdom'; printers' indices (☞) used to mark Lovelace's annotations to a letter by Anna; the skewed and rotated type of the verse fragments drawn up by Clarissa after the rape (see Fig. 1); the unusual scriptorial typeface used for two of Clarissa's signatures in the first edition (a 'counterfeit signing' in which, the *Gentleman's Magazine* protested, 'there appears to be some degree of affectation'); and the thematically loaded 'Rape of Europa' ornament, which Richardson appears to have had cut expressly for the volume containing the rape.[48]

This imaginative use of print resources also prepared the way for comparable exploitation, so far little explored, in other Richardson-printed novels of the period by Sarah Fielding, Charlotte Lennox, and others. Imitators of Henry Fielding, including the stable of writers employed by William Owen, also got in on the act. *Ephraim Tristram Bates* is relatively low key in visual terms, though it does look forward to *Tristram Shandy* in its wittily overzealous interpolation of blocks of asterisks when conversation drops to a whisper, as though in some pedantic effort not to violate

[47] J. Paul Hunter, 'From Typology to Type: Agents of Change in Eighteenth-Century English Texts', in Margaret J. M. Ezell and Katherine O'Brien O'Keefe (eds.), *Cultural Artifacts and the Production of Meaning* (Ann Arbor: University of Michigan Press, 1994), 41–69 (at 43); Christopher Flint, 'In Other Words: Eighteenth-Century Authorship and the Ornaments of Print', *Eighteenth-Century Fiction*, 14 (2002), 621–66; see also Geoffrey Day, *From Fiction to the Novel* (London: Routledge, 1987), 93–9, 156–66.

[48] *Clarissa*, 2: 54 (music); 5: 30–46 (indices); 6: 308 (skewed type); 5: 358 (Europa ornament, repeated at 8: 250). The simulation of manuscript in the first edition (as objected to in the *Gentleman's Magazine*, 19 (Aug. 1749), 349) was not repeated at the corresponding points in the third (7: 408; 8: 113).

me fly to the fuccour of fuch a poor diftreffed—With what pleafure would I have raifed the dejected head, and comforted the defponding heart!—But who now fhall pity the poor wretch, who has encreafed, inftead of diminifhed, the number of the miferable!

PAPER X.

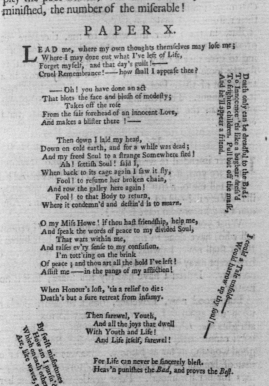

LEAD me, where my own thoughts themfelves may lofe me;
Where I may doze out what I've left of Life,
Forget myfelf, and that day's guilt!——
Cruel Remembrance!——how fhall I appeafe thee?

——Oh! you have done an act
That blots the face and blufh of modefty;
Takes off the rofe
From the fair forehead of an innocent Love,
And makes a blifter there !——

Then down I laid my head,
Down on cold earth, and for a while was dead;
And my freed Soul to a ftrange Somewhere fled !
Ah ! fottifh Soul ! faid I,
When back to its cage again I faw it fly,
Fool ! to refume her broken chain,
And row the galley here again !
Fool ! to that Body to return,
Where it condemn'd and deftin'd is to mourn.

O my Mifs Howe ! if thou haft friendfhip, help me,
And fpeak the words of peace to my divided Soul,
That wars within me,
And raifes ev'ry fenfe to my confufion,
I'm tott'ring on the brink
Of peace ; and thou art all the hold I've left !
Affift me——in the pangs of my affliction !

When Honour's loft, 'tis a relief to die :
Death's but a fure retreat from infamy.

Then farewel, Youth,
And all the joys that dwell
With Youth and Life !
And Life itfelf, farewel !

For Life can never be fincerely bleft.
Heav'n punifhes the *Bad*, and proves the *Beft*.

*Death only can be dreadful to the Bad;
To Innocence 'tis like a bugbear drefs'd
To frighten children. Pull but off the mafk,
And he'll appear a friend.*

*I could a Tale unfold,
Would harrow up thy Soul!*

*By fwift misfortunes
How am I purfu'd!
Which on each other
Are, like waves, renew'd!*

AFTER all, Belford, I have juft fkimmed over thefe tranfcriptions of Dorcas ; and I fee there are method and
good

Fig. 1. Skewed type in Richardson's *Clarissa*, octavo 4th edn. (1751), 5: 59: 'some of the scraps and fragments, as either torn through, or flung aside, I will copy, for the novelty of the thing, and to shew thee how her mind works now she is in this whimsical way.'

plausibility by assuming the narrator can hear. An example of this device—one the narrator eventually tires of, resolving to 'try no more Secretaries of *****' (*ETB* 181)—is reproduced as Fig. 2. (Compare the whispering at *TS* 3.17.221 and 7.29.624; see also 6.34.560, where, as in *Ephraim Tristram Bates*, the jokily clumsy obliteration of what is said seems to satirize the automatic—and, in the more relaxed post-Walpole climate, increasingly gratuitous—convention of using asterisks to indicate clandestine matter.) *Ephraim Tristram Bates* also anticipates the black page of *Tristram Shandy* with its offset '*Alas! poor* Bates' exclamation, and with other arresting visual indicators, which include an oversized black sunflower ornament used twice as a melancholy emblem. William Toldervy (who also compiled the first major English collection of funerary inscriptions, *Select Epitaphs* (1755)) gloomily punctuates his otherwise comic novel with epitaphs set out in facsimile style, and these alternate incongruously with at least nine fold-out sheets of printed music that the characters compose on their journey. As Hunter briefly notes, 'the folded calling card in an experimental 1755 novel called *The Card*' (written by John Kidgell, and published by Newbery) anticipates 'specially designed individual pages like the blank, black, and marbled ones in *Tristram Shandy*'.[49]

Kidgell's work, indeed, goes rather further. Though limited in its commercial success (*The Card* seems to have been a flash in the pan, having reportedly 'had a great run among the Circulating Libraries of the day' but no second edition[50]), it shares with *Tristram Shandy* the distinction of playing more systematically on its own material format than any other novel before the flurry of single-minded metafiction that developed in the 1960s—works such as B. S. Johnson's disbound novel *The Unfortunates* (1969) or William Gass's multicoloured, typographically riotous *Willie Masters' Lonesome Wife* (1971). Its unconventional title page identifies the work as 'Printed for the MAKER', and with this substitution for the usual 'Author' Kidgell invites readers to approach *The Card* more as a printed artefact than merely a literary composition, with part of its meaning metatextually produced by its own material features. The self-conscious typographical presentation of Kidgell's preface ('I have . . . intreated my printer not to croud it into *Italicks*') reinforces the significance of every detail of format in much the way Sterne was to do in *A Political Romance* (where the entreaty becomes a threat made, he tells his printer, 'at

[49] Hunter, 'From Typology to Type', 43.
[50] MS note (written before 1844) in the William Andrews Clark Memorial Library copy of *The Card*. I am grateful to Jennifer Schaffner, reference librarian, for this information.

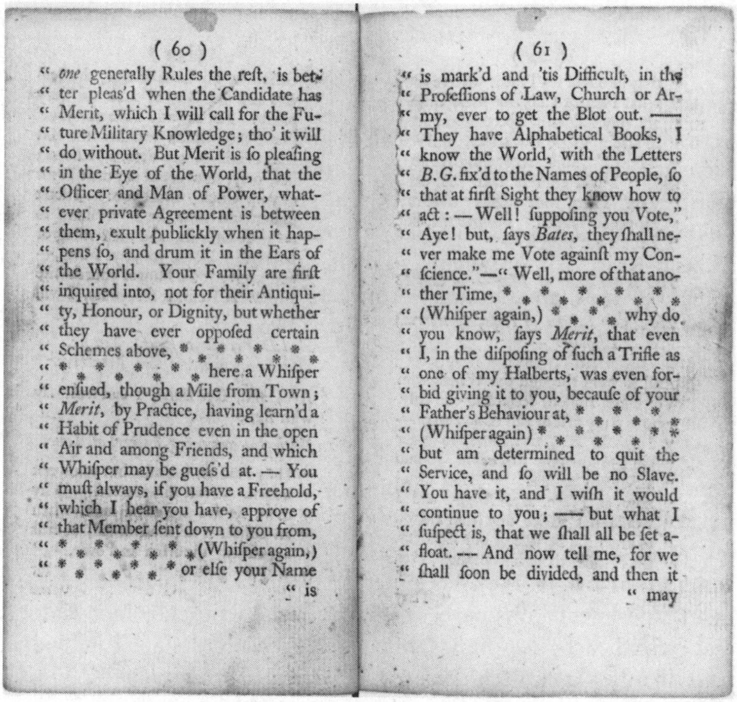

" *one* generally Rules the reſt, is bet-
" ter pleas'd when the Candidate has
" Merit, which I will call for the Fu-
" ture Military Knowledge; tho' it will
" do without. But Merit is ſo pleaſing
" in the Eye of the World, that the
" Officer and Man of Power, what-
" ever private Agreement is between
" them, exult publickly when it hap-
" pens ſo, and drum it in the Ears of
" the World. Your Family are firſt
" inquired into, not for their Antiqui-
" ty, Honour, or Dignity, but whether
" they have ever oppoſed certain
" Schemes above, * * * * * *
" * * * * * * * here a Whiſper
" enſued, though a Mile from Town;
" *Merit*, by Practice, having learn'd a
" Habit of Prudence even in the open
" Air and among Friends, and which
" Whiſper may be gueſs'd at. — You
" muſt always, if you have a Freehold,
" which I hear you have, approve of
" that Member ſent down to you from,
" * * * * * * * (Whiſper again,)
" * * * * * * * or elſe your Name
" is

" is mark'd and 'tis Difficult, in the
" Profeſſions of Law, Church or Ar-
" my, ever to get the Blot out. ——
" They have Alphabetical Books, I
" know the World, with the Letters
" *B. G.* fix'd to the Names of People, ſo
" that at firſt Sight they know how to
" act : — Well! ſuppoſing you Vote,"
" Aye! but, ſays *Bates*, they ſhall ne-
" ver make me Vote againſt my Con-
" ſcience."—" Well, more of that ano-
" ther Time, * * * * * * *
" (Whiſper again,) * * * why do
" you know, ſays *Merit*, that even
" I, in the diſpoſing of ſuch a Trifle as
" one of my Halberts, was even for-
" bid giving it to you, becauſe of your
" Father's Behaviour at, * * * *
" (Whiſper again) * * * * * *
" but am determined to quit the
" Service, and ſo will be no Slave.
" You have it, and I wiſh it would
" continue to you; —— but what I
" ſuſpect is, that we ſhall all be ſet a-
" float. —— And now tell me, for we
" ſhall ſoon be divided, and then it
" may

Fig. 2. Whispered asterisks in
*The Life and Memoirs of Mr.
Ephraim Tristram Bates* (1756),
60–1: 'here a Whisper ensued,
though a Mile from Town;
Merit, by Practice, having learn'd
a Habit of Prudence even in the
open Air and among Friends,
and which Whisper may be
guess'd at.'

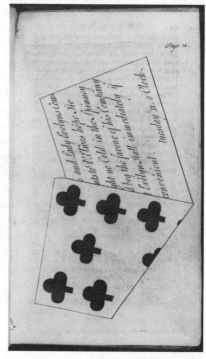

Fig. 3. The eponymous device in
John Kidgell's *The Card* (1755),
facing 1: 12: 'Miss *Evelyn* obtained
the Favour of *the ten of Clubs*, to
wait upon Doctor *Elwes*, on the
fairer Side of which (etched in
beautiful Manuscript) was this
important Commission.'

your peril').[51] And Kidgell's point is more conspicuously displayed by a hand-coloured knave of clubs placed opposite the title page, which in its motley presence enigmatically distorts (as Janine Barchas has recently noted) the conventions of frontispiece portraiture.[52] A few pages later the narrative is interrupted, even more unconventionally, by a plate representing a ten of clubs, folded over, with a partially legible come-hither message etched aslant on the reverse, as though Kidgell is determined to cram as much visual gimmickry as possible on a single illustrative leaf (see Fig. 3). This second card is immediately followed by a second preface, which, the narrator acknowledges, must be thought of as displaced from its proper textual position, 'either through the Inaccuracy of the Transcriber, or a Neglect of the Corrector of the Press, or a Design in the Author to excite the Curiosity of the Reader . . . by a certain Ornament of Rhetorical Figure, formerly distinguished by the Apellation of *Hysteron, Proteron*, but now called with vulgar Simplicity, the *Cart before the Horse*' (*Card*, 1: 13).

Here and elsewhere Kidgell wittily defamiliarizes elements of published fiction that are normally transparent or functional. As the second preface confesses, his very title must now be seen as a red herring, and as merely opportunistic in denoting an object that disappears from the narrative, 'crumbled into a great Variety of Particles' (*Card*, 1: 17), within a few pages—at which point the generic expectations hitherto encouraged, that the book will be a fashionable novel of circulation like Francis Coventry's *Pompey the Little* (1751) or Susan Smythies's *The Stage-Coach* (1753), are abruptly dropped. The facsimile card itself is no more than a ruse to save at least a fragment of the book from the usual fate of print:

by this Artifice doth the *Author* ingeniously project a Method to preserve himself from total *Oblivion*; humbly conceiving, that when this *neglected Treatise* under the Character of Waste-Paper, shall be doomed to share the Fate of it, some little *Master* or *Miss* may be kindly advertised of the Picture of that harmless *Card* which adorns one happy Leaf of it. (*Card*, 1: 13)

The card, by this account, is worth more than *The Card* as a whole, the materiality of the book more significant than its narrative content; and it is true enough that much of Kidgell's best matter lies outside his narrative text (which was decoded by contemporaries as a libellous *roman à clef* about Edward Young[53]). Paratextual jokes include a cast list burlesquing

[51] John Kidgell, *The Card*, 2 vols. (1755), 1: 8; *PR* 50.

[52] Janine Barchas, 'Prefiguring Genre: Frontispiece Portraits from *Gulliver's Travels* to *Millenium Hall*', *Studies in the Novel*, 30 (1998), 260–86 (at 276–7).

[53] Samuel Johnson, *Lives of the English Poets*, ed. G. B. Hill, 3 vols. (Oxford: Clarendon Press, 1905), 3: 389.

Richardson's list in *Grandison*, and there even appear to be bogus entries in the 'Errata' table, which as well as correcting misprints lists pedantic inserts that, like the transposed preface, have an oddly Shandean ring: 'After *Barebones*, add, as *Rapin* in his History of *England* has thought it expedient to record' (*Card*, 1: xviii).

As well as adroitly positioning itself as a book about the material form of books, *The Card* also skilfully parodies a range of the period's fictional styles, 'from the celebrated Author of *Clarissa*, to Writers of *inferior* Note innumerable' (*Card*, 1: 14). The process begins with a nicely judged letter from 'Nerissa': 'Every the minutest Circumstance, my Dear, is to a friendly Correspondent material' (*Card*, 1: xii). In common with the novels analysed by Booth, *The Card* then seems unable to sustain its metafictional aspect throughout the main body of its text, which settles down into the usual bantering, sub-Fieldingesque style for most of its pages. But this feature returns strongly in the final chapters, which culminate in a riot of narrative metalepsis and jumbled mimetic levels. At the wedding celebration that rounds off the plot, Roderick Random attends in company with 'Mrs. *Booby*, late Miss *Pamela Andrews*', David Simple squires Betsy Thoughtless, and even the most recent and obscure fictional titles (by William Guthrie and William Dodd) are registered when two masquerading couples appear, 'the Gentlemen call[ing] themselves the *Friends*, and the Ladies the *Sisters*'. The party ends acrimoniously when 'Mr. *Thomas Jones*, in waiting on Miss *Harlowe* to her Chair, had the Imprudence to be rude to her; and Sir *Charles Grandison*, for interposing, the Misfortune to *have his Ears boxed*' (*Card*, 2: 294–6).

TRISTRAM'S WORDLESS PAGES

Years later, in the long hiatus that followed publication of *Tristram Shandy*'s third instalment, the *Court Magazine* carried an item in which 'Tristram Shandy' writes Kidgell an unsolicited letter, requesting his advice and suggesting that they collaborate on the fourth instalment. Primarily, this ironic item plays on the notoriety as a pornographer that Kidgell had gained by cashing in (with *A Genuine and Succinct Narrative of a Scandalous, Obscene, and Exceedingly Profane Libel*) on the salacious potential of Wilkes's 'Essay on Woman': Tristram is unsure how to handle Toby's amours in volumes 7 and 8, and wants Kidgell's help in rendering 'the substance of these amours . . . in the same inoffensive manner you have done with the ESSAY ON WOMAN'.[54] But the author of this anonymous item (possibly Hugh Kelly, novelist-editor of the *Court Magazine*) may also have been remembering *The Card*, and the way in which Kidgell had pioneered the post-Fielding leap—a leap we now think of as distinctively Shandean—from self-reflexive narrative fiction to self-referential printed artefact. Above all, *The Card* is a work that anticipates Sterne's in the clarity and wit with which it registers the conditions of authorship and technologies of production now determining modern writing. By insisting on its own identity as a highly specialized kind of manufactured commodity, in which an author unable to reach his audience with the intimacy of speech or manuscript resorts to increasingly showy gimmicks to gain passing attention, *The Card* defamiliarizes the very idea of the book, while also displaying the apparent inability of the new generation of novelists to be original through words alone. It reminds us, as the *Monthly Review* complained when reviewing *The Bracelet* (1759), that at a time when 'Most *novels* have no character at all . . . the superior merit of some, is owing merely to the *genius* of the printer'. Or it reminds us that, as another commentator on *Tristram Shandy* was shortly to put it, 'the art of writing' is now one 'by which you are to understand that of printing and publishing'.[55]

Yet even *The Card*—the extreme case of the compulsion to outdo Fielding in self-referential sophistication that dominates the fiction of the 1750s—fails to perform in full what *Tristram Shandy* at last achieves, after so many false starts from so many hands. Now all Fielding's narratological insights and literary games—his play with narrative time, with formal and material features of organization, with the vagaries of communication and interpretation—are fully absorbed, and become the assumed, unspoken backdrop against which takes place a yet more radical interrogation of narrative representation and the capacity of print to stabilize experience and meaning. It may not be coincidence that in staging this interrogation *Tristram Shandy* restored to the novel genre the market success of Richardson and Fielding in their heyday—a success apparently closed to novels that failed either to innovate formally (like the unsaleable *Histories of Some of the Penitents*, which, as the elderly Richardson sourly noted, had 'no *Shandying* in it'[56]) or to pursue their self-consciousness (like that

---

[54] *Court Magazine*, 2 (Dec. 1763), 583; see also Howes, *Yorick and the Critics*, 17.

[55] *Monthly Review*, 20 (Mar. 1759), 276 (reworking the famous opening of Pope's *Epistle to a Lady*); *The Life, Travels, and Adventures of Christopher Wagstaff, Gentleman, Grandfather to Tristram Shandy*, 2 vols. (1762), 1: 34.

[56] To Lady Bradshaigh, 20 June 1760, Forster MSS, XI, fo. 269.

half-baked ur-*Tristram* of 1756, *Ephraim Tristram Bates*) beyond the level of incidental decoration.

Crucially, the interrogation proceeds through visual as well as verbal means, and with an attentiveness to the material and commercial conditions of printing and publication already heralded in *A Political Romance*, informed as that work avowedly is by 'the Information of Persons conversant in Paper and Print' (*PR* 52). Indeed, *Tristram Shandy*'s studious defamiliarization of printed meaning may be traced back even further in Sterne's career, with the cryptic symbols (analogous to Dr Slop's '†' in the unhorsing scene) used to denote key terms in his poem of 1743, 'The Unknown World' (or, as it was in Sterne's fair manuscript copy, 'The Unknown $\odot$').[57] There are many ways in which *Tristram Shandy* pursues the standard topics of representation, interpretation, and reading, but the most arresting is its dramatization of narrative aporia through creative deformations of print conventions. Much of this adopts and flippantly reworks typographical experiments from other recent novels, such as Tristram's mock-Richardsonian use of printers' indices to flag points of wisdom and information (as at 2.12.131, 4.25.375, and elsewhere), or his style (as at 6.14.521) of asterisking mid-sentence conversational lacunae, which is closer to *Ephraim Tristram Bates* than to *A Tale of a Tub*, and, in its interpolation of stray unsubstituted words, more cleverly teasing than both. Other features are almost certainly unprecedented, such as the famous flourish of Trim's stick (9.4.743) or the cancelled chapter and temporarily inverted page numbering in the last eight chapters of volume 4 (4.25.361–72). But all embody the same reminder, that, both as an object in its own right and as a representation of a fictional world, the novel rests on conventions and assumptions that, once visually or verbally defamiliarized, start to look shakily arcane. The blithe ease with which Tristram traces Trim's flourish with the stick implies, by contrast, the lumbering poverty of even the most studiously particularized description; yet in itself Tristram's line remains only a trace, and never the thing itself. For all his protestations to the contrary, the absent chapter implies the arbitrariness of narrative selection and the necessary incompleteness of even the most prolix representation—an implication that lingers in the skewed page numbering of the chapters to follow, which engenders a naggingly literal sense that Tristram has got his material the wrong way round. Cumulatively, these features of Sterne's text disrupt the transparency and

---

[57] The poem was conventionally printed in the *Gentleman's Magazine*, 13 (July 1743), 376: see *EMY* 152–4.

continuity of narrative language, and, though small in themselves, they constitute, collectively, a radical fragmentation of novelistic communication and coherence. The narrative representation of Shandy Hall is systematically exposed as ill seen, and—words never being enough—even more ill said.

It has long been a standard move of *Tristram Shandy* criticism to read Sterne's pseudo-Lockean play on 'the imperfection of words' (5.7.429)— an imperfection acute enough, within the novel's world, to put lives in jeopardy and turn black to green—as spilling beyond this represented world to infect the efficacy of its representation. Far from connecting Tristram with his reader's conception, as he complains in his transposed preface, the 'tall, opake words' (3.235) to which he entrusts his life and opinions sturdily thwart communication. In this context there is an undertow of desperation to his most celebrated moments of resort to the visual: the black page for Yorick's death in the first instalment, the blank one for Widow Wadman's beauty in the third, and, between the two, the marbled page that stands for the work as a whole. Each of these pages looks back to comparable moments from recent novels, reworking their material gestures much as the text reworks their literary tropes, but fulfilling a so far largely unrealized potential in such gestures for emblematizing impasse.

The intertextual relationship is clearest with the black page, which picks up the jocoserious ending (quoted above) of *Ephraim Tristram Bates*. There the joke is rather simple, a dive into bathos reminiscent of Fielding's burlesque Shakespearian echoes in *The Tragedy of Tragedies* ('wherefore art thou *Tom Thumb?*'), so that the sentimental vision of strangers enquiring for the hero's tomb and striking their breasts is indecorously disrupted by the ensuing '*Alas! poor* Bates' (*ETB* 238).[58] Sterne's version closely tracks this passage, but, in explicitly restoring the Shakespearian name, Sterne also recalls the very different situation in *Hamlet*, in which the original Yorick is casually disinterred from an unmarked grave. His own Yorick, by contrast, has 'a plain marble slabb' on which is inscribed his borrowed epitaph, so that 'not a passenger goes by without stopping to cast a look upon it,——and sighing as he walks on, | Alas, poor YORICK!' (1.12.35–6). Yorick is preserved from oblivion in the laments of passers-by, and in this respect the marmoreal inscription performs its traditional function (which is to confer a certain permanence on transitory, mutable life) while also mirroring Tristram's project of fixing in print the remembrance of a

---

[58] Henry Fielding, *The Tragedy of Tragedies*, ed. James T. Hillhouse (New Haven: Yale University Press, 1918), p. 109 (II.iii).

generation now dead. The black page that follows seems to reinforce this effect, exceeding in its melancholy insistence both the black sunflower ornament of *Ephraim Tristram Bates* and Hamlet's equivocal lament. Yet the black page also implies the insufficiency of words, including even the unforgettable three-word inscription—admirably Lockean in its communicative plainness—to which Yorick's elegy is entrusted. Tristram feels impelled to go further, and in the context of his anxieties about the opacity of words it is not fanciful to see in the page something more than a simulacrum of Yorick's plain slab or a decoration of the kind sometimes found (as the Florida editors note at this point) in Jacobean elegy printing. In contrast with the economical wording of Yorick's inscription, the surfeit of printers' ink that follows takes the effort to memorialize him to opposite extremes, as though in some infinitely prolix inscription and reinscription, on a single page, of every tall opaque word that might possibly have been brought to bear.

Tristram's later remark (in the context of the marbled page) that 'many opinions, transactions and truths . . . lie mystically hid under the dark veil of the black one', which 'the world with all its sagacity' has not unravelled (3.36.268), brings to the surface this hint that the black page might mark not an absence but an illegible excess of words. Now the page seems to mimic the modern nonsense of *A Tale of a Tub*, passed off by Swift's hack as 'wondrous *Deep*, upon no wiser a Reason than because it is wondrous *Dark*';[59] or it becomes, in its blackness, the evil twin of those 'vacant Spaces' of narrative that, in *Tom Jones*, let Fielding's reader productively employ his 'wonderful Sagacity' (*TJ* 3.1.116). To this extent, the page stands as a lament not only for Yorick, but also for the imperfection, in Tristram's hands, of printed words. Coalescing to the pure unbroken black of mourning, they give up their feeble struggle for expressive meaning for the sake of mere visual impact.

Five volumes later, the blank page pursues a radically opposite strategy, entirely banishing opaque words in the pursuit (as Tristram would have it) of clear understanding. 'To conceive this right,—call for pen and ink—here's paper ready to your hand', he announces, as though forfeiting his own control over the reader's image of Widow Wadman: 'paint her to your own mind . . . 'tis all one to me——please but your own fancy in it' (6.38.566). With 'paint', 'conceive', and 'fancy' in particular, Tristram's wording recalls the difficulty of conjuring up a represented world and communicating it to the reader with which he has been wrestling all along.

---

[59] Jonathan Swift, *A Tale of a Tub*, ed. A. C. Guthkelch and D. Nichol Smith, 2nd edn. (Oxford: Clarendon Press, 1958), 208.

Even in the opening volumes he worries that, unless he spends paragraphs fussily specifying in what posture the sermon is delivered, readers 'would be apt to paint *Trim*, as if he was standing in his platoon ready for action:— His attitude was as unlike all this as you can conceive' (2.17.140). Only a few chapters before the blank page, he continues to fret that for all his efforts of minute description 'the reader has not a clear conception' of Toby's bowling-green (6.21.534), and that in striving 'to keep all tight together in the reader's fancy' he has lost his own way (6.33.557–8). Now the reader's fancy must do the job alone, and so conceive the picture more adequately than Tristram's words can do.

But this invitation to the reader also has resonance beyond *Tristram Shandy*. The idea of images more easily conceived than described is a commonplace trope of mid-eighteenth-century fiction, which, with characteristic sophistication, Sterne now makes wittily literal. Sometimes it is a comic device for signalling exaggerated appearances or expressions, as when a Smollett character stares 'with a certain stolidity of apprehension, which is easier conceived than described'; sometimes it is a mock-decorous way of handling erotic material, as when a Haywood character takes liberties with a woman 'which may better be conceived than described'.[60] Tristram's delegation of the decision leaves open both these possibilities for the reader to conceive, but perhaps especially the second. Like his notorious asterisks, his blank page at once disavows and stimulates the bawdy potential of his text, inviting the reader to imagine for himself a 'concupiscible' Wadman in much the way he later preserves the purity of his text (as opposed to the reader's completion of it) with a smaller blank, a 'void space' left empty 'that the reader may swear into it' (7.37.639). Overleaf, his follow-up remark that at least one page will now be impervious to the usual attacks on his bawdry was a red rag to the *Critical Review*, which was reminded by the blank page 'of a puritan who slept all Sunday that he might not break the Sabbath, and then boasted of his having committed no sin on the seventh day, though he had cheated all the other six'. In taking his break from verbal transgression, Sterne had merely compounded his offence.[61]

It is not only narrative language that now seems insufficient. Though in one respect the blank page of the third instalment matches the black and marbled pages of the previous two, it also picks up, ironically, another

---

[60] Tobias Smollett, *Peregrine Pickle*, ed. James L. Clifford, rev. Paul-Gabriel Boucé (Oxford: Oxford University Press, 1983), 260; Eliza Haywood, *The History of Miss Betsy Thoughtless*, ed. Beth Fowkes Tobin (Oxford: Oxford University Press, 1997), 270.

[61] *Critical Review*, 13 (Jan. 1762), 67.

sequence. Given that the first and second instalments had been adorned by illustrative frontispieces, keyed to particular pages in the text and engraved to designs by Hogarth, the invitation to the reader to illustrate the third instalment himself also implies a commentary on the inadequacy of graphic representation. Just as Tristram's pen no longer seems enough, nor does Hogarth's pencil—a point repeated another way pages later, when Tristram pompously identifies the engraved plotlines that close volume 6 as 'Inv. T. S | Scul. T. S' (6.40.570), as though to imply that the designer and engraver of the earlier plates ('W. Hogarth inv.ᵗ . . . S. Ravenet Sculp.'') have now been sacked. Perhaps Sterne knew that years earlier two illustrative frontispieces designed for *Pamela* by Hogarth had been rejected by Richardson, a decision Richardson excuses by quoting a reader who preferred to use his own imagination. 'I am so jealous . . . in Behalf of our *inward* Idea of Pamela's *Person*, that I dread *any* figur'd Pretence to Resemblance', this reader had written, adding that thanks to Richardson's powers of description a better picture 'will be sure to find place in the *Fancy*'.[62] No such confidence can survive several volumes of *Tristram Shandy*, and by this point the blank page can only reinforce the emphasis on representational impasse. Here is another of Tristram's unavailing or self-cancelling gestures, which for all its efforts to clarify the reader's conception means absolutely nothing. Like the Lockean *tabula rasa* of the newborn mind, it is rich in its potential for inscription, but void as it stands. In this context, Sterne may also have remembered a well-known verse exchange surrounding the Earl of Orrery's gift to Swift of a giltbound writing book. Its 'spotless Leaves' constitute a '*Rasa Tabula*', in Orrery's presentational poem, ripe for Swiftian inscription; but Swift glumly refuses the challenge in reply, resolving to leave the pages blank 'As Trophies of a Muse deceas'd'.[63] By the same token, the blank page of *Tristram Shandy* is the trophy of a narrative blocked—or, as another writer of the period saw, of meanings unrealized. 'The reader is to suppose that these asterisks must certainly mean something of the utmost consequence', writes Cuthbert Shaw of an indecipherable lacuna in his verse satire *The Race* (1766): 'It is exactly of the same kind with the blank page in *Tristram Shandy*.'[64]

---

[62]　*Pamela*, 518. The reader was Aaron Hill.

[63]　*The Poems of Jonathan Swift*, ed. Harold Williams, 3 vols. (Oxford: Clarendon Press, 1937), 2: 609–11. Additionally in play may be the little subgenre of extempore poems typified by Aaron Hill's verses 'Writ on a Blank Leaf of an Obscene Poem', or by the anonymous 'Verses Wrote in the Blank Leaf of Mrs. Haywood's Novel', a paean to love first printed in the 1722 edition of *Love in Excess*.

[64]　Cuthbert Shaw, *The Race* (1766), 14 n.

Sandwiched between these two illegible pages, wordlessly black and blank in succession, is the most widely discussed visual device in the entire work, the marbled page (3.36.269). Explicitly presented as a hermeneutic challenge—the reader must draw on all his reading and knowledge to penetrate its 'moral' as a 'motly emblem of my work'—it discloses no certain meaning, but offers multiple options. Its motley evokes the carnivalesque tradition behind *Tristram Shandy*, the tradition of folly and jest; but it also (like the dead and buried Yorick) yokes this tradition with death, marble being pre-eminently the material of funerary sculpture—of 'marbled Effigies and monumental Deposits', in the words of Henry Brooke.[65] In this respect the marbled page resumes the implications of the black page, which at its simplest level had seemed to illustrate Yorick's 'plain marble slabb'. But it also does more, for in its material form the marbled page suggests another oxymoron. Marble is an emblem of permanence or endurance, and a standard resource for poets concerned to promote the idea of printed verse as rendering immutable an otherwise fugitive life. In the classic statement of Shakespeare's sonnets, 'Not marble nor the gilded monuments I Of princes shall outlive this pow'rful rhyme, I But you shall shine more bright in these contents I Than unswept stone, besmeared with sluttish time'; and this trope—that printed words might prove more genuinely marmoreal than the real thing—is regularly echoed closer to Sterne's day. One example is by Robert Gould, who writes that, because even stone becomes dust, 'We must on *Paper*, not on *Marble*, write'; another is by Thomson, who writes of meanings eternally impressed, as though in some crescendo of increasing durability, 'on monumental Brass, I On sculptur'd Marble, on the deathless Page'.[66]

Marbled paper, however, renders this familiar trope palpably flimsy, and the surrounding context of *Tristram Shandy* affords little confidence in the capacity of printed volumes to bestow immortality on a life that, manifestly, is failing to fix on the page. Language too is decadent and mortal, and that recognition is everywhere in *Tristram Shandy*, from Walter's lament that the very names of antiquity 'are falling themselves by piece-meals to decay' (5.3.422) to Tristram's plangent last apostrophe to Jenny, in which 'every letter I trace tells me with what rapidity Life follows my pen' (9.8.754). Destined as it is for the gutter of time, the disintegrating

---

[65] Henry Brooke, *The Fool of Quality*, 5 vols. (1766–70), 4: 227.

[66] *Shakespeare's Sonnets*, ed. Stephen Booth (New Haven: Yale University Press, 1977), 48 (sonnet 55, ll. 1–4); Robert Gould, *Works* (1709), 68 ('Epitaph, on Mrs. Jane Roderick', l. 10); James Thomson, *Liberty, The Castle of Indolence and Other Poems*, ed. James Sambrook (Oxford: Clarendon Press, 1986), 137 (*Liberty*, pt. 5, ll. 389–90).

narrative Tristram writes is no place in which to look for marmoreal utterance, and here the marbled page suggests as much in another way. For it is also, vividly, a figure of disorder. By the 1730s marbled paper was widely used to cover books—'The paper gilt, & Cover marbled', as Swift puts it in another poem—and shortly afterwards for endpapers as well.[67] Positioned as it is in mid-volume, the marbled page thus does something comparable to the inverted numbering of pages in the volume to follow, identifying *Tristram Shandy* as a book turned inside out. This implication was clear to the reader who mockingly suggested, shortly after the publication of Sterne's second instalment, that 'Tristram's two pictures' should have been used to bind a particular half-mournful, half-jesting collection of verses, 'with a black cover on one side, and a marbled one on the other'.[68]

This idea of inversion apart, the swarming colours of the page also make it a figure of chaos (albeit controlled chaos), like the mid-twentieth-century 'poured paintings' by Jackson Pollock to which it is sometimes compared. Sterne may be asking us here to think about the process of marbling paper, much as other contemporary or near-contemporary writers turned to the technologies that materially produced their works as metaphors for literary effect.[69] The ability of the marbler to control the general design (by swirling, combing, or—as in most lifetime editions *Tristram Shandy*—just placing the spots of colour) cannot be exact, and each impression taken alters the next by disturbing the gelatinous fluid on which the colours float. The page thus emblematizes not only Tristram's efforts to fix on the page the flux of consciousness and experience, thereby creating a still image of something mobile and unstable—as mobile and unstable, perhaps, as consciousness in Hume's account of 'different perceptions . . . in a perpetual flux and movement'.[70] It also emblematizes the unpredictable flux of the text itself, in which intended structures go interminably awry, and an unruly pen governs the author (6.6.500). A further effect—that no one marbled page is identical with any other, so that, until

[67] *Poems of Swift*, 2: 463; see also Diana Patterson, 'Tristram's Marblings and Marblers', *Shandean*, 3 (1991), 70–97.

[68] See Peter de Voogd, ' "O. C." and the Marbled Page', *Shandean*, 2 (1990), 231–3 (at 231, quoting an item from the *London Chronicle*, 29 Jan. 1761).

[69] Smart uses type-founding to describe his poetic technique of giving 'an impression upon words by punching, that when the reader casts his eye upon 'em, he takes up the image from the mould which I have made' (*Jubilate Agno*, ed. Karina Williamson (Oxford: Clarendon Press, 1980), 69, l. B404). Blake's visionary writing, like the etchings that give it material form, works 'by corrosives . . . melting apparent surfaces away' (*The Marriage of Heaven and Hell*, ed. Geoffrey Keynes (Oxford: Oxford University Press, 1975), plate 14).

[70] David Hume, *A Treatise of Human Nature*, ed. L. A. Selby-Bigge, rev. P. H. Nidditch (Oxford: Clarendon Press, 1978), 252.

Fig. 4. MS inscription on the marbled page of the 'New Edition' (1768) of
Tristram Shandy, 3: 169: 'Mr. Tristram Shandy might much better imploy himself
in wrighting than sending a Marble Paper Leave in to the World.' Reproduced by
kind permission of Geoffrey Day.

our age of photographic reproduction, every set of *Tristram Shandy* is un-like the next—reflects this pervasive sense in Sterne's writing that recep-tion is unpredictable, that interpretative coherence is in the hands of the reader alone, and that hobby-horsical individuals will read to their own minds. From this point of view the page and the book it represents look more like Hermann Rorschach's inkblot test, a psychiatric tool in which interpretation of a randomly generated image displays only the inter-preter's mind. Or, as Elizabeth W. Harries less anachronistically adds, it re-sembles Alexander Cozens's late-eighteenth-century 'new method' of teaching drawing, in which chance blots suggest to the pupil a drawing to be realized.[71]

Amidst the proliferating connotations and interpretative possibilities of *Tristram Shandy*, no transcendent, authorially sanctioned meaning rises above the rest, either for the marbled page or for the work as a whole. And here is the final salient hint of this motley emblem: to look for definitive and authorized meaning, as Tristram here suggests we might, is to come up against a hard surface. Any effort 'to penetrate the moral of the next marbled page' is doomed from the start, as Sterne's carefully worded play on yet another proverbial quality in marble quietly tells us—marble being known above all (as in the passage from Sarah Fielding's *Remarks on Clarissa* cited above, p. 37) for its sheer impenetrability. The effort at inter-pretation must end in frustration—a frustration felt with resentment by the early reader who wrote as follows across the page (see Fig. 4): 'M[r]. Tristram Shandy might much better imploy himself in wrighting than sending a Marble Paper Leave in to the World.'[72] But this reader was wrong, and had missed the largest point of the marbled page, and of the work it emblematizes, which is that writing—even in the most accomplished or prolix instances of its 'new species'—can never quite do enough.

[71] Elizabeth W. Harries, *The Unfinished Manner: Essays on the Fragment in the Later Eighteenth Century* (Charlottesville, Va.: University Press of Virginia, 1994), 46.

[72] I am grateful to the owner of this copy, Geoffrey Day, for permission to reproduce the page; see also Day's comments on it in *From Fiction to the Novel*, 162.

PART TWO

The Serialization of *Tristram Shandy*

3

The Practice and Poetics
of Serial Fiction

No less significant than Sterne's experiments with the material resources
of print technology were his use of, and play on, a commercial innovation
that had been fuelling book-trade expansion since the 1730s: serial publication. Modern editions of *Tristram Shandy*, by rendering it stable and
complete as a material object, inevitably obscure this key dimension of the
work, and the radical fluidity thereby entailed. We can hold *Tristram
Shandy* entire in our hands from start to finish, consume it without
enforced interruption, move around it at will. It is easy to forget that its
original conditions of composition, transmission, and reception were very
different—that it was not only irregularly written across a period of more
than seven years, but also irregularly published in the intermissions of
writing, at every stage of which process the future shape and direction of
the text remained largely, or even wholly, unfixed.

Tristram Shandy's serialization is more than some mere nicety of bibliographical documentation, its very low profile as a topic in criticism
notwithstanding. The protracted and erratic accumulation of its original
volumes, and the protracted and interrupted experience of its original
readers, have major interpretative implications. Through the mechanism
of serialization, Sterne engineered something we need to view more as an
unstable process than as a static product—a process that, in the ongoing
story it performs about Tristram's struggle to write his life before interrupted by death, relies substantially for its meaning and effect on the time
it takes to unfold. This process or performance is now irrecoverable as
such; yet it is worth the effort of imaginatively reconstructing the experience of its first audience, for whom access to *Tristram Shandy* came in five
distinct stages of reading, phased over eighty-five months. To make this
effort is to see how Sterne renders open and active many of the themes that
dominate modern readings of the work: the resistance of memory and ongoing experience to textual capture; the human consciousness of time, and

the manipulation of time in narrative; 'the infirmities of ill health', and the shortfalls of 'this Fragment of Life' (*TS* 1, dedication). It is also to get a new perspective on the much-debated question of *Tristram Shandy*'s ending. The prolonged drama of digressive writing and progressive disease that serialization originally staged, in which Tristram fails to record his life in the past while watching it waste in the present, is brought in its seventh year, with death impending, to a climax that lends weight—albeit with important modifications—to the argument of Wayne Booth and others that Sterne contrives an ambiguous kind of closure in volume 9.

Yet to read *Tristram Shandy* as I do in the following two chapters—as a novel finished off in such a way as to simulate an unfinished memoir, the implied conclusion being the serial memoirist's death—is not to assimilate Sterne's work to the ideals of structural coherence and pre-planned unity that underlie the formalist case about closure. Though outline trajectories may have been envisaged by Sterne from the start, serialization entails an alternative set of characteristics—contingency, malleability, elasticity, improvisation—which dominate the progress of his text. It is hard to overestimate the effects on the work we now have of a process that mixed the normally distinct sequence of writing, printing, and reading into a tangle of overlapping, mutually imbricated events. Through the mechanism of serialization, *Tristram Shandy* could accumulate in a rolling state of openness to determination from without, and the consequences are both local and large. In its wittily haphazard registration of its own reception, the work exploits the inherent contingency and reciprocity of serial composition to brilliant effect, its dialogic inscriptions of response and counter-response making something palpable of Tristram's initial sense that writing must resemble conversation. Public and private events demonstrably condition the pace, and perhaps even the direction, of key elements of plot, the end of the Seven Years War between volumes 6 and 7 bringing Toby's campaigns to a matching end, and the decline of Sterne's health in the same interval producing a matching decline in Tristram's. Crucially, serialization also provided Sterne with a vehicle flexible and capacious enough to respond to unrelated texts and trends as they emerged during publication, endlessly renewing the fashionability of *Tristram Shandy* and its ongoing status as a cultural barometer.

Sterne was only one among several novelists to have experimented with serial publication in the period, when conditions, as argued in Chapter 2 above, seem to have required innovations not only in the form but also in the marketing of fiction. He produced, however, a uniquely exaggerated and self-conscious example, using methods distinctive enough to be recalled as a practical model, a century later, in the period we often mistakenly assume to have pioneered serial publication.[1] Victorian and eighteenth-century serialization, however, were markedly different in character, in ways evidently attributable to differences in the technologies and infrastructures that governed production and transmission in each period. (By the same token, serial fiction as driven now by Internet technology and dot.com entrepreneurship is different again, not least in the facility with which its interactive or participatory gestures outdo even Sterne's.[2]) Though *Tristram Shandy* was subject to a range of market pressures during production (from booksellers, readers, reviewers, and even writers of spurious instalments), Sterne could exercise a degree of authorial agency that was unavailable to his Victorian counterparts, many of whom saw the mode as constraining rather than empowering their writing, or as subordinating artistic freedom to an unyielding, quasi-industrial kind of discipline. The shift is epitomized by George Eliot during the writing of *Middlemarch*, when she looked incongruously back to *Tristram Shandy* for an ideal of creative autonomy that eluded her in practice.

The paradox is that Sterne used the freedom and control he enjoyed as a serialist to dramatize, in Tristram's writing, a condition of entrapment and chaos. From this point of view, *Tristram Shandy* can look uncannily like a

---

[1] Serial fiction is most simply defined as 'a continuing story over an extended time with enforced interruptions' (Linda K. Hughes and Michael Lund, *The Victorian Serial* (Charlottesville, Va.: University Press of Virginia, 1991), 1) or 'the division of narrative into separately issued instalments, usually for commercial convenience but occasionally for art' (John Sutherland, *Victorian Fiction: Writers, Publishers, Readers* (Basingstoke: Macmillan, 1995), 87). I use the term to denote all fiction first published this way, irrespective of variations in length of instalment, interval and regularity of issue, or vehicle of publication. A taxonomy of possible relevance to *Tristram Shandy* is attempted in Robert D. Mayo's history of early magazine fiction, which distinguishes between 'the *serial tale*, in which a story with a single intrigue or narrative action is simply divided into several installments, and published (usually) in successive numbers until completed', and '*episodic narrative*, which was very much more loosely organized than the serial tale and could presumably be resumed or abandoned by the author at will' (*The English Novel in the Magazines 1740–1815* (Evanston, Ill.: Northwestern University Press, 1962), 41–2). As the evidence in this chapter suggests, however, it is impossible in practice to sustain firm distinctions between planned, continuous, closed writing, on the one hand, and improvised, discontinuous, open-ended writing, on the other. We need to think in terms of a broad continuum of serial types, in which an irregular text like *Tristram Shandy* holds a position distant, but not categorically distinct, from a regular text like Smollett's *Sir Launcelot Greaves*.

[2] A trashily postmodern example is the collaborative mystery story, 'Murder Makes the Magazine', which accumulated in forty-six daily increments on the Amazon.com web site in summer 1997, topped and tailed by John Updike, but with forty-four intervening instalments contributed by visitors competing online for a daily cash prize. On interactive electronic fiction in general, see George P. Landow, *Hypertext 2.0* (Baltimore: Johns Hopkins University Press, 1997); David J. Bolter, *Writing Space: Computers, Hypertext, and the Remediation of Print*, 2nd edn. (Mahwah, NJ: Erlbaum, 2000).

parody of Victorian fiction, though not in the way alleged in Shklovskian readings of Sterne's work, which concentrate on representational technique to the neglect of publishing mode. Very specifically, the parodic exposure is of Victorian *serial* fiction, and of the organizational, temporal, and commercial dilemmas in which it entangled its exponents. This is not a chance effect, but one traceable to the special varieties of paradox and impasse thrown up by earlier exercises in serialization—and in the serialization not only of fiction but also of other genres, including autobiography, historiography, and encyclopaedias. The effect can be historicized, in other words, just as surely as we can historicize (along the lines argued in Chapters 1 and 2 above) *Tristram Shandy*'s parodic exposure of narrative conventions and mimetic illusions. Serializing *Tristram Shandy* enabled Sterne to explore the conflicts and contradictions inveterate in the serial mode—conflicts between openness and closure, continuation and totalization, expansiveness and coherence—while keeping pace and interacting, over seven years, with the changing literary and cultural environment through which he wrote.

PUBLISHING *MIDDLEMARCH*, 1871–1872

On 7 May 1871 George Henry Lewes reported to John Blackwood, George Eliot's publisher, that her novel in progress was running over length. Four volumes would be needed instead of the usual three—an idea that made Lewes wince, he admits, 'but the story must not be spoiled for want of space'. Acknowledging the conflict between authorial and publishing imperatives that Eliot's prolixity was generating, his letter proposes a scheme 'suggested by the plan Victor Hugo followed with his long *Misérables*—namely to publish it in *half-volume parts* either at intervals of one, or as I think better, two months'. Each half-volume would have 'a certain unity and completeness in itself', and sufficient matter

to furnish the town with talk for some time, and each part thus keep up and swell the general interest. *Tristram Shandy* you may remember was published at irregular intervals; and great was the desire for the continuation. Considering how slowly the public mind is brought into motion, this spreading of the publication over 16 months would be a decided advantage to the sale—especially as each part would contain as much as one ought to read at a time.[3]

---

[3] *The George Eliot Letters*, ed. Gordon S. Haight, 9 vols. (New Haven: Yale University Press, 1954–78) (hereafter *GEL*), 5: 145–6.

This was not the first time *Tristram Shandy* had been urged on Blackwood as a model, specifically in its form of publication, for maximizing currency and sales. As John Sutherland has noted, a similar situation had arisen two decades earlier, while Bulwer-Lytton was writing *My Novel; or, Varieties in English Life*. Realizing that this work too was outgrowing the standard three-decker format (to such an extent that he privately called it *The Boa Constrictor*), Lytton invoked Sterne, Richardson, and Cervantes to support his request for staggered publication in small volumes. 'For great *sales . . .* something great might be done by a popular book in a new shape,' he urged: 'Tristram Shandy and Clarissa Harlowe came out volume by volume—Don Quixote was published in parts.'[4]

It is hard to feel that any of these examples could have struck a pragmatic publisher as particularly auspicious. Hugo was already a byword for baggy digressiveness, and *Les Misérables* had been criticized by Lewes himself (in a review for *Blackwood's Magazine* in 1862) on just this issue.[5] *Clarissa* had been crammed into seven long volumes only by the messy expedient of switching to a smaller typeface in volume 6, and in its swollen third edition exceeded 3,000 pages. *Don Quixote* is no lightweight, and a full decade had intervened between its two massive parts of 1605 and 1615 (which a century later became the subject of separate experiments in instalment publication in English, once in a penny newspaper and once in monthly numbers).[6] *Tristram Shandy* is the work we know.

Yet with neither proposal does Blackwood seem to have smelled a rat. Though rejecting Lytton's request, he agreed to experiment with *Middlemarch* along the lines proposed by Lewes (so infuriating Lytton, who claimed intellectual property and wrote to protest).[7] Beginning in December 1871, the work came out a book at a time to a total of eight books, each designed to be bound with its pair into an accumulating four-volume set. The parts came out bi-monthly, accelerating to monthly intervals for the final two parts, so that the whole process was completed a year to the day from its start.

---

[4] Bulwer-Lytton, 12 Nov. 1849 (National Library of Scotland Blackwood MSS, 4086), cited in J. A. Sutherland, *Victorian Novelists and Publishers* (London: Athlone, 1976), 195. The following account is indebted to Sutherland's chapters on *Middlemarch* both here (pp. 188–205) and in his *Victorian Fiction* (pp. 107–13); also the editor's introduction to *Middlemarch*, ed. David Carroll (Oxford: Clarendon Press, 1986), and, on Eliot's earlier publications, Carol A. Martin, *George Eliot's Serial Fiction* (Columbus, Oh.: Ohio State University Press, 1994).

[5] Martin, *George Eliot's Serial Fiction*, 183–4, 313.

[6] R. M. Wiles, *Serial Publication in England before 1750* (Cambridge: Cambridge University Press, 1957), 34, 97–8.

[7] Sutherland, *Victorian Novelists and Publishers*, 203. *My Novel* was conventionally serialized in *Blackwood's Magazine* (1850–3) prior to book publication as a four-volume set (1853).

But why, in the Victorian heyday of serial fiction, should Lewes and Eliot (or Lytton before them) have felt the need to cite *Tristram Shandy*? Though Sterne and Richardson were not alone in serializing fiction in the mid-eighteenth century, the method never became standard practice, whereas a century later it had become a pervasive and familiar publishing mode for novels and much else besides. The answer seems to lie in the relatively haphazard, improvisatory character of the book trade in Sterne's day, as compared with the inflexible systems of what had genuinely become, by Eliot's time, a publishing industry.[8] Two distinct permutations of serial fiction—publication in parts and serialization in magazines—had become entrenched, neither having the flexibility that *Middlemarch* seemed to need. Inaugurated to massive success by *Pickwick Papers* (1836–7), the publication of novels in independent monthly parts was rapidly imitated by Dickens's competitors, and this (as Robert L. Patten writes) 'became for thirty years a chief means of democratizing and enormously expanding the Victorian book-reading and book-buying public'.[9] Dickens was to use this mode for nine of his novels; Thackeray published *Vanity Fair*, *Pendennis*, and other novels by numbers in the 1840s and 1850s; Trollope revived the method in the 1860s. 'Serialisation in monthly parts accounts for a rich slice of our canonised Victorian fiction,' John Sutherland writes, adding that all three of these authors, with now forgotten rivals like Harrison Ainsworth and Charles Lever, made the greatest gains of their literary careers by using this mode.[10]

Yet Dickens was already calling novels in numbers 'the old form' in 1841, and by the time George Eliot's career began the part-issued novel, commercially risky and never statistically predominant as a publishing mode, had been superseded by the monthly miscellanies and other fiction-carrying periodicals that thrived in its wake.[11] It was with this development—the magazine serialization of original fiction, which would only later appear in book form—that Victorian serial fiction hit its stride. Here again Dickens was to the fore with the piecemeal appearance in *Bentley's Miscellany* of *Oliver Twist* (1837–9) and his editorship from 1850 onwards of weekly papers (*Household Words* and then *All the Year Round*), which be-

---

[8] See Simon Eliot's overview, 'Some Trends in British Book Production, 1800–1919', in John O. Jordan and Robert L. Patten (eds.), *Literature in the Marketplace: Nineteenth-Century British Publishing and Reading Practices* (Cambridge: Cambridge University Press, 1995), 19–43.

[9] Robert L. Patten, *Charles Dickens and his Publishers* (Oxford: Clarendon Press, 1978), 45.

[10] Sutherland, *Victorian Novelists and Publishers*, 21; Sutherland, *Victorian Fiction*, 106.

[11] Sutherland, *Victorian Fiction*, 105 (quoting Dickens's notice 'To the Readers of "Master Humphrey's Clock"'), 102–3.

tween them carried *Hard Times*, *A Tale of Two Cities*, and *Great Expectations*, as well as several major novels by Gaskell and Collins. Magazine serialization reached its peak when in 1860 Blackwood's long-established monthly, *Blackwood's Magazine*, was challenged for pre-eminence by the lavishly financed *Cornhill*. Edited by Thackeray and opening with instalments of Thackeray's own *Lovel the Widower* and *Framley Parsonage* (the first of thirty-four novels that Trollope was to publish in one or the other version of serial form), the *Cornhill* burst on the scene with a six-figure monthly sale.[12] All the while the conventional three-decker product remained central to the Victorian fiction industry, feeding the circulating libraries with their undemanding staple diet while also accommodating some major non-serial novels. But it is little exaggeration to say that between *Pickwick Papers* and *Middlemarch* it was serial publication, either in shilling numbers or in magazines like the *Cornhill*, that most signally energized the production of fiction while also crucially shaping its forms and techniques.

Yet this was not what Lewes and Eliot wanted. Following the commercial failure of the three-decker *Felix Holt*, they shared Blackwood's sense of the need to contrive 'some innovation in form of publication' (20 Mar. 1867; *GEL* 4: 452). But they also wanted a more expansive and flexible mode, suitable to the scope and complexity of *Middlemarch*, than monthly magazine instalments or separate shilling numbers seemed to offer. Experience had associated monthly parts inseparably for Eliot with artistic compromise and personal crisis, and the idea of longer, slower *livraisons* was intended to circumvent the problems of space and time that had plagued her previous efforts as a serialist. Eliot was temperamentally no Lever, a novelist whose relish for market-led improvisation once made him ask his publisher, as *The O'Donoghue* (1845) neared completion, to choose for himself between an ending of 'Demosthenic abruptness in eleven numbers' or a more leisurely, romantic alternative 'with love and marriage licenses in thirteen numbers'.[13] Still less was she an eleventh-hour chancer like J. F. Smith, whose reputation was for turning up at the

---

[12] Mayo, *English Novel in the Magazines*, 11–12; see also John Sutherland, '*Cornhill*'s Sales and Payments: The First Decade', *Victorian Periodicals Review*, 19 (1986), 106–8. For Trollope, see Mary Hamer, *Writing by Numbers: Trollope's Serial Fiction* (Cambridge: Cambridge University Press, 1987), 182–6.

[13] Cited in Sutherland, *Victorian Novelists and Publishers*, 103. Sutherland notes that Lever's subsequent contract for *The Knight of Gwynne* (1847), specifying twelve parts but requiring him to stretch his material 'to twenty or any less quantity of numbers' if requested during publication, was not unusual (p. 102): commercial imperatives dictated an unyielding uniformity of unit length and regularity in Victorian serial production, but could vary the number of units.

printer's, scanning the end of his previous instalment, and locking himself away with a bottle of port to thrash out the next through the night.[14] Even scrupulous craftsmen like Collins and Dickens (for all their complaints that *The Woman in White* involved a 'weekly race' or that with *Hard Times* 'the difficulty of the space is CRUSHING'[15]) could thrive on the temporal and spatial constraints of serial form, fully aware that exigencies of production might assume as large a role as the creative will in shaping their output. Eliot could neither flourish in these conditions nor accept their power to enslave her muse in the unrelenting technologies and economies of the serial production line.[16] She never submitted to weekly publication like Collins and Dickens, resisting Dickens's efforts to procure from her a novel for *All the Year Round* on the grounds 'that *Time* is an insurmountable obstacle' (18 Nov. 1859; *GEL* 3: 205). Even the lighter discipline of monthly publication was oppressive. Blackwood was unusually flexible when running *Scenes of Clerical Life* through his magazine, but as serialization progressed, her appetite for leisurely contemplation forced him to issue one urgent warning, as his fear of a missed instalment grew, that 'it would be a serious disadvantage to baulk the public expectation now fairly raised' (10 Feb. 1857; *GEL* 2: 293). With *Adam Bede* Eliot confronted another of serialization's constraints, the impossibility of going back to alter chapters already in the public domain, and resisted 'the idea of beginning to print till . . . I know the end as well as the beginning' (17 Aug. 1859; *GEL* 3: 133).[17]

Eventually Eliot had Blackwood publish both *Adam Bede* and *The Mill on the Floss* as single-issue three-deckers, insisting that what she termed 'the Nightmare of the Serial' (20 Dec. 1859; *GEL* 3: 236), with its unyielding monthly timetable and its fragmentation of the whole into atomized parts, would harm both herself and her art. 'She fears the nervous excitement of the trial and thinks her story will tell better in a mass,' Blackwood reported (15 Dec. 1859; *GEL* 3: 236). Similar problems returned with the se-

[14] Hamer, *Writing by Numbers*, 17.

[15] Pierpont Morgan Library Collins MSS, cited in Sutherland, *Victorian Fiction*, 43; *The Letters of Charles Dickens*, ed. Walter Dexter, 3 vols. (London: Nonesuch, 1938), 2: 543, cited in John Butt and Kathleen Tillotson, *Dickens at Work* (London: Methuen, 1957), 203.

[16] See the materialist argument of Bill Bell, 'Fiction in the Marketplace: Towards a Study of the Victorian Serial', in Robin Myers and Michael Harris (eds.), *Serials and their Readers, 1620–1914* (Winchester: St Paul's Bibliographies, 1993), 124–44.

[17] Eliot's worry chimes with the criticism made of Thackeray by Trollope (who was unusual in tending to complete his serial novels before publication began): 'an artist should keep in his hand the power of fitting the beginning of his work to the end' (Anthony Trollope, *An Autobiography*, ed. Michael Sadleir and Frederick Page (Oxford: Oxford University Press, 1950), 138).

rialization of *Romola* in 1862–3, when Eliot's distaste for arbitrary division into bite sizes made her resist a *Cornhill* proposal for sixteen monthly instalments of twenty-four pages each. Despite negotiating a more flexible scheme, Eliot soon fell behind schedule, produced instalments of erratic length, and overshot by two the stipulated number of units. Partly the problem was poor health, but more crucial was her disinclination to parcel *Romola* into portions dictated by contractual obligation and production needs. Later she recalled that it was only the offer of 'a varying and unusual number of pages' that had made her assent to magazine serialization, adding that, 'if I could gain more by splitting my writing into small parts, I would not do it, because the effect would be injurious as a matter of art' (20 Oct. 1875; *GEL* 6: 179).

All such trouble would be avoided by *Middlemarch*'s Shandean plan— or that was the idea. The commercial advantages of serialization would be had (Lewes stresses the capacity of the mode to extend, or periodically renew, the metropolitan voguishness of new fiction), but without the aesthetic costs. Unlike the thirty-two-page units and twenty-part run of the typical serial novel, the five-shilling parts proposed for *Middlemarch* would let an unusually lengthy text appear in only eight instalments, thus avoiding the tendency of 'tea-spoonfull' measurements (the term is Dickens's)[18] to fragment overall structure. Each instalment would have the 'unity and completeness in itself' described by Lewes, and would share the capacity of her non-serial novels to 'tell better in a mass'. The parts, moreover, would be large enough to vary in length as artistic judgement dictated, the onus falling on Blackwood to disguise short measure in the briefer instalments by printing on bulkier paper. Bi-monthly publication would minimize the capacity of publishing deadlines to rush Eliot's writing, and this method would also let readers ponder *Middlemarch* at the intervals she thought fitting: 'the slow plan of publication', she later wrote, 'has been of immense advantage to the book in deepening the impression it produces' (4 Aug. 1872; *GEL* 5: 297). Here was another acknowledged benefit of serialization (which Lewes had earlier urged on Eliot when stressing the advantage to *Romola* 'of being read slowly and deliberately, instead of being galloped through in three volumes' (5 July 1862; *GEL* 8: 304)), stripped of the corresponding danger of fragmented access. In its slow expansiveness and ongoing accretions, as one influential reviewer saw, *Middlemarch* would simulate for its readers 'the only way in which human life itself . . . can be studied'.[19]

---

[18] *Letters of Charles Dickens*, 3: 131, cited in Sutherland, *Victorian Fiction*, 55.
[19] R. H. Hutton (*Spectator*, 7 Dec. 1872), cited in Hughes and Lund, *Victorian Serial*, 10–11.

And so, with breach of convention and irregularity of execution being the order of the day, what better precedent to cite than *Tristram Shandy*? Lewes perhaps cited it too in wry tacit acknowledgement of the trouble Eliot was having in organizing her plot, confining its length, and fighting her fear 'that I have too much matter, too many "momenti" ' (19 Mar. 1871; *GEL* 5: 137). It was only when serialization began, however, that the Shandean dilemma really hit her. Planning in her writing to keep three books (or six months) ahead of the press, she found herself behind from the start, and when recording in her journal the publication of book 1 she adds that she ought 'by this time to have finished the fourth Part, but an illness . . . has robbed me of two months.' Book 4 took three full months to compose, cutting her buffer from six to four months, and setting a trend that, if continued, would mean that the final instalment (book 8) would have to be printed before it had been written. 'It is now the last day but one of January,' a later entry in Eliot's journal records: 'I have finished the Fourth Part . . . and the Second Part will be published the day after tomorrow.'[20] Writing book 5 took three further months, whittling the buffer down more. Where an expert serialist like Trollope would hold himself obsessively to hourly rates of production, monitoring his output on special charts,[21] Eliot could drift for days without writing a sentence. *Middlemarch* never suffered the involuntary interruption that occasionally affected serial novels: *Pickwick Papers* on Dickens's bereavement in 1837, for example, or Thackeray's *Pendennis* during a life-threatening illness of 1849. But the struggle to keep up took its toll. By 13 February Lewes reports Eliot '*thin* with misery' (*GEL* 5: 246). In May she is still in a 'swamp of illness with only here and there a bit of firm walking', her journal laments: 'I have still three Books to write.'[22]

Time was not the sum of Eliot's troubles, however, and in other ways *Middlemarch* typifies the pressures crowding in on Victorian serial writers. Part-publication exercised special demands of plot, requiring the novelist to reconcile the rival structural claims of part and whole, ensure that all storylines remained in view across each instalment, and keep readers hooked through effective serial breaks. In the opening books she struggled to hold these competing imperatives in balance, concentrating on the integrity of each individual instalment while Blackwood worried about 'the want of . . . continuous interest' between them (20 July 1871; *GEL* 5: 168). Later Blackwood's anxieties were recognized when Lewes reported her de-

---

[20]   1 Dec. 1871, cited in *Middlemarch*, ed. Carroll, p. xl; 30 Jan. 1872, cited on p. xliii.
[21]   Hamer, *Writing by Numbers*, 41.
[22]   8 May 1872, cited in *Middlemarch*, ed. Carroll, p. xlv.

cision to transpose passages from book 2 into book 1, explaining that 'this new arrangement not only pitches the interest forward . . . but also equalizes quantities better' (7 Sept. 1871; *GEL* 5: 184). A growing sense of the need to keep readers in touch with all the threads of a multiple plot posed subsequent problems, however. Bits of text kept turning up in the wrong place, or would seem from different points of view to have rival potential right places. Chapters were moved from instalment to instalment as Eliot's original emphasis on distinctness of units gave way to more frequent switches between competing storylines (and it has required a book-length study to trace the shifting combinations of the novel's parts[23]). Sometimes the changes were last minute, as when Eliot belatedly decided that four chapters from book 3 belonged properly in book 2, and Lewes was forced to send Blackwood urgent instructions as the type was being set.[24] Here the reorganization marked a retreat from Eliot's original plan to exclude her heroine entirely from book 2, and shows her growing sense of the serial's special demands. As time went on she made skilful use of even its most lowbrow conventions, notably in the cliffhanger endings to book 3 (Featherstone's death) and book 7 (Dorothea's melodramatic resolution to 'find out the truth and clear him!'). But Eliot contrived these endings with some reluctance, attributing the suspenseful conclusion of book 3 to Lewes's insistence, and noting with anxiety that it made the instalment disproportionately short. Blackwood's remedy for the short-weight instalments was not only bulkier paper but also copious endpaper advertisements for, among other things, another great incremental product of the age, the Mutual Life Assurance Society's Scottish Widows' Fund.[25]

As if all these organizational problems were not enough, *Middlemarch*'s serial timetable also meant that Eliot's struggles with the structure, content, and length of instalments involved a fourth dimension. More than half the novel was unwritten when publication began, exposing the work as a result to the characteristic reciprocity and contingency of serial fiction—its capacity to be marked or swayed in the writing by its own reception, and by other matters arising. Trollope famously describes the dramatic effect on *The Last Chronicle of Barsetshire* of an overheard conversation about Mrs Proudie that made him resolve to 'go home and kill her off before the week is over'.[26] It is hard to imagine Eliot shaping her

[23] Jerome Beaty, *Middlemarch from Notebook to Novel: A Study of George Eliot's Creative Method* (Urbana, Ill.: University of Illinois Press, 1960).

[24] *Middlemarch*, ed. Carroll, pp. xl–xlii.

[25] Martin, *George Eliot's Serial Fiction*, 200, 185.

[26] Trollope, *An Autobiography*, 275.

plots with such exuberant opportunism, and no difference will have been made to *Middlemarch* by the early pressure she experienced to bump off Mr Casaubon. Carol Martin has plausibly argued, however, that the eleventh-hour resumption of Dorothea's story in book 2 was in reaction to reviews of book 1, which impressed on Lewes and Eliot the inadvisability of leaving her in limbo for a whole instalment. Elsewhere the writing of *Middlemarch* was demonstrably complicated or changed by reader response to previous parts, or by coincidental developments at the time. Book 5 hastily incorporates legal information supplied by a barrister who had written to correct a technical error. Earlier Eliot had become engrossed in a celebrated inheritance scandal in the civil courts, the Tichborne case, which affected the prominence belatedly given to Featherstone's will in book 3, appearing as it did when public interest in the case was at its peak.[27]

Other developments compounded the pressure as Eliot continued to write: a marked decline in sales between books 1 and 2, which, though it then levelled, left numbers thousands short of expectations. Then there was Eliot's lingering anxiety that, for all the short measure of individual instalments, the novel overall, like *Romola*, might still overshoot its projected space. 'Still,' she wrote as the fifth part of *Middlemarch* appeared, 'I shudder to think what a long book it will be—not so long as Vanity Fair or Pendennis, however, according to my calculation' (4 Aug. 1872; *GEL* 5: 297). The comparison was not casual, since Thackeray's novels were prime examples of the inherent enmity between serialization and ideal form.[28] *Vanity Fair* had begun with an open-ended contract, almost came to a premature end after disastrous sales of the third instalment, and was still unfixed in length as late as the fifteenth: the result was that Thackeray had no incentive to plan or compose ahead. 'At the end of the month I always have a life-&-death struggle to get out my number of Vanity Fair,' he wrote.[29] *Pendennis* was likewise written close to each deadline and with constant improvisation, and in the end Thackeray opportunistically stretched its run by four numbers. 'This book began with a very precise plan, which was entirely put aside,' he serenely observes in the volume edi-

[27] Martin, *George Eliot's Serial Fiction*, 27, 191–8, 13–14, 199–201.

[28] Sutherland, *Victorian Novelists and Publishers*, 101–4; Sutherland, *Victorian Fiction*, 95–7.

[29] *The Letters and Private Papers of William Makepeace Thackeray*, ed. Gordon N. Ray, 4 vols. (Oxford: Oxford University Press, 1945–6), 2: 346, cited by Edgar F. Harden, *The Emergence of Thackeray's Serial Fiction* (Athens, Ga.: University of Georgia Press, 1979), 8.

tion, attributing to its serial origins its tendency to 'fail in art, as it constantly does and must'.[30]

Few would accuse Eliot of being lured by serialization into Thackeray's baggy forms (though Henry James thought *Middlemarch* 'a mere chain of episodes, broken into accidental lengths and unconscious of the influence of a plan'[31]). Eliot would never have sacrificed structure to gratify the kind of reader demand once archly expressed by Elizabeth Gaskell, who wished that 'Mr Trollope would go on writing Framley Parsonage for ever'.[32] In many ways the novel triumphantly reconciles Eliot's long-term ambitions for the work with the transient imperatives of serialization, and in the process she conquered her aversion to the form. Eventually, indeed, she was far enough ahead to bring forward publication of the ending, and afterwards remained strongly enough attached to the original serial divisions to retain them (as was highly unusual) in volume editions of the novel.

Yet for most of the period of production, and whatever the poise and control of the text itself, *Middlemarch* had been a strenuous and sometimes frantic exercise in crisis management. As the process drew to its close, Eliot resumed her figures of swamps and bad dreams to write of the year 'having been a sort of nightmare in which I have been scrambling on the slippery bank of a pool, just keeping my head above water' (19 Aug. 1872; *GEL* 5: 301). Far from lifting her clear of the frenzied conditions in which Victorian serialists worked, her Shandean plan for *Middlemarch* had simply plunged her further in. The only surprise is that both Eliot and Lewes knew *Tristram Shandy* well,[33] and should have known what to expect.

PUBLISHING *TRISTRAM SHANDY*, 1759–1767

There are huge differences, of course, between the publishing histories of *Middlemarch*, which occupied a year, and *Tristram Shandy*, which

[30] W. M. Thackeray, *The History of Pendennis*, ed. John Sutherland (Oxford: Oxford University Press, 1994), p. lv.

[31] Henry James, *The Critical Muse: Selected Literary Criticism*, ed. Roger Gard (London: Penguin, 1987), 75.

[32] 'I don't see any reason why it should ever come to an end, and every one I know is always dreading the *last* number,' she adds (*The Letters of Mrs Gaskell*, ed. J. A. V. Chapple and Arthur Pollard (Manchester: Manchester University Press, 1966), 602).

[33] Eliot and Lewes read *Tristram Shandy* together at least twice, in 1859 (*GEL* 2: 493) and 1873 (*GEL* 5: 368 n.).

occupied seven. Nor are these simply a matter of relative pace and duration. *Middlemarch* had its number of instalments, intervals of publication,
and overall length prescribed before publication started, and meticulous
plans for its extrapolation had been prepared in line with Eliot's determination never to publish an opening until sure that her ending would fit. No
firm structures seem to have been in place when *Tristram Shandy* began its
run. Even choice of publisher was a matter of ongoing improvisation, with
Sterne bringing out the inaugural volumes himself and negotiating instalment by instalment thereafter. (The result is that a true first edition of
Tristram Shandy mixes, properly speaking, the output of three publishers:
Sterne himself, the brothers Dodsley, and Becket and Dehondt.[34]) Here
Lewes's term for the publication of *Tristram Shandy*—'irregular'—barely
catches its haphazard, intermittent, opportunistic progress through the
press. It has been influentially argued that Sterne always knew how
Tristram Shandy would end, and I address this debate in the chapter to
follow.[35] Setting aside the whimsical suggestions of Tristram himself,
however, there is no good evidence that Sterne knew from the start, or even
at much later stages, how many volumes he would fill before reaching this
end, how many years the process would take, or just what would come in
between. Plenty of evidence points the opposite way.

The basic facts are that *Tristram Shandy* came out in four long instalments of two volumes apiece and a fifth and final instalment of a single
volume; the dates respectively December 1759, January 1761, December
1761, January 1765, January 1767; the intervals respectively thirteen months,
eleven months, thirty-seven months, twenty-four months. Irregular
indeed; and, as Sterne's letters on the subject clearly show, the result of an
open-ended process of improvisation in which alternative possibilities, alternative futures or non-futures for *Tristram Shandy*, were always potentially in play. From start to finish, indeed, the work typifies and exaggerates
the characteristic elasticity of serial writing—its capacity to be suspended,
interrupted, protracted, or curtailed as commercial or personal exigencies
might require. Sterne's first recorded proposals (in letters to Dodsley)
speak of *Tristram Shandy* as a semi-annual publication of one or two volumes at a time. On 23 May 1759 he urges immediate publication of a single
volume, already seeing some kind of serial or time-lapse method as necessarily implied by his subject: 'If You publish it now—a 2ᵈ Volume will be

[34] On the composition and publication of *Tristram Shandy*, see *TS Notes*, 814–31; *EMY*
278–97; *LY, passim*.
[35] Wayne Booth, 'Did Sterne Complete *Tristram Shandy?*', *Modern Philology*, 48 (1951),
172–83.

ready by Christmas, or Nov^r—the Reason for some such Interval, you will better see in reading the Book' (*Letters*, 74). In October he proposes to publish a pair of volumes himself and then 'bargain with you, if possible, for the rest as they come out, which will be every six months' (*Letters*, 80); in January 1760 the same implication of relentless recurrence returns when he mentions his design in *Tristram Shandy* 'of raising a tax upon the public' (*Letters*, 89). Thereafter, however, Sterne quietly drops the ideas first of such rapidity, and then of such regularity, as this. Tristram forecasts a pattern of annual publication (1.14.42), and this promise is roughly fulfilled by Sterne's timing of the first three instalments. But the process then becomes flexible enough to be suspended by two much longer intervals, as dictated by the rhythms of authorial health, inclination, travels, and (notably in 1762–4) bouts of writer's block. The only consistent pattern to be found lies in the appearance of a *Tristram Shandy* instalment every winter between 1759–60 and 1766–7 that Sterne chose to spend in England. (This was of course the season for publishing novels, which 'generally usher in the Winter as snow-drops do the Spring', as the *Critical Review* once wearily put it.[36])

As for the number of volumes to be written, here again improvisation is the key. Though clearly hoping that *Tristram Shandy* will accumulate on a large scale, Sterne in his surviving letters nowhere commits himself to a final total (though Tristram is sure of finding enough Gaskells in his public to fantasize about eighty volumes). Instead he presents the work as an ongoing process of indefinite extent, forever liable to be pursued or dropped at will. His first letter to Dodsley talks only of a future '2^d Volume', and his next unspecifically of 'the rest' as they appear. When four are in print, he declares that *Tristram Shandy* is his 'hobby-horse', which—echoing Tristram (1.14.42)—he will continue 'as long as I live' (21 Sept. 1761; *Letters*, 143). While writing the ninth and last volume five years later, he announces that he will publish 'but one this year, and the next I shall begin a new work of four volumes, which when finish'd, I shall continue Tristram with fresh spirit' (23 July 1766; *Letters*, 284). Weeks later, however, he seems to have changed his mind, and talks of publishing 'the 9th & 10 of Shandy the next winter' (30 Aug. 1766; *Letters*, 288). Then, when winter arrives, he regrets (in a favourite trope of composition as childbirth) that he has just 'miscarried of my tenth Volume by the violence of a fever' (?7–9 Jan. 1767; *Letters*, 294). Internal evidence suggests that elements from this abortive volume 10 may in fact have been salvaged to round off volume 9, but the

---

[36] *Critical Review*, 2 (Oct. 1756), 276.

prospect of again attempting this volume is explicitly revoked in no surviving source from Sterne's own pen.

Yet if on the one hand *Tristram Shandy* could be kept going *sine die*,
Sterne's thinking is clearly that on the other it could be curtailed at any
point, as reception, death, or just plain boredom might dictate. His first
letters present the first instalment as experimental, a testing of the market
or '*coup d'essai*' to be extended only 'if this 1st Volume has a run' or, again, 'if
my book sells and has the run our critics expect' (*Letters*, 81, 74, 80). In a
memorandum drawn up in December 1761 'in Case I should die abroad', he
envisages the work as it might be cut off by his own demise after volumes 5
and 6, the copyright to which he bequeaths (*Letters*, 146–7). Thereafter, his
anxious enquiries to Becket about sluggish sales of these two volumes in
1763–4—'Have you sold any Shandys since Christmas? how many?'
(*Letters*, 211)—do much to explain his simultaneous failure to produce
their successors, which must for a while have seemed unmarketable; and
when he does at last make progress in autumn 1764 it is not clear whether
he means this fourth instalment alone or the serial as a whole when he talks
of being now at work 'to finish Tristram' (*Letters*, 228). In the event,
Tristram Shandy of course continues into a fifth instalment and ninth volume of January 1767, and it is only the following September that we hear,
in a letter by Sterne's friend Richard Griffith, of his subsequent resolution
'never to write any more *Tristrams*' (*LY* 261). Griffith's credibility, however,
is not enhanced by his subsequent career as a forger of Sterneiana (*LY*
307–8), and for all the internal evidence of implied closure in volume 9 it
remains possible, and certainly unfalsifiable, that it is only Sterne's death a
few months later that deprives us of volume 10, or indeed of volume 80.

Always represented by its author as an open-ended, ongoing sequence,
and not as some marmoreal text of fixed extent, *Tristram Shandy* was
understood by even its most hostile early readers in just this way. In *A
Funeral Discourse, Occasioned by the Much Lamented Death of Mr. Yorick*
(1761), 'Christopher Flagellan' floats the idea that only Dodsley's greed was
perpetuating a text that now might already have ended: 'I gave him two
Volumes of pretty good stuff', Sterne is made to declare, 'and the unexpected sale of them made him yawn after twenty' (*CH* 133). After the third
instalment, it became a standard complaint that Sterne had invented a
'method of *protraction* or art of *continuation*' designed as a way 'of retain-
ing the reader *ad infinitum*',[37] and in the anonymous *Jack and His Whistle*

---

[37] *The Life, Travels, and Adventures of Christopher Wagstaff, Gentleman, Grandfather to
Tristram Shandy*, 2 vols. (1762), 1: xi, 1: 35; cited by René Bosch, *Labyrinth of Digressions:
Tristram Shandy in Engeland in de Achttiende Eeuw* (Utrecht: Gottmann & Fainsilber Katz,
1999), 93.

. . . *To Which is Added, A Paper Dropt from Tristram Shandy's Pocket-Book* (1762), Sterne is given the exuberant boast that 'to testify my contempt of the public taste . . . ten thousand [volumes], if I should live to write them, would not suffice' (*CH* 148). When Hume more soberly comments at around this time that the six-volume *Tristram Shandy* 'may perhaps go on a little longer', he recognizes its status as a serial of adjustable length and duration, and William Rider does the same when pronouncing it 'absurd to continue a Work of so ludicrous a Nature so long' (*CH* 147, 151). The point returns after the fourth instalment of 1765, when Ralph Griffiths in the *Monthly Review*, though expecting Sterne to move on now to volumes 9 and 10, advises him to 'stop where you are', the reason being that the public 'will have *had enough*, by the time they get to the end of your eighth volume' (*CH* 167).

As for Johnson's famous comment of 1776 ('Nothing odd will do long. *Tristram Shandy* did not last'), Johnson cannot have been referring, as is often assumed, to the waning popularity of a work that was republished in at least seventeen London and Dublin editions of the 1770s. His words make sense only as describing the curtailment in volume 9 (at a time when sales really were in decline) of a potentially longer project, 'last' being used here in the sense of 'continue' rather than 'endure'.[38]

Where serial publication leaves Eliot scrambling on the banks of a pool, in short, we find Sterne instead riding a wave—steering an improvised course, at any rate, through the ebbs and flows of market forces and authorial impulse. Their rival priorities as serialists are sharply divergent, and come close to enacting the famous distinction between completed text and continuous writing that for Northrop Frye defined 'an age of sensibility'.[39] Where Eliot keeps in view a specific final product that the serialized text will progressively disclose, serialization offers Sterne a more amenable kind of process, something flexible, open-ended, potentially interminable indeed, and always responsive to whatever shifts of circumstance or priority might come into play. Ever the opportunist, ever the extemporist, he remains non-committal about the shape and scale of the text as it erratically grows under his hands. This is not necessarily to say that *Tristram Shandy* had no plan; but it is to say that any such plan could never have been more than provisional, that it had contingency built into its structure, and was always ready to accommodate change or chance.

There is a practical difference here, which aligns Sterne rather more with the average Victorian hand-to-mouth hack than with Eliot herself.

---

[38] *CH* 219; see also Johnson's *Dictionary* (1755), s.v. 'To Last'. On the reduced print run, slow sales, and unenthusiastic reception of volume 9, see *LY* 265–6.

[39] Northrop Frye, 'Towards Defining an Age of Sensibility', *ELH* 23 (1956), 144–52.

When any given instalment of *Middlemarch* was published, Eliot (for all her fear of falling behind) had already completed at least one instalment to follow, and was writing further ahead. Whatever her deviations on points of detail, moreover, she was doing so along the lines of a predetermined plan. Sterne was never ahead of himself like this, and seems never to have begun composing an instalment until months after its predecessor had appeared. The only possible exception to this pattern comes at the very outset, in mid-1759, when Sterne may have had among his papers (if we credit an anonymous but plausible report dated 15 April 1760) 'more than would make four such volumes as those two he has published' (*CH* 57). But most if not all of this putative material, satirizing learned divinity and the controversy about Job, was never used, and if any small part of it did ever get recycled, it was transformed with a thoroughness measurable by the enormous gulf in style and mode between the 'Rabelaisian Fragment' as posthumously published in 1775 (or, more accurately, in Melvyn New's transcription of 1972) and *Tristram Shandy* proper.

The result of this improvisatory process was a free-wheeling text able to generate its own continuation (at least in part) from audience responses to each preceding instalment, as well as from other ongoing events. Far from wishing to contrive the impression of a self-contained whole, indeed, Sterne revelled in opportunities to base later parts of the work on material he could not have envisaged until earlier parts were out. Conspicuously, *Tristram Shandy* is a work that responds to its own reception, and it uses the serial form to make something far less abstract than is often assumed of Tristram's initial sense that writing should become 'a different name for conversation' (2.11.125). Reception acts most obviously on the text in Tristram's allusions to reviews of preceding instalments, to which reviewers could then respond when reviewing the next, thereby perpetuating a genuinely conversational dynamic that peaks with the fourth instalment, when both the *Critical* and *Monthly* reviewers pick up and play on Tristram's idea of meanings left 'to be settled by | The REVIEWERS OF MY BREECHES' (7.32.632; see *CH* 160, 164). The whole trajectory of the serial could be affected by this conversation, notably in a shift of emphasis towards benevolence and pathos (reaching its climax, however equivocal, in the Maria episode of volume 9), which has long been thought to answer calls from the *Monthly Review* and elsewhere for the injection of a more sentimental tone.[40]

---

[40] Rufus Putney, 'The Evolution of *A Sentimental Journey*', *Philological Quarterly*, 19 (1940), 349–69 (at 363–5); see also Frank Donoghue's reformulation of this case in *The Fame*

The same applies to more local details, some of which appear to rework imitations and parodies of the first instalment, which reflected back to Sterne, and suggested new potential for developing, his original emphases. His gleeful response to the earliest pamphlet attacks—'I wish they would write a hundred such' (*Letters*, 107)—stems not only from a modern sense that no publicity can ever be bad, but also from the opportunities presented within them for generating further new text. It is likely that *Yorick's Meditations*, in responding to ideas of reader intervention from the first instalment (the author is shown 'labouring with a thought; and I could wish some judicious critic would lend his kind obstetric hand to help to deliver me of it'[41]), in turn inspired the new twist given these ideas in the second, when Tristram asks critics to help him get Walter and Toby off the stairs (4.3.340–1). Other instances are itemized by Anne Bandry, including two examples of missing chapters in imitations of the first instalment (the spurious volume 3 of *Tristram Shandy*, and *The Life and Opinions of Jeremiah Kunastrokius*), both of which anticipate Sterne's much wittier development of this device in volume 4 (4.25.372). Bandry puts it nicely when describing 'une sorte de chassé-croisé entre les revues, les volumes de Sterne et les imitations', in which *Tristram Shandy*—famously (or notoriously) a text that generates itself by recycling the texts of others—now extends the intertextual loop by imitating its own imitations, or stealing back from the thieves.[42]

Nor was the plasticity of *Tristram Shandy* responsive only to printed sources. If rumour is true, private interventions could determine major elements of plot as serialization went on, as when Bishop Warburton reportedly took fright at rumours that he was to be lampooned as Tristram's tutor and pre-empted potential whole volumes by buying Sterne off (*LY* 5–8). On a smaller scale, Warburton could also generate text (albeit involuntarily), when a passage in the third instalment mockingly reworks the letter of advice he sent to Sterne on publication of the first (*TS* 5.20.453; see Florida note to ll. 5–6). At the same time, *Tristram Shandy* could respond to unrelated developments in the external world, as the dedication to volume 9 jestingly does by playing on the fact that the commoner to whom volume 1 is dedicated has in the interim become a peer: 'Having, *a priori*,

Machine: Book Reviewing and Eighteenth-Century Literary Careers (Stanford, Calif.: Stanford California Press, 1996), 56–85.

[41] *Yorick's Meditations upon Various Interesting and Important Subjects* (1760), 38.

[42] Anne Bandry, 'Imitations of *Tristram Shandy*', in Melryn New (ed.), *Critical Essays on Lawence Sterne* (New York: G. K. Hall, 1998), 39–52 (at 49); Anne Bandry, *Tristram Shandy: Créations et imitations en Angleterre au XVIIIe siècle* (Paris: Université de la Sorbonne Nouvelle, 1991), 245.

intended to dedicate *The Amours of my uncle Toby* to Mr. [Pitt]——I see more reasons, *a posteriori,* for doing it to Lord [Chatham]' (9, dedication, 733). It could draw on developing personal experience, including experience directly attributable to publication of the earlier parts. In the second and third instalments, apostrophes to 'my dear friend *Garrick*' (3.24.246; 6.29.549) address a celebrity whose friendship was gained only when Sterne speculatively sent him the first (*LY* 4). In the fourth instalment, a whole volume draws on a journey through France that Sterne did not undertake until the previous instalments were published, and that he could not have undertaken without the proceeds he had gained from these instalments. Here *Tristram Shandy* beautifully anticipates, and exaggerates, the innovative cost-effectiveness of Victorian serial fiction—its capacity to recirculate a publisher's cashflow, so that sale of each succeeding part would finance production of the next.[43] Now even the imaginative content of the serial arises from the success of earlier parts, the income generated by volumes 1 to 6 serving in turn to generate the plot of volume 7.

For Sterne, in short, all the difficulties of schedule and organization that bedevilled the serialization of *Middlemarch,* and all the contingent pressures that simultaneously threatened its integrity as a unified whole, were not problems but opportunities—opportunities to engineer a publishing process, a reading experience, and an incrementally growing text that could thrive on contingency. He cheerfully discarded the compartmentalized model of literary production to which Eliot always at heart subscribed, in which a text crafted in Parnassian isolation is only then handed down, unmodified by mode of publication or readerly desire, to be printed, sold, and read in the world below. The neat categories of this traditional model are ceaselessly disrupted by the overlapping composition, publication, and reception of serial fiction, and Sterne embraced the results. If Eliot thought *Tristram Shandy* a recipe for escaping the Thackerayan instability of serial writing, indeed, she could hardly have been more wrong. The work, on the contrary, is an uncanny anticipation of all the tendencies she most deplored.

It is also a very knowing anticipation—for to turn from Sterne's experience to that of his narrator is to see that serial writing is not only the method of *Tristram Shandy,* but also a part of its subject. Here is a work that brilliantly dramatizes, indeed satirizes, the various pressures involved in writing *pari passu* with publication. Assailed as he proceeds by 'lets and confounded hinderances' and other 'unforeseen stoppages' (1.14.41–2),

⁴³ Patten, *Dickens and his Publishers,* 54.

Tristram's role is precisely that of the frantic and disorganized serialist, whose struggles to produce a viable text in the face of a publishing process already in train wittily exaggerate the problems that Victorian novelists like Eliot were later to face. The difference is that *Tristram Shandy* gleefully displays on its surface all the technical tricks, obstructions, and interferences that his successors strove to conceal.

Consider, for example, the serial breaks. Like Eliot, Tristram is keenly aware of the need to keep his readers hooked and buying, but his own efforts to arouse suspense have none of her dexterity. At the end of the first instalment he bossily writes that 'the reader will be content to wait for a full explanation of these matters till the next year,—when a series of things will be laid open which he little expects' (2.19.181). The second break is similarly vague, promising next year to 'lay open a story to the world you little dream of' (4.32.402). This time Tristram does at least try to raise specific expectations, eagerly insisting on his ability to maintain continuity: 'the first chapter of my next volume, if I live, shall be my chapter upon WHISKERS, in order to keep up some sort of connection in my works' (4.32.400). But a year later he finds himself trapped by his advance commitment, regretting 'as inconsiderate a promise as ever entered a man's head' (5.1.409).

Tristram's lack of finesse as a serialist further appears in his treatment of reviews—an area of textual management in which, as so often, the gap between Sterne and the incompetent persona he adopts is immense. Like many Victorian novelists who used reviews to tailor their developing texts to audience expectations and tastes, Eliot absorbs the content of early reviews and where necessary modifies her plan—more modestly than most of her contemporaries, however, and always silently. Tristram's contrasting failure to conceal the reviewers' power over his text brings this feature ludicrously to the surface. In the second instalment, he peevishly protests at the cruelty of 'Messrs. the monthly Reviewers' (3.4.190) and thinks aloud about how to please them in future (3.20.229). The competition he then sets up to remedy the impasse on the staircase—'I am very willing to give any one of 'em a crown to help me' (4.13.340)—carries him far from the compositional method he later attributes to himself, of writing one sentence and then 'trusting to Almighty God for the second' (8.2.656). In the true fashion of the market-led serial, it is the reviewers who come to hold sway; and in this respect Sterne presciently registers, in Tristram's fatuous thoughts aloud, a determining condition of novel production that, newly influential in his own day, would become more so in the century to follow.

More extensively treated in *Tristram Shandy* are the issues of time and space that pressed on even the most organized serial writers. Like Eliot with her 'too many "momenti"', Tristram finds himself burdened by too much raw material for his allotted space, so that his text threatens, more even than hers, to proliferate out of control. 'In short, there is no end of it,' he sees within pages: 'for my own part, I declare I have been at it these six weeks, making all the speed I possibly could,—and am not yet born' (1.14.42). Already he has plans for a twentieth volume (1.13.40), and he soon begins to talk of going on at two volumes a year for forty years (1.22.82). Perplexed throughout by 'what he is to put into it,—and what he is to leave out' (3.23.244), he eventually finds himself assailed by too much material for even the most capacious text. One expanding topic is compressed into 'a sketch, and will be finished, if I conjecture right, in three pages (but there is no guessing)'; the full version 'will take up as many books', and must wait for a separate work (6.21.536). Other topics fare worse. The text is littered by unfulfilled promises of future inclusion, involving not only chapters of opinion that Tristram then apologizes for failing to deliver (5.8.434) but also central parts of his life: 'who my *Jenny* is', for example (4.32.401), or his continental travels of 1741 (a year his narrative never gets near) 'with Mr. *Noddy*'s eldest son . . . of which original journey perform'd by us two, a most delectable narrative will be given in the progress of this work' (1.11.26). With hostages to fortune like this, ineradicable from the text at later stages because of part-publication, Tristram is made to resemble the hapless serialist once imagined by Thomas Hardy, who struggles to develop ill-considered openings that 'may, in a rash moment, have been printed in some popular magazine before the remainder is written'.[44] Elsewhere his efforts to cram everything in lead only to panic and chaos. In a well-known passage, the linear flow of his narrative is interrupted by exponential proliferations of detail: 'fifty things more necessary to let you know first . . . a hundred difficulties . . . a thousand distresses and domestic misadventures crouding in upon me thick and three-fold' (3.38.278). Incompatible levels of narrative time jockey for position in the text—'a cow broke in (to-morrow morning) to my uncle *Toby*'s fortifications'—while the time of Tristram's own narration fails to keep pace: 'but there is no time to be lost in exclamations.——— I have left my father lying across his bed, and my uncle *Toby* in his old fringed chair, sitting beside him, and promised I would go back to them in

---

[44] Thomas Hardy, 'Candour in English Fiction' (1890), cited in Bell, 'Fiction in the Marketplace', 127.

half an hour, and five and thirty minutes are laps'd already.——Of all
the perplexities a mortal author was ever seen in,—this certainly is the
greatest' (3.38.278).

With so much matter to narrate, Tristram's predicament mockingly
encapsulates the serialist's abiding problem of how to keep different elements of a multiple plot simultaneously in view. Like Eliot, he has to keep
his audience in touch with its various threads as they develop across instalments, while at the same time maintaining the integrity of separate
parts. Here again he is frank about his dilemma from an early stage, thinking it 'so long since the reader . . . has been parted from the midwife, that
it is high time to mention her again to him, merely to put him in mind that
there is such a body still in the world'. The mention is made more necessary, he adds, by the potential he now sees for further delay: 'fresh matter
may be started, and much unexpected business fall out betwixt the reader
and myself, which may require immediate dispatch' (1.13.39). At this stage
Tristram seems confident enough of his organizational powers: of the origins of Toby's wound, 'it would be running my history all upon heaps to
give it you here.——'Tis for an episode hereafter; and every circumstance
relating to it in its proper place, shall be faithfully laid before you' (1.21.75).
Gradually, however, the confidence slips. One piece of information comes
'a little out of its due course;—for it should have been told a hundred and
fifty pages ago', he later confesses; 'but that I foresaw then 'twould come in
pat hereafter, and be of more advantage here than elsewhere.—Writers
had need look before them to keep up the spirit and connection of what
they have in hand' (2.19.169). Keeping up this spirit and connection increasingly distresses Tristram's invention as he progresses, however, and in
contemplating the gap between his second and third instalments he mod-
erates the ambition: now it is merely 'to keep up some sort of connection'
(4.32.400).

Even this more modest goal involves constant changes of tack. Tristram
must move passages from place to place, as Eliot was to do, anxiously aware
all along of the need to uphold 'that necessary equipoise and balance . . .
from whence the just proportions and harmony of the whole work results'
(4.25.374). One set of reflections 'croud in upon me ten pages at least too
soon, and take up that time, which I ought to bestow upon facts', he acknowledges in volume 6 (6.29.550), restating his earlier sense of suffoca-
tion ('croud in') by narrative circumstance. The disruptive 'chasm' created
by the absence of pages torn out to make 'the book . . . more perfect and
complete by wanting the chapter, than having it' (4.25.372) anticipates later
feats of textual juggling in volume 9, where further chapters come out of

sequence owing to 'the necessity I was under of writing the 25th chapter of my book, before the 18th' (9.25.785). In perhaps his most self-conscious encounter with this problem, Tristram is paralysed by the rival claims of three different volumes as the appropriate home for an adventure of Trim's: 'for it will do very well in either place;——but then if I reserve it for either of those parts of my story,—I ruin the story I'm upon,—and if I tell it here—I anticipate matters, and ruin it there' (3.23.244).

Like Eliot again, Tristram finds that such decisions have as much to do with the technical exigencies of instalment size as with purely aesthetic concerns. Matter must frequently be carried from instalment to instalment, simply to equalize parts. As early as the opening volume, he breaks off from a speech of Walter's to worry 'whether I shall be able to find a place for it in the third volume or not' (2.7.119). At the end of the eighth, he interrupts Toby's departure for Widow Wadman's in order to resume it in a new instalment, boasting that 'the account of this is worth more, than to be wove into the fag end of the eighth volume' (8.35.729). Where the result of such manœuvres in Victorian fiction is simply to withhold an episode from the reader for a month or two, however, Tristram's mismanagement involves his audience in a wait of two full years. For the modern reader, able to turn the page and continue the narrative at once, the teasing effect is largely lost; for Sterne's first readers, however, the ludicrous disparity between reading time (twenty-four months) and narrated time (a few seconds) is reinforced by the closing words of the instalment, which implicitly invite them to '*look through the key-hole* as long as you will' (8.35.729). The full effect is yet more extreme, since Toby's amours have already been trailed for several years as the 'choicest morsel' of the work (4.32.401): in a grotesque exaggeration of the suspense on which serial fiction thrives, then, Tristram's failure 'to get into that part of my work, towards which, I have all the way, looked forwards, with so much earnest desire' (4.32.400) leaves anticipation hanging for half a decade. The trick is repeated with Trim's comic anecdote of the Jew's widow and the sausage, promised in the first instalment of 1759 (2.17.144), recalled in the second a year later (4.4.329), but only delivered in volume 9, after a wait of eighty-five months (9.4–7.742–52).

As many of these passages already indicate, what heightens all these problems of organization on Tristram's part is the ongoing movement of the clock—the tiny, persistent increments of 'tick, tick, tick' that, in Stuart Sherman's fine account of chronometric technology and literary form in the period, made newly insistent and palpable the relentless sliding of present into past.[45] Here once more his trouble anticipates and exaggerates Eliot's, and here again it is easy to miss the full effect that Sterne originally contrived by having narrated time stand frustratingly still over seven years while Tristram goes on writing, readers go on reading, and everyone goes on ageing. As Eliot was to do, yet far more extremely, Tristram finds that time distressingly outstrips his power to tell a long and complex story. On the one hand, he is acutely aware of every fleeting moment, and he regularly monitors a growing gap between the time of writing and the time described: a line from the first instalment, he tells us, was written 'this very rainy day, *March* 26, 1759' (1.21.71), one from the third 'this day (*August* the 10th, 1761)' (5.17.449), and one from the fifth 'this 12th day of August, 1766' (9.1.737). Yet, as the years pass, Tristram's promised *Life* fails to get itself told; his tour with Mr Noddy and the identity of Jenny remain undescribed. Crisis point arrives in a passage that, like several others cited here, is usually read as touching universal issues of narrative representation, as opposed to the more specific and peculiar predicament of the serial writer:

I am this month one whole year older than I was this time twelve-month; and having got, as you perceive, almost into the middle of my fourth volume—and no farther than to my first day's life—'tis demonstrative that I have three hundred and sixty-four days more life to write just now, than when I first set out; so that instead of advancing, as a common writer, in my work with what I have been doing at it— on the contrary, I am just thrown so many volumes back—was every day of my life to be as busy a day as this—And why not?—and the transactions and opinions of it to take up as much description—And for what reason should they be cut short? as at this rate I should just live 364 times faster than I should write—It must follow, an' please your worships, that the more I write, the more I shall have to write—and consequently, the more your worships read, the more your worships will have to read. (4.13.341–2)

The dilemma, of course, is insoluble. Even if Tristram now ups the pace to 'twelve volumes a year, or a volume a month, it no way alters my prospect'. He will never write enough, or fast enough, to exhaust the endless raw materials that press upon him. Even if he could, more raw matter would continue to be lived, demanding continuing writing. It is a bind that Johnson—a writer more Shandean in many of his insights than he would

---

[45] Stuart Sherman, *Telling Time: Clocks, Diaries, and English Diurnal Form, 1660–1785* (Chicago: University of Chicago Press, 1997), 1–28.

have admitted—poignantly caught when warning Hester Thrale of 'an intemperate attention to slight circumstances which is to be avoided, lest a
great part of life be spent in writing the history of the rest'.[46]

Surrounded all the while by cautionary instances of non-production—
'*Slawkenbergius* . . . spending so many years of his life upon this one work'
(*TS* 3.38.273); Walter struggling to complete the 'Tristapædia' while its
reader grows too old to use it—Tristram has reason enough to worry. The
more comprehensive he tries to make his book, the less likely he is to complete it: as he puts it of the 'Tristapædia', tellingly, we 'eternally forego our
purposes in the intemperate act of pursuing them' (5.16.448). Further anticipations of Eliot's difficulty arise as he finds his losing race to tell his tale
jeopardized on one side by the failing health that slows his power to write,
and on another by the declining readership to which serial works are
always prone. His panic comes to a head when, in volume 8, he fails to rec-
ollect 'any one opinion or passage of my life, where my understanding was
more at a loss to make ends meet, and torture the chapter I had been writing, to the service of the chapter following it, than in the present case'.
Compounding the literary entanglement now is the pressure of external
troubles:

Is it not enough that thou art in debt, and that thou hast ten cart-loads of thy fifth
and sixth volumes still—still unsold, and art almost at thy wit's ends, how to get
them off thy hands.

To this hour art thou not tormented with the vile asthma thou gattest in skating
against the wind in Flanders? and is it but two months ago, that in a fit of laughter,
on seeing a cardinal make water like a quirister (with both hands) thou brakest a
vessel in thy lungs, whereby, in two hours, thou lost as many quarts of blood . . .
(8.6.662–3)

Here is crisis indeed; and here, with uncanny prescience, Sterne sets out
the Shandean dilemma of the serial writer. All the practical problems that
Eliot experiences in the writing of *Middlemarch*, yet of course conceals in
the text itself, come to the surface as explicit comic topics for *Tristram
Shandy*. They are compellingly dramatized, moreover, by a mode of publication—a seven-year performance of ongoing crisis—that locates and expresses Tristram's failure in time as well as space.

Shklovsky's famous contention that *Tristram Shandy* could be read as
a deconstructive exposure of the forms and conventions of nineteenth-

---

[46] *The Letters of Samuel Johnson*, ed. Bruce Redford, 5 vols. (Oxford: Clarendon Press,
1992), 3: 61 (6 Sept. 1777).

century realism—a parody, as it were, of *War and Peace*—must be ad-justed. It is a deconstructive exposure, specifically, of Victorian serializa-tion—a parody of *Middlemarch*, and of the letters and journals that surround it. While exploiting the characteristic opportunities of serial fiction (improvisation and flexibility, responsiveness to reception, pro-gressiveness of disclosure through time), it wittily foregrounds the characteristic difficulties (aesthetic, technical, calendrical, economic) en-countered by Victorian practitioners of the mode. Yet, for all the many par-allels between Tristram's dilemma and Eliot's in *Middlemarch*, perhaps the crowning similarity lies in the end with Thackeray in *Denis Duval*, Gaskell in *Wives and Daughters*, and Dickens in *Edwin Drood*. Here the gasping for breath that Eliot experienced is felt with a vengeance, all these novels being cases of serial fiction cut off in mid-flow by unscheduled authorial death. The most striking instance is *Edwin Drood*, while writing which Dickens is reported to have 'found himself hopelessly entangled, as in a maze of which he could not find the issue. . . . the anxiety and subsequent excite-ment materially contributed to his sudden and premature death.'[47] By this account (Rudolf Lehmann's), Dickens's life was put in jeopardy by words; it ended only hours after he had completed his twenty-third chapter, ter-minally interrupting a novel that was then one-quarter published but half unwritten.

And so it is, perhaps, with Tristram and his eighty volumes. So much at-tention has been paid to the timing of Sterne's own death by scholars de-bating Wayne Booth's question 'Did Sterne Complete *Tristram Shandy*?' that few have considered what the ending implies about Tristram himself. Yet *Tristram Shandy* is unmistakably the story of a writer not just strug-gling with literary form but doing so under pressure of worsening disease; and we need to understand the blank pages at the end of volume 9, and the non-appearance of volume 10, as inherent parts of this story. Dramatized in the continuous present of serialization, the novel's unfolding tale of fail-ing health not only gives Tristram's losing battle with narrative language its peculiar urgency and weight; it also supplies in advance an internal, fic-tionalized reason for the premature close of his work. Here a change of context is needed. Illusions of proleptic parody in Sterne always derive, on inspection, from his conscious parody of existing texts or trends; and so it is with his anticipation of the hazards and pitfalls of Victorian serial fic-tion. Though relatively unexplored, and varying widely in its conventions

---

[47] Rudolf Lehmann, *An Artist's Reminiscences* (1894), 231–2, cited in Charles Dickens, *The Mystery of Edwin Drood*, ed. Margaret Cardwell (Oxford: Clarendon Press, 1972), p. xxvii.

and procedures from the Victorian norm, serial publication was a vital part of mid-eighteenth-century print culture. Its resources were also creatively used, by many writers, to amplify and generate meaning, one such resource being the serial's capacity to perform narratives of developing or fluctuating selfhood, or the different stages and outcomes of disease.

4

Serializing a Self

In Addison's inaugural number of the *Spectator*, the presiding persona of the new journal efficiently describes his life, starting three months after conception and ending at the present day. He then outlines an ambitious scheme for conveying his opinions (to which will be added 'other Particulars in my Life and Adventures . . . as I shall see occasion'). The wording of his proposal is arresting: wishing 'to communicate the Fulness of my Heart', he intends using the serial 'to Print my self out, if possible, before I die'. In the incremental form of diurnal instalments, his language seems to promise, the private will become public, the impalpable will be made material, the fugitive will be fixed. Accumulating in regular bulletins ('I shall publish a Sheet-full of Thoughts every Morning'), the taciturn self of Mr Spectator will be transformed into an eloquent text—or will be so transformed 'if possible'.[1] The confidence of Addison's persona is only fleetingly disrupted by this qualification, however, and whatever factors might jeopardize his chances of printing out the self before death are left unmentioned. He does not speculate about any possible mismatch between the fluidity of subjectivity and the linearity of prose, or between the endlessness of opinions and the finiteness (even when repeated daily) of a single folio half-sheet. He does not even worry about the possible effect on his project of sudden death (a prospect that leaves him 'not at all sollicitous'[2]); and though other casualties arise during the *Spectator*'s run (Sir Roger de Coverley is the notable case), Mr Spectator himself is immune. Ongoing reports of his ongoing opinions and life accumulate serenely for a further twenty-one months, and little sense of incompleteness or failure on his part colours the journal's close. It was left to imitators

---

[1] *Spectator*, ed. Donald F. Bond, 5 vols. (Oxford: Clarendon Press, 1965), 1: 5 (no. 1, 1 Mar. 1711); see also Stuart Sherman's chapter on Addison in *Telling Time: Clocks, Diaries, and English Diurnal Form, 1660–1785* (Chicago: University of Chicago Press, 1997), 109–58.

[2] *Spectator*, 1: 34 (no. 7, 8 Mar. 1711).

like Edward Moore's weekly *World* (1753–6) or the fortnightly *Ladies Magazine, or the Universal Entertainer* (1749–53) to contrive, when winding up their journals, a more playful effect of business left undone. The first ends abruptly, and in an imported persona, when its fictional manager, Adam Fitz-Adam, fatally crashes his chaise; the second breaks off in midflow when its ailing editor, 'Jasper Goodwill', dies of that most Shandean disorder, consumption.[3]

None of these periodicals, of course, makes any serious move towards fictional autobiography. At most they gesture in that direction by using sketchy fictional situations and progressions to frame their miscellaneous matter—a characteristic perhaps exaggerated by Michael G. Ketcham, who finds in the *Spectator* 'a proto-Shandeanism where . . . a faintly comic narrator moves through a series of associations, shifting between incidents and reflections'.[4] Yet in articulating the ambition of turning the self into a text while also intimating the possibility of failure, Addison momentarily pinpoints the fundamental problem for all autobiographical writing, which is that completeness, one way or another, must always elude it. The difficulty is directly encountered in more genuine serial autobiographies of the period, which in their very mode of production conveyed a sense that to represent identity in all its shifting complexities—to print the self out in full—required a form of writing more flexible and extensive than conventionally seamless memoirs could provide, and a form of writing, too, that would never end. Underpinned by a sense of flux that was commonplace at the time (Sterne is not unusual in his observation that 'in the same day, sometimes in the very same action, [men] are utterly inconsistent and irreconcileable with themselves' (*Sermons*, 11.104)), these serials were able to register identity with new alertness to its ongoing twists and turns. Inherently, the subjects and meanings they sought to define were never closed or resolved. In avoiding false closure of their own, however, works of this kind inevitably courted arbitrary closure from without—the kind of closure Sterne describes in a more famous sermon, 'Job's Account of the Shortness and Troubles of Life', preoccupied as it is by the unpredictability with which 'cruel distemper or unthought of accident' arrives to cut off life (*Sermons*, 10.98). As several of these works were to demonstrate, to document one's life in serial form was to cultivate a mode

    [3] Morris Golden, 'Periodical Context in the Imagined World of *Tristram Shandy*', *The Age of Johnson*, 1 (1987), 237–60 (at 248); Robert D. Mayo, *The English Novel in the Magazines 1740–1815* (Evanston, Ill.: Northwestern University Press, 1962), 212.
    [4] Michael G. Ketcham, *Transparent Designs: Reading, Performance, and Form in the Spectator Papers* (Athens, Ga.: University of Georgia Press, 1985), 98.

more responsive than others to the instability of identity over time, but one also more vulnerable to the very contingencies it sought to catch.

In the extracts from his *Journal* that John Wesley issued in twenty-one instalments between 1739 and 1791 (the year of his death), the patterned certainties of spiritual autobiography are discarded for a more provisional and discontinuous mode of writing, in which a spiritual life of unceasing struggle is monitored and held up for inspection in ongoing interim reports. As Isabel Rivers writes, 'serialization effectively emphasized that Wesley's quest was never complete': he had engineered a form in which the experience described could never be final, stability and conclusiveness were never on offer, and spiritual recognitions could never accumulate fully enough to complete the work of self-examination.[5] Serial autobiography could also lend itself to less high-minded purposes, as in the case of *An Apology for the Conduct of Mrs. Teresia Constantia Phillips*, the notorious (and probably ghostwritten) serial memoir that Phillips published and sold from her own address in seventeen shilling numbers in 1748–9. Although Philips complained in successive instalments about the ruses practised by her enemies to curtail or delay publication (she also feared piracy, and anticipated Sterne's unusual precautions against forgery by announcing that 'to prevent Imposition, each Book will be signed with her own Hand'), the work proved successful enough in broadcasting Phillips's intended message about herself while also spinning out a lucrative scandal.[6] A more troubled case exists in the contemporaneous *Memoirs of Laetitia Pilkington*, even though Pilkington shared much of Phillips's exuberant ingenuity in exploiting the plasticity of the mode (notably when threatening, in her opening instalment, that 'if every married Man, who has ever attack'd me, does not subscribe to my *Memoirs*', these men would be named and shamed in later instalments[7]). Published in three

---

[5] Isabel Rivers,' "Strangers and Pilgrims": Sources and Patterns of Methodist Narrative', in J. C. Hilson et al. (eds.), *Augustan Worlds* (Leicester: Leicester University Press, 1978), p. 194; see also Isabel Rivers, *Reason, Grace, and Sentiment: The Language of Religion and Ethics in England, 1660–1780* (Cambridge: Cambridge University Press, 1991), ch. 5. The term 'serial autobiography' is Felicity Nussbaum's: see *The Autobiographical Subject: Gender and Ideology in Eighteenth-Century England* (Baltimore: Johns Hopkins University Press, 1989), 1–29 and (on Wesley) 80–102.

[6] R. M. Wiles, *Serial Publication in England before 1750* (Cambridge: Cambridge University Press, 1957), 143–6, 355; for Paul Whitehead's likely authorship of Phillips's *Apology*, see Virginia Blain, Patricia Clements, and Isobel Grundy (eds.), *The Feminist Companion to Literature in English* (London: Batsford, 1990), 852. Sterne's signature in every copy of volume 5 (see *LY* 113) prompted the *Critical Review* to note that he was following 'a precaution first used' by Philips (*CH* 138–9).

[7] *Memoirs of Laetitia Pilkington*, ed. A. C. Elias, Jr., 2 vols. (Athens, Ga.: University of Georgia Press, 1997), 1: 93.

volume-length parts of 1748, 1749, and 1754, Pilkington's autobiography is discontinuous in chronology and digressive in style, its fractured structure and inclusive instincts posing a conspicuous ongoing threat to any prospect of reaching adequate closure. 'In the narrative, written a decade before Sterne's *Tristram Shandy*, the trivial is always disrupting the linear description of the past,' as Felicity Nussbaum puts it.[8] Description of the past was then more conclusively disrupted by Pilkington's death in 1750, which left her third volume unpublished, and perhaps unwritten. 'The Author intended another Volume of these Memoirs, but died before she had compleated it; and . . . no such Third Volume will ever be published,' reads a note in the 1751 reissue of volumes 1 and 2. The posthumous volume of 1754, which brings Pilkington's interrupted narrative to an off-the-peg providentialist conclusion, was at least augmented, and perhaps substantially forged, by her son.[9]

But what of *Tristram Shandy*, that work so finely attuned to all that is most hostile to first-person writing: the impenetrability of identity ('Don't puzzle me' (7.33.633)); the insufficiency of language ('Well might *Locke* write a chapter upon the imperfections of words' (5.7.429)); the un-availability of permanence ('Time wastes too fast' (9.8.754))? Serialization gave Sterne the ideal medium in which to work out such concerns, specifically by dramatizing the way Tristram's struggle to control his writing co-exists, with ever more desperate imbrication, with the struggle to prolong his life. That Tristram is progressively ailing as he writes, losing his life even as he endeavours to write it, gives urgency to what might otherwise seem a merely playful meditation on the impossibility of fixing the self (or the memories and opinions that constitute a self) in serial print. In contriving this unfolding tale, Sterne had a wealth of serial precedents to play on.

The boom in eighteenth-century serialization can be pinpointed with reference to the original and revised versions of Fielding's book-trade satire, *The Author's Farce*. The original play of 1730 makes no allusion to the trend; the 1734 revision, however, adds a new trick to the cynical repertoire of Mr Bookweight, a Curll-like dealer in false imprints, cribbed translations, and bogus pamphlet-wars. 'Write me out proposals for delivering five sheets of Mr. Bailey's English Dictionary every week, till the whole be finished,' he orders Mr Quibble, who should use as his model 'the propos-

---

[8] Nussbaum, *Autobiographical Subject*, 193.
[9] 3rd edn., 2 vols. (1751), 2: 364; for Jack Pilkington's role, see introduction to the Elias edn., 1: xxvii. The posthumous volume of 1754 appears as lot 2492 in the sale catalogue of Sterne's library (on the status of which, see above, p. 60).

als for printing Bayle's Dictionary in the same manner'.[10] His finger on the pulse as ever, Fielding was adjusting his satire to register an innovation that (in the words of its historian, R. M. Wiles) 'accelerated the book trade more than any other single force affecting the reading habits of our ancestors between 1700 and 1750'.[11] By making prestigious books available in cheap instalments ('in Scraps', sneered one contemporary, 'that the Purchaser may not feel the Price'[12]), serial publication not only expanded the book-buying market but also made its exploitation newly efficient. Costs could be spread and returns speeded and recycled; purchasers could be locked in by systems of subscription, with demand accurately predicted; slender packets of sheets could be distributed to provincial areas that had once seemed commercially inaccessible (this being the decade when an expanding post-road network was first used for monthly magazine distribution on a national scale).[13]

The trend towards piecemeal issue of large multi-volume works peaked in the early 1730s (Wiles identifies 1732 as the crucial year) with several immensely successful publications that Sterne would later use. The five-volume second edition of Bayle's *Dictionary Historical and Critical* (1733–8), which Sterne borrowed from York Minster Library and used in 'Slawkenbergius's Tale', had originally been published in 148 fortnightly parts. In the sale catalogue of his library (lot 2) is the ten-volume rival version in monthly parts, *A General Dictionary, Historical and Critical* (1733–41), which took even longer to appear.[14] As this protracted project reached its close, the fifth edition of Chambers's *Cyclopaedia* (1741–3) came out in weekly sixpenny numbers of three sheets each, as opposed to the lump-sum price of four guineas for the simultaneously available fourth edition of 1741; and this pattern was repeated when the sixth edition of 1750

---

[10] Henry Fielding, *Dramatic Works*, 3 vols. (London: Smith, Elder & Co., 1882), 1: 215 (II.iv). Samuel Foote picks the same target in *The Author* (1757) with passing reference to a sozzled hack named 'Master *Clench*, in *Little Britain*', who 'has a Folio coming out in Numbers' (I.i).

[11] Wiles, *Serial Publication*, 2; see also John Feather, *A History of British Publishing* (London: Croom Helm, 1988), 114–15.

[12] *Comedian*, 6 (Sept. 1732), referring to John Kelly's translation (in rivalry to Nicholas Tindal's) of Rapin's *History of England*; cited in Wiles, *Serial Publication*, 108.

[13] See Thomas Keymer, introduction to *The Gentleman's Magazine*, 16 vols. (London: Pickering & Chatto, 1998), 1: vii–xl (at pp. xvi–xx).

[14] C. B. L. Barr and W. G. Day, 'Sterne and York Minster Library', *Shandean*, 2 (1990), 18–19; Wiles, *Serial Publication*, 287, 175; see also, on the serialization of Bayle and other biographical dictionaries on the Baylean model, Isabel Rivers, 'Biographical Dictionaries and their Uses from Bayle to Chalmers', in Isabel Rivers (ed.), *Books and their Readers in Eighteenth-Century England: New Essays* (Leicester: Leicester University Press, 2001), 137–69 (at 149–52).

was accompanied by a serialized seventh in 1751–2.[15] Although it is the second edition (1738) that Sterne may have owned (lot 236), the Florida editors use the serialized text of 1741–3 in annotating *Tristram Shandy*, and Judith Hawley has shown that he used this edition specifically (s.v. 'Circumcision') in a mock-learned passage in volume 5.[16] Chambers as much as Bayle must have been in Sterne's mind as he contrived, in 'the slow progress my father made in his *Tristra-pædia*' (5.16.448), his domestic analogue for the situation in which the hapless compilers of these serial encyclopaedias were caught, their openings becoming obsolete before their endings could appear.

Probably the most spectacular success of all was Sterne's principal source for the campaigns of Uncle Toby, Nicholas Tindal's long-running translation and continuation of Rapin de Thoyras's *History of England*. Although the relevance of this work for *Tristram Shandy* was not documented until 1936, the popularizing effect of serialization had made it one of the best-known histories of the century (and netted its publishers, even before the continuation began, as much as £10,000): 'no Book in our Language had ever more Buyers or Readers,' as the *Daily Gazetteer* averred.[17] When Tristram thinks better of his plan to transcribe a lengthy passage from Rapin, there are complex resonances to his joke that this would be to charge the reader 'for fifty pages which I have no right to sell thee' (7.6.584). Here was a work notorious for the quarrels about copyright that had surrounded its lucrative run; a work that had already been extensively plagiarized elsewhere;[18] and a work that many of Sterne's readers would already have owned. First launched in monthly octavo numbers that sold at a rate of thousands weekly, and grew into a fifteen-volume first

---

[15] On the complex bibliography of the *Cyclopaedia*, see L. E. Bradshaw, 'Ephraim Chambers's *Cyclopaedia*', in Frank Kafker (ed.), *Notable Encyclopaedias of the Seventeenth and Eighteenth Centuries* (Oxford: Voltaire Foundation, 1981), 123–40; also Wiles, *Serial Publication*, 8, 327.

[16] Judith Hawley, 'Laurence Sterne and the Circle of Sciences: *Tristram Shandy* and its Relation to Encyclopaedias' (diss., University of Oxford, 1990), 188, referring to *TS* 5.27.459–5.28.463.

[17] Theodore Baird, 'The Time-Scheme of *Tristram Shandy* and a Source', *PMLA* 51 (1936), 803–20; Wiles, *Serial Publication*, 237. A total print run of 18,000 copies in the thirty years after 1725 is estimated by Philip Hicks, who calls the work 'England's most successful book serialization, the groundbreaking one for the entire industry' (*Neoclassical History and English Culture: From Clarendon to Hume* (London: Macmillan, 1996), 147; see also p. 148, citing the *Gazetteer* of 12 Mar. 1736). For the complex bibliography of the various Rapin editions before 1750, see app. B of Wiles's study.

[18] See e.g. Fielding's *Journey from This World to the Next*, in *Miscellanies, Volume Two*, ed. Bertrand A. Goldgar and Hugh Amory (Oxford: Clarendon Press, 1993), 86–97: chs. 20–1 are closely based on Tindal's Rapin, which Fielding owned in the folio edition of 1732–3.

edition of 1725–31, Rapin's *History* was so successful that by the end of its run rival publishers were cashing in with a serial translation of their own. Tindal's publishers responded with a second edition in weekly folio numbers (1732–5), and his continuation began in 1736. Two combined editions of the history and continuation are listed in the sale catalogue of Sterne's library, the second weighing in at twenty-eight octavo volumes.[19]

The handsome editions that resulted from these processes could never wholly erase their serial origins, and occasionally Tindal makes explicit the relentless pressures of the mode. Like many similar publications, his work got off to a shaky start (one witness reports that he 'was for some Time not a little dubious, as to its success; and strongly inclin'd to drop his Design; and yet it is well known to what a vast Account it turn'd at last'), and he used a sequence of dated volume dedications to document his progress.[20] The impression left is of a frantic ongoing juggling act between his various duties as translator-historian, parish priest, and naval chaplain. In July 1726 he is in the Baltic, dedicating to his admiral a volume on the Norman conquest; September 1728 sees him back in his Essex parish, dedicating to the British merchants of Lisbon the volume of medieval history he wrote while ministering there; in March 1747 he is in another parish, dedicating to the Duke of Cumberland a volume on the 1720s.[21] Altogether this herculean task occupied Tindal for several decades, not least because, once the commitment to continuation had been made, it became, more accurately, sisyphean (and tantalizing with it). He began with intentions of abridging his massive source, but 'soon dropt his Design, and resolv'd not only to give the Publick a full and fair Translation, but also to add some *Notes* and *Observations* relating to *Antiquities, Curiosities, remarkable Occurrences, Characters* . . . and several other Particulars and Circumstances'. Even when he had finished translating and begun his own continuation, Tindal was still doggedly adding opinion to transaction, so that 'nothing is omitted to render the Work as comprehensive and useful as possible'.[22] The result was predictable. In 1736–7 his first effort at continuation promised on its title page to fill the gap '*from the Revolution to the Accession of King*

---

[19] Lot 7, in five folio volumes, probably combines the second edition of 1732–5 with the first edition of the continuation (1735–6); lot 1019, in twenty-eight octavo volumes, probably combines the first edition of 1725–31 with the uniform octavo continuation in thirteen volumes of 1744–7. Also in the catalogue is Thomas Lediard's rival continuation in weekly folio numbers of 1735–6 (lot 278).

[20] *A Letter to the Society of Booksellers* (1738), cited in Wiles, *Serial Publication*, 136.

[21] *The History of England*, 15 vols. (1725–31), 2: A2; 6: A2; *The History of England . . . Continued from the Revolution to the Accession of King George II*, 13 vols. (1744–7), 13 [28]: A4ᵛ.

[22] *The History of England*, 1: A3; *The History of England . . . Continued*, 1 [16]: A2ᵛ.

George I', yet by the time this update drew to a close, in 1747, he had spent ten years describing no more than thirteen, and was only just at the point getting George II crowned. The more he wrote, the more he had to write; and the manufacturers of paper were profiting indeed. In the 1750s two further editions of the continuation advertised coverage '*from the Revolution to the Accession of King George II*', but as *Tristram Shandy* entered gestation the title of a newly extended fourth edition (1758–60) was revised to read '*A Continuation of Mr. Rapin de Thoyras's History of England, from the Revolution to the Present Times*'. For the first time, Tindal had explicitly embraced the Shandean project of describing a subject that would accumulate without limit, dooming his work to a rolling state of incompleteness no matter how fast he produced it. Volume 21 of this continuation appeared in September 1760, to be sneered at by Smollett (who was now doing well himself as a writer of serial history) in the *Critical Review*.[23] Undeterred, Tindal's publishers (who now included the printer of *Tristram Shandy*'s later instalments, William Strahan) launched a further update almost as soon as its predecessor was complete. By the time this fifth edition drew to a close in 1763, Tindal's work had been kept a-going for almost forty years—its only serious rival in bulk and longevity being a publishers' venture partly owned and printed by Richardson, the twenty-volume *Universal History from the Earliest Account of Time to the Present* (1736–50), several volumes of which Sterne borrowed from York Minster Library in 1754. At the same crucial stage for *Tristram Shandy*, this massive serial was revived in the form of a forty-four-volume *Modern Part of an Universal History* (1759–66), about a third of it compiled by Smollett, who at one stage wrote in desperation to Richardson of having to fill sheets with material 'which all the art of man cannot spin out to half the number'.[24]

The phenomenal success of serial publications like Tindal's Rapin attracted much conservative hostility, partly because it was attributed to marketing more than merit, and partly because it gave a dangerous currency to knowledge. Complaining that 'you have Bayle's *Dictionary* and Rapin's *History* from two Places, with the daily Squabbles of Book sellers and Translators about them', the *Grub-Street Journal* worried about the democratization of reading entailed by serial form. Poor men now 'spend Six-pence upon a Number of Rapin' while their families starve, the journal

---

[23] James G. Basker, *Tobias Smollett: Critic and Journalist* (Newark, Del.: University of Delaware Press, 1988), 260; see also, on the serialization and profitability of Smollett's historical works, pp. 104–9.

[24] Barr and Day, 'Sterne and York Minster Library', 10, 16; *The Letters of Tobias Smollett*, ed. Lewis M. Knapp (Oxford: Clarendon Press, 1970), 78 (4 Apr. 1759).

protested, adding that to extend this sort of material to men 'designed by Nature for Trade and Manufactures . . . was the Way to do them Harm, and to make them, not wiser or better, but impertinent, troublesome, and factious'.[25] Fielding (whose various comments on the Whig-Republican extremism of Tindal's Rapin partly explain the strength of this anxiety) was more amusingly scathing about serials, but his hostility was no less real. *Tom Jones* sarcastically admires the miracle of literary commodification through which 'the heavy, unread, Folio Lump, which long had dozed on the dusty Shelf, piece-mealed into Numbers, runs nimbly through the Nation'. *Joseph Andrews* fakes up a classical provenance for the practice, reporting that Homer not only divided his work into books 'but, according to the Opinion of some very sagacious Critics, hawked them all separately, delivering only one Book at a Time, (probably by Subscription)'. He thereby pioneered the art 'of publishing by Numbers, an Art now brought to such Perfection, that even Dictionaries are divided and exhibited piecemeal to the Public; nay, one Bookseller hath . . . contrived to give them a Dictionary in this divided Manner for only fifteen Shillings more than it would have cost entire'.[26]

Serial works like this were an easy target. Although the contemporaneous example of Chambers's *Cyclopaedia* (which cost much the same whether bought outright or in parts) suggests fairer dealing than Fielding alleges, there were obvious disadvantages to users. The publishers of one medical dictionary in weekly numbers, 'alphabetically digested', pulled the plug midway through the letter 'B', presumably without compensating buyers, and such abrupt curtailments were not uncommon. Even a multivolume work by the indefatigable Tindal fell behind schedule after one number and collapsed after two.[27] Moreover, as Fielding well knew, text in this early phase of serial publication would be divided to suit the needs of production, not reception, so that a subscriber's weekly or monthly purchase would be simply a fascicule of so many sheets, utterly lacking the integrity of a Homeric book, and often beginning or ending in midsentence. Distinct in kind from the serialization in volumes that Sterne would later practise, this primitive mode of serialization never lost its dual reputation for cozenage and dumbing down: in the 1760s Hume preferred 'publishing in Volumes than in Numbers' because the latter method 'has somewhat of a quackish Air', while Samuel Bishop wrote scathingly that

[25] *Grub-Street Journal* (19 Sept. 1734), cited in Wiles, *Serial Publication*, 236–7.

[26] *TJ*, 13.1.684; *JA*, 2.1.77. On the politics of Tindal's Rapin, see *JA*, 3.1.162; *TJ*, 6.2.273.

[27] See Wiles, *Serial Publication*, 8 (Chambers); 121–2 (*Dr. Colbatch's Legacy, or, The Family Physician*, 1732); 119–20 (Tindal's *History of Essex*, 1732).

'*Scribblers,* from hand to mouth, who write and live, | In weekly *Numbers,* mental *Spoon-meat* give'.[28] Even so, it remains surprising that Fielding—a prolific writer of periodical journalism, and a novelist adroit in his games with fictional time—could see no redeeming potential in the serialization of books.[29] By the simple expedient of harmonizing printers' units with authorial divisions, thereby giving each number of a part-issued work an integrity of its own, serialization had more than commercial opportunities to offer, not least in the medium it established for manipulating through time the experience of reading. Here was an opportunity that novelists in particular could exploit.

Far more of the period's fiction than we commonly suppose reached its full extent through part publication, sometimes a volume or two at a time, sometimes in units that anticipate the more slimline Victorian norm. As J. Paul Hunter has argued, this tendency implies a grounding assumption in eighteenth-century fiction 'that stories are interwoven, seamless, continuous, and relatively endless', and encouraged readers to look for continuation more than resolution in the novels they consumed.[30] Well-known works like *Robinson Crusoe* and *Pamela* generated sequels, and Defoe was especially assiduous in scattering continuation nodules along his path as he wrote, most of which (like the volumes on Moll's 'governess' and highwayman husband tentatively projected in the preface to *Moll Flanders*) he never returned to exploit.[31] Other works inhabit a grey area between serial fiction and *roman fleuve.* Trilogy may be the best term for Sarah Fielding's linked publications of 1744–53, *The Adventures of David Simple, Familiar Letters between the Principal Characters in David Simple,* and *Volume the Last,* but there are closer connections between the three parts of Aphra Behn's *Love-Letters between a Nobleman and His Sister* (1684–7) or Eliza Haywood's *Love in Excess* (1719–20), which William Beatty Warner has de-

---

[28] Hume to Andrew Millar, 17 May 1762, cited by Basker, *Tobias Smollett,* 109; Bishop, 'The Book', ll. 51–2, in Samuel Bishop, *Poetical Works,* 2 vols. (1796), 1: 229.

[29] Mayo illustrates 'the reluctance of the journals to emulate the novel' with reference to Fielding's *Champion.* Here connected narrative never develops: even 'the "Voyages of Mr. Job Vinegar," which appeared in thirteen instalments between March and October, 1740, studiously seems to avoid a narrative structure' (*English Novel in the Magazines,* 76).

[30] J. Paul Hunter, 'Serious Reflections on Farther Adventures: Resistances to Closure in Eighteenth-Century English Novels', in Albert J. Rivero (ed.), *Augustan Subjects: Essays in Honor of Martin C. Battestin* (Newark, Del.: University of Delaware Press, 1997), 276–94 (at 282).

[31] Defoe's groundwork was not wasted, and shortly before *Tristram Shandy* an enterprising writer picked up the loose threads in a thee-part work, *Fortune's Fickle Distribution . . . Containing First, The Life and Death of Moll Flanders. Part II The Life of Jane Hackaway Her Governess. Part III The Life of James McFaul, Moll Flanders' Lancashire Husband* (1759).

scribed as using serialization to open the amatory novel 'to a potentially endless repetition on the market'.[32] Decades later, Henry Brooke's *The Fool of Quality* (1766–70) is a genuine serial novel in five more or less annual volumes. Several translated works are relevant, most obviously Marivaux's *La Vie de Marianne*. Written and published in eleven parts between 1731 and 1742, and serially translated in a three-stage English edition of 1736–42, the text plays explicitly on the dilatoriness of its own production, provoking complaints at the time (as W. H. McBurney and M. F. Shugrue report) 'that if a month of Marianne's life occupied six parts of the novel, the reader would need more than a lifetime to finish the work'. Eventually, Marivaux abandoned the novel without a conclusion, prompting a second English translator, Mary Collyer, to round off her version in fortnightly numbers, *The Virtuous Orphan* (1742), with a twelfth and final part of her own devising.[33]

More journalistic in character, though moving towards serial fiction in their limited continuities of focalization and setting, were open-ended satirical sequences like John Dunton's six-part ramble *The Night Walker* (1696–7) and Ned Ward's fictionalized journal *The London Spy* (1698–1700). Published in sixpenny numbers of four sheets each, *The London Spy* was designed to go on 'Monthly, as long as we shall find Encouragement', and ran eventually to eighteen numbers and two volumes. (The continuing vigour of its mode in Sterne's day is shown by Goldsmith's satirical essay series *Chinese Letters*, which began almost simultaneously with *Tristram Shandy*, attacked Sterne's first instalment in June 1760, and was fleetingly mocked in return in Sterne's third instalment of December 1761.)[34] Preceding *The Night Walker* was another Dunton periodical, *A Ramble round the World* (1689), which collapsed very soon, but was later revived (as *A Voyage round the World*, 1691) into an experimental fusion of autobiographical and fictional material that Dunton 'had been sweating at the best part of this seven Years', as his prologue declares. In a passage that looks forward to Tristram's glee at galloping amongst the critics and splashing a bishop (*TS* 4.20.306–7), Dunton adds: 'I first send out this *First Volume* by way of *Postilion*, to slapdash, and spatter all about him, (if the Criticks come in his way) in order to make Elbow-room for all the rest

[32] William Beatty Warner, *Licensing Entertainment: The Elevation of Novel Reading in Britain 1684–1750* (Berkeley and Los Angeles: University of California Press, 1998), 116.

[33] Marivaux, trans. Mary Collyer, *The Virtuous Orphan*, ed. W. H. McBurney and M. F. Shugrue (Carbondale, Ill.: Southern Illinois University Press, 1965), p. xxxvii.

[34] Wiles, *Serial Publication*, 77, 80–1; *TS Notes*, 146, 371. For further interaction between Sterne and Goldsmith's vehicle, the *Public Ledger*, see Anne Bandry, '*Tristram Shandy*, the *Public Ledger*, and William Dodd', *Eighteenth-Century Fiction*, 14 (2002), 309–22.

of his *little Brethren* that are to come after.' Twenty-four of these little brethren are envisaged altogether, but the project then peters out after three, closing with the narrator's lament that because of his digressiveness—'How many Miles (*alias* Pages) *am I again out of my way?*'—he must now suspend his present thread and 'reserve it for the next Volume'.[35]

The same period also saw begin to develop the tradition of magazine fiction described by Robert D. Mayo, who traces its inauspicious origins back to the failure, after six chapters in three instalments, of a projected twenty-four-part Cervantic imitation of 1681 entitled 'Don Rugero'. In the early eighteenth century, periodicals often ran intermittent background fictions, spun out over time and dropped when convenient. The inaugural *Tatler*, for example, promises 'from time to time . . . to be very exact in the progress' of the lovelorn Cynthio, who is eventually killed off six months and eighty-four numbers later. Mayo establishes the 1740s as the decade in which more sustained kinds of fiction written expressly for magazine publication (and sometimes making serious efforts to exploit the advantages of periodicity) become significant. The richest period comes in the early 1760s, but a noteworthy prior example exists in 'A Story Strange as True': this skilfully managed serial tale ran intermittently through seven numbers of the *Gentleman's Magazine* in 1737–8, terminating (though with unfulfilled hints about future resumption) in the same number as a contribution that has been attributed to Sterne.[36]

Sometimes there could be a compelling logic to serialization. It was perfectly appropriate for publication of Antoine Galland's *Arabian Nights' Entertainments* to be an extended event, both in the Grub Street translation that closely followed the first French edition (1704–17) and in unauthorized newspaper serializations of the 1720s.[37] The work's framing situation (in which a narrator staves off execution by repeatedly deferring narrative closure) catches to perfection the characteristic elasticity of serial writing, as well as the hovering threat of sudden curtailment.[38] Scheherezade's

[35] John Dunton, *A Voyage round the World*, 3 vols. (1691), 1: 26; 3: 416; see also J. Paul Hunter, *Before Novels: The Cultural Contexts of Eighteenth-Century English Fiction* (New York: Norton, 1990), 336.

[36] Mayo, *English Novel in the Magazines*, 24–6, 34–5, 6, 273–98, 165–6; Kenneth Monkman, 'Did Sterne Contrive to Publish a "Sermon" in 1738?', *Shandean*, 4 (1992), 111–33.

[37] Antoine Galland, *Arabian Nights' Entertainments*, ed. Robert L. Mack (Oxford: Oxford University Press, 1995), p. xxv; Wiles, *Serial Publication*, 35, 38; Mayo, *English Novel in the Magazines*, 59. An eight-volume *Arabian Nights* in French (The Hague, 1714) is in the sale catalogue of Sterne's library (lot 2262).

[38] The point is nicely caught in Hilary M. Schor's study of Gaskell's serial fiction, *Scheherezade in the Marketplace: Elizabeth Gaskell and the Victorian Novel* (Oxford: Oxford University Press, 1992).

dilemma is not exactly Tristram Shandy's—where he lives 364 times faster than he writes, she has only a day to live, and narrates 1,001 times more slowly—but in each case the proliferation of gratuitous narrative that typifies the work could not have been better enacted. By the same token, the halting publishing process that so infuriated Marivaux's early readers could intensify a series of games with narrative time that anticipates *Tristram Shandy*. By recurrently promising, from part 3 onwards, an inter- polated tale that fails to materialize until part 8 ('I am not in a condition to undertake it present'; 'I find I must defer it'), *La Vie de Marianne* looks for- ward to Tristram's seven-year procrastination of his 'choicest morsel' (*TS* 4.32.401). Serialization could also enrich a fictional exploration of subjec- tive duration and objective time that is incipiently Shandean. 'These vari- ous sensations and reflections, though so long in relating, passed through my mind almost in an instant':[39] when Marianne makes this remark in Marivaux's second instalment, for which readers had already waited thirty months, her words set up an intricate three-way discrepancy between relative rates of thinking, writing and reading. Sterne plays similarly with anisochrony in *Tristram Shandy*'s famous chapter on consciousness and time, which begins when 'two hours, and ten minutes . . . since Dr. *Slop* and *Obadiah* arrived' seem 'almost an age' to Walter (3.18.222)—the dif- ference being that here Sterne brings Walter's imagination into jokey harmony with the real-time experience of his readers, for whom Slop's arrival in the previous instalment had happened a year ago.

At this earlier point, Tristram talks of synchronizing the rates of action and reading, thus preserving 'the unity, or rather probability, of time'. Because it is 'about an hour and a half's tolerable good reading' since Obadiah was sent for Slop, Obadiah has now had 'time enough, poetically speaking . . . both to go and come', and his return can be described (2.8.119). Here Sterne makes Tristram as absurdly fussy as ever. Yet in aspiring to equivalence of duration between narrated time and reading, he seeks only to replicate an effect that serialization had already made commonplace. Again, the *Arabian Nights* provides an arresting example, its three-year serialization from 1723 in 445 thrice-weekly numbers of *Parker's London News* tracking rather closely the 1,001 nights in which Scheherezade's narrative prolongs its flight from death. No doubt as much by chance as design, a similar effect was often achieved by newspaper

---

[39] Marivaux, trans. Collyer, *The Virtuous Orphan*, 163, 201, 57; see also the comments by McBurney and Shugrue on this second resemblance (introduction, p. xxxvii), and by Wayne Booth on the first ('The Self-Conscious Narrator in Comic Fiction before *Tristram Shandy*', *PMLA* 67 (1952), 163–85 (at 174)).

piracies of diary or epistolary fiction. When *Robinson Crusoe* was serialized thrice weekly in the *Original London Post* (1719–20), the duration of reading did not exactly match an isolation that lasted decades, but the sense given of Crusoe's steady notching of days must still have been enhanced by the reader's slow-paced access to the text. Similarly, when Behn's *Love-Letters between a Nobleman and His Sister* was run over four months in the *Oxford Journal* (1736), or when Richardson's *Pamela* was serialized in *Robinson Crusoe's London Daily Evening Post* (1741–2), the diurnal rhythms of each narrator's life and writing could be replicated in the reading.[40] Just as these epistolary narrators write 'to the moment', so their readers were required to read to the moment. It is worth noting that the *Pamela* controversy generated a spate of serials in various media, as though anything connected with the novel was recognized in the trade as best delivered and accessed in serial form. When Sterne's sometime book-seller Caesar Ward and his London partner published their opportunistic *Pamela's Conduct in High Life* in volume-length instalments of May and September 1741, they appropriated the novel, in effect, as an open-ended serial, thus anticipating not only the plan of *Tristram Shandy*—Richardson described their intention 'to try the Success of one first (and still more and more Volumes . . . so long as the Town would receive them)'—but also the difficulties later presented to Sterne by spurious continuations.[41] Other serializations include a second unauthorized continuation, *Pamela in High Life* (published in three parts of autumn 1741 to match a three-part piracy of the original); *Pamela Versified* (a fifteen-part serial dropped after two instalments); and unlicensed serializations of *Anti-Pamela* and *Joseph Andrews* in a farthing newspaper, *All-Alive and Merry* (1741–3).[42]

Perhaps it was because of this capacity to simulate in the reading the undifferentiated continuum of time in *Pamela* that Fielding refused to see any potential in part-published narrative. In *Tom Jones* he distinguishes himself from 'the painful and voluminous Historian' who narrates the past

---

[40] Wiles, *Serial Publication*, 27, 69, 51–2. It was probably this *Pamela* serialization that first generated the famous story about villagers ringing the church bells on hearing of Pamela's marriage: see Thomas Keymer, 'Reading Time in Serial Fiction before Dickens', *Yearbook of English Studies*, 30 (2000), 34–45 (at 38–9).

[41] *Selected Letters of Samuel Richardson*, ed. John Caroll (Oxford: Clarendon Press, 1964), 44 (Aug. 1741); on the spurious *Tristram Shandy* volumes, see LY 87–8, 264; also Anne Bandry, 'The Publication of the Spurious Volumes of *Tristram Shandy*', *Shandean*, 3 (1991), 126–37.

[42] See the chronology of publications in *The Pamela Controversy: Criticisms and Adaptations of Richardson's Pamela 1740–1750*, ed. Thomas Keymer and Peter Sabor, 6 vols. (London: Pickering & Chatto, 2001), 1: xxi–xxix.

at a constant rate whatever its eventfulness, and likens such histories to 'a News-Paper, which consists of just the same Number of Words, whether there be any News in it or not'. With this talk of a drudging seriality analogous to newspaper journalism, Fielding may have been pointing at Tindal. Yet in his use of the term 'Historian' to include a novelist like himself, as opposed to that lesser historian who 'seems to think himself obliged to keep even Pace with Time', it is hard not to detect a sideswipe against Richardson (as well as a hint that Sterne would develop in Tristram's own painful accretions). He, by contrast, would follow a strategy that Richardson had ignored (and that Tristram, later, would fail to get near) by mixing 'some Chapters . . . that contain only the Time of a single Day, and others that comprise Years' (*TJ* 2.1.75–7).

In using serialization to enhance and dramatize the distinctive effects of 'writing to the moment', Richardson may even have taken his cue from serial appropriations of *Pamela*. In *Clarissa*, too, narrators progressively disclose themselves in the increments of epistolary exchange, and Richardson now chose to reinforce this gradualist effect by spreading publication over a period corresponding to the action. *Clarissa* came out in three instalments (two volumes in December 1747, two in April 1748, three the following December), and this schedule tracked the pace of a fiction covering a calendar year. Richardson thereby enhanced the potential of non-retrospective epistolary narration to stage intimate periodic reports of what he called 'the unfoldings of the Story, as well as of the heart', prolonging an effect so addictive that one reader thought *Clarissa* had 'no other Fault but its not continuing as long as the Faculty is left for Reading'.[43] By timing instalment breaks to coincide with moments of unresolved crisis, moreover, Richardson showed as keen a sense of the cliffhanging pause as any Victorian serialist, so replicating the more local effects created when narrators tease their addressees by breaking off (as Lovelace puts it to Belford) 'without giving thee the least hint of the issue of my further proceedings'. Awaiting the second instalment, one provincial reader lamented that 'we are left wholly in the dark as to the catastrophe. Miss Clarissa is a most amiable character, but we leave her in so perplexing circumstances that I think long for the other volumes'.[44]

[43] *Selected Letters of Richardson*, 289 (14 Feb. 1754); Forster MSS, xv, 2, fo. 34 (commentary by Jane Collier).
[44] *Clarissa*, 6: 280; *'Your Affectionate and Loving Sister': The Correspondence of Barbara Kerrich and Elizabeth Postlethwaite, 1733–1751*, ed. Nigel Surry (Dereham: Larks Press, 2000), 83 (2 Mar. 1748).

Behind all this lay a dramatization of decline and death that, though wholly unlike *Tristram Shandy* in tone, pioneered its effects of prolongation. By involving readers so intimately with his heroine, and then leaving them an interval of several months to imagine her flourishing future, Richardson used serialization to render her untimely death with dramatic force. At the same time, he involved his narrators in an incipiently Shandean struggle to compensate for Clarissa's death by first enshrining her life in narrative, slowing the final volumes with exhaustive accounts by Belford and others, even as Clarissa herself despairs of the capacity of language to organize and render meaning.[45] Richardson cannot have foreseen the doggedness with which readers would exploit the apparent openness of the novel (which, unusually for serial fiction, had been fully drafted years beforehand) by besieging him with requests for a happy ending, and was soon complaining of the trouble arising 'from publishing a work in Parts which left everyone at liberty to form a catastrophe of their own'.[46] But he was able, in response, to turn to advantage the capacity of serial writing to pursue a conversation with readers. By hearing in the gap between instalments the case for a happy ending, he was able to revise the third instalment, and append an answering postscript, in light of their responses and desires: with this move, like *Tristram Shandy*, *Clarissa* inscribes within itself the history of its own reception.

Different anticipations of Sterne's project arise from the serialization in 1753–4 of *Sir Charles Grandison*, which Richardson was forced by copyright infringements to compress into four months.[47] Even so, the time-lapse method enabled him to restage several of *Clarissa*'s main effects, such as his incremental drawing out, in the reading, of Clementina's emotional and mental breakdown. Yet there was also an interesting departure from *Clarissa*'s method. Where the relentless logic of the earlier novel could lead to only one outcome (albeit one that readers tried to avert by besieging Richardson between instalments with requests for a happy ending), in *Sir Charles Grandison* he sought to experiment with a soap-opera-like continuity of action that frustrated the desire for closure of any kind. The final volume tails quietly off with several plotlines unresolved, prompting readers to plead for further volumes and Richardson himself to

[45] On this Shandean dimension, see Thomas Keymer, *Richardson's Clarissa and the Eighteenth-Century Reader* (Cambridge: Cambridge University Press, 1992), 222–9.

[46] *Selected Letters of Richardson*, 117 (17 Dec. 1748).

[47] See T. C. D. Eaves and B. D. Kimpel, *Samuel Richardson: A Biography* (Oxford: Clarendon Press, 1971), 375–86.

propose a participatory scheme in which members of his circle would continue writing the novel by assuming a narrator apiece.[48] Privately anxious that 'some other officious Pen (as in Pamela in High Life, as it was called) will prosecute the Story', he sometimes suggested that the open-endedness of *Grandison* made formal resumption an option: eighteen months later he was still asking a correspondent to 'give me your Opinion, should the Humor return, as to proceeding, or closing, as at present'.[49] But publicly he insisted that the work, though strictly speaking unconcluded, could not be taken further. In a open letter to a reader *who was solicitous for an additional volume to . . . Sir* CHARLES GRANDISON; *supposing it ended abruptly*, he observed 'that in scenes of life carried down nearly to the present time . . . all events cannot be decided, unless, as in the History of *Tom Thumb the Great*, all the actors are killed in the last scene; since persons presumed to be still living, must be supposed liable to the various turns of human affairs'. From these assumptions, *Sir Charles Grandison* became literally interminable, but would have to continue in the imagination of readers rather than on the page. It would be up to them to marry Clementina to Jeronymo or not, as the fancy might take them. Halving matters amicably, he asks his addressee: 'Do you think, Madam, I have not been very complaisant to my Readers to leave to them the decision of this important article?' (*SCG* 3:467; 3:470; 3:468).

Commenting on the relative absence of major novelists from the sale catalogue of Sterne's library, Nicolas Barker notes the presence of the volume of *Grandison* in which Richardson reprinted this teasing document (lot 2486).[50] But he misses the significance of lot 1481, 'British Magazine, or Monthly Repository for Gentlemen and Ladies, 2 vols . . . 1760', a fiction-bearing periodical that (like Lennox's *Lady's Museum* in the same year) may have been launched by its founder-editor, Smollett, as a way round the adverse market conditions affecting novels at the time. Its leading item, *Sir Launcelot Greaves*, marks the culmination of all the traditions and processes described above, and remains the leading product of a minor boom in magazine fiction in the *Tristram Shandy* years that, though it proved a false start, significantly anticipates the Victorian serial mode. These years saw the first appearance as magazine or newspaper serials of works by leading writers like Goldsmith and Lennox, as well as

<hr />

[48] Ibid. 384–6, 403–13.

[49] *Selected Letters of Richardson*, 296 (25 Feb. 1754); Liverpool Public Library MSS, cited by Eaves and Kimpel, *Samuel Richardson*, 412 (letter of 12 Sept. 1755).

[50] Nicolas Barker, 'The Library Catalogue of Laurence Sterne', *Shandean*, 1 (1989), 9–24 (at 17).

anonymous Shandean imitations like *The Disasters of Tantarabobus* (1762) or, a few years later, *A Sentimental Journey, by a Lady* (1770–7).[51] The vogue began with Smollett's novel, which started its run through the first two volumes of the *British Magazine* in January 1760, a few weeks after volumes 1 and 2 of *Tristram Shandy* appeared. Coexisting in the magazine's pages with other serial items like 'The History of Omrah' (an oriental tale by Goldsmith) and a lengthy history of Canada (which was probably also by Smollett),[52] it closed after twenty-five parts in December 1761, the month which also saw published volumes 5 and 6 *Tristram Shandy*.

Each successive part was termed a chapter, but Smollett was doing more here than string out something otherwise indistinguishable from non-serial fiction in the Fielding mould. On the contrary, he saw (as Fielding had missed, and as modern theorists of narrative time repeatedly miss) that serialization, by subjecting the temporal experience of the reader to limited but definable regulation, could further complicate the kind of interplay between *Erzählzeit* (the time of narrating) and *erzählte Zeit* (the narrated time) for which *Tom Jones* is often praised.[53] The duration and interruptions of reading are always on Smollett's mind as he writes, as is the elasticity of his publishing mode. His novel never commits itself to a specified length until its final month, and, although it does reach conventional closure at this point (unlike 'The History of Canada', which peters out unfinished after more than three years), Smollett begins joking about premature curtailment as early as Chapter 3, which (placed pointedly below the conclusion of Goldsmith's short-lived 'Omrah' tale) is headed 'Which the reader, on perusal, may wish were chapter the last'.[54] In a sense, the whole work unfolds as an ingenious set of variations, practically enacted, on the seminal chapter from *Joseph Andrews* in which Fielding mocks the practice of serialization while defining the strictly spatial divisions between his own chapters as places for readerly repose. Now, in Smollett's hands, chapters become units of time as well as space, and

[51] Charlotte Lennox's *Harriot and Sophia*, originally serialized in Lennox's *Lady's Museum* (Mar. 1760–Jan. 1761), was separately published as *Sophia* (1762); Oliver Goldsmith's *Chinese Letters* was serialized in the *Public Ledger* (Jan. 1760–Aug. 1761) and separately published as *The Citizen of the World* (1762). *The Disasters of Tantarabobus* was in the *Universal Museum* (Jan.–Aug. 1762), and *A Sentimental Journey, by a Lady* (1770–7) was in the *Lady's Magazine* (which after eighty parts and 270,000 words abandoned the work uncompleted 'on account of the desire of *many* Correspondents'): see Mayo, *English Novel in the Magazines*, 341–4.

[52] Louis L. Martz, *The Later Career of Tobias Smollett* (New Haven: Yale University Press, 1942), 180. For Goldsmith's authorship of 'Omrah', see Basker, *Tobias Smollett*, 195.

[53] See Keymer, 'Reading Time', 34–5.

[54] *British Magazine*, 1 (Mar. 1760), 124.

opportunities for the manipulating novelist to procrastinate, withhold, and frustrate. His first instalment breaks mischievously off at its critical point, asking the reader to 'wait with Patience' for the 'comfort and edification' provided in the following number. Another picks up the mock solicitude with which *Joseph Andrews* acknowledges that a chapterless volume 'fatigues the Spirit', concluding that, 'as the ensuing scene requires fresh attention in the reader, we shall defer it till another opportunity, when his spirits shall be recruited from the fatigue of this chapter'.[55] The underlying joke is always the same: that Smollett's reader cannot simply, like Fielding's, resume reading at will the next day, but instead has been stranded for a month.

There are other ways in which *Sir Launcelot Greaves* wears its serial origins on its sleeve. There is no authority for Sir Walter Scott's account of Smollett despatching scribbled instalments from Berwickshire to London ('when post-time drew near, he used to retire for half an hour, to prepare the necessary quantity of copy . . . which he never gave himself the trouble to correct, or even to read over'[56]), but the novel was clearly written *pari passu* with publication, and its instalments play not only on their own discontinuous mode of production but also on intervening texts and events. That Smollett was monitoring Sterne and his imitators as he wrote is clear not only from his annotated listings of new publications in the *British Magazine* but also from the novel's madhouse scene, written at a time when volumes 1 to 4 of *Tristram Shandy* had already established Toby's hobby horse and its effect on communication as central themes. When one inmate rants about sieges ('why don't you finish your second parallel?—send hither the engineer Schittenbach—I'll lay all the shoes in my shop, the breach will be practicable in four and twenty hours—don't tell me of your works—you and your works may be damn'd'), another starts off about doctrine: 'Assuredly, (cried another voice . . .) he that thinks to be saved by works is in a state of utter reprobation.'[57] The whole exchange— not only the shoemaker's besieging obsession but also the methodist's hobby-horsical misprision—flows straight from Uncle Toby. Evidently, Smollett grasped very well Sterne's Lockean intimation that the

<hr>

[55] *JA*, 2.1.76; *Sir Launcelot Greaves*, ed. David Evans (Oxford: Oxford University Press, 1973), 7 (ch. 1, Jan. 1760), 119 (ch. 14, Jan. 1761).

[56] Lionel Kelly (ed.), *Tobias Smollett: The Critical Heritage* (London: Routledge, 1987), 354.

[57] *Sir Launcelot Greaves*, 185–6 (ch. 23, Oct. 1761). See also Basker's demonstration that, having reviewed a Shandean imitation (*Yorick's Meditations*) in the *Critical Review* for July 1760, Smollett plagiarized it in chapter 10 (Sept. 1760) of *Sir Launcelot Greaves* (*Tobias Smollett*, 259).

association of ideas 'is really Madness', and that anyone giving in to its motions will 'be thought fitter for *Bedlam*, than Civil Conversation'.[58]

It may also be that the relationship of influence or borrowing between these overlapping texts could work in both directions, with serialization establishing an ongoing dynamic of mutual exchange. Sterne's teasing suspension of Toby's amours at the end of the 1765 volumes ('but the account of this is worth more, than to be wove into the fag end of the eighth volume of such a work as this' (8.35.729)) had obvious precedents in *Sir Launcelot Greaves*, which, though starting later, was now completed: 'But the scene that followed is too important to be huddled in at the end of a chapter, and therefore we shall reserve it for a more conspicuous place in these memoirs.' Perhaps an even more intricate dynamic was at work, given the launch and development during the first year of both *Sir Launcelot Greaves* and *Tristram Shandy* of Lennox's *Harriot and Sophia*, which pioneered the style of sentimental instalment break that is now a standard convention in television soaps. Typically, Lennox uses the break to freeze her action at suspenseful moments, leaving a character 'motionless with astonishment' at the end of one month's instalment, or 'reliev[ing] her labouring heart with a shower of tears' at the end of another.[59] The technique irritated as many readers as it pleased, or so it would seem from the announcement of a rival magazine when launching a six-part imitation of its own in July 1760: this novel, *The Fortune-Hunter*, would be 'divided in such a manner that the portion, in each number, shall make a complete story, in itself, without torturing curiosity, by abruptly breaking off, in the most affecting parts, (the design of which conduct is too plain)'.[60] Smollett's flippant obstructions of reading playfully court this same objection, and Sterne's habit of freezing characters in awkward postures while Tristram breaks off—the conspicuous instance is the end of volume 8, which leaves Mrs Shandy bending at a keyhole for two years—renders parodically literal Lennox's device.

DYING BY NUMBERS

The directness with which *Tristram Shandy* plays on individual serial works, as opposed to the generic conditions they all expose, will always be

---

[58] John Locke, *An Essay Concerning Human Understanding*, ed. Peter H. Nidditch (Oxford: Clarendon Press, 1975), 395.

[59] *Lady's Museum*, 1 (Mar. 1760), 44; 1 (Nov. 1760), 666.

[60] *Royal Female Magazine*, 2 (July 1760), p. ii, cited by Mayo, *English Novel in the Magazines*, 286.

debatable. But in many cases the points of contact are close and suggestive. It would be possible, for example, to read *Tristram Shandy* as an elaborate comic subversion of the Spectatorial project, in which the lucubrations that Addison's urbane persona offers for 'the Diversion or Improvement' of his readers give way to the crack-brained efforts of a provincial buffoon 'to write my life for the amusement of the world, and my opinions for its instruction' (*TS* 3.28.253). Certainly, Tristram's decision to mingle life with opinions as he writes—'expecting that your knowledge of my character, and of what kind of a mortal I am, by the one, would give you a better relish for the other' (*TS* 1.6.9)—calls to mind the famous premiss from which the *Spectator* begins, which is 'that a Reader seldom peruses a Book with Pleasure 'till he knows whether the Writer of it be . . . of a mild or cholerick Disposition, Married or a Batchelor, with other Particulars of a like nature, than conduce very much to the right Understanding of an Author'.[61] Tristram's more teasing strategy is to keep his readers guessing, and after twelve further chapters he is still warning them 'not to take it absolutely for granted . . . "That I am a married man"' (*TS* 1.18.56). Later Sterne brings to the surface the absurdity of Tristram's pretensions to a Spectatorial lineage by having him compare a banal observation 'struck out by me this very rainy day, *March* 26, 1759' with a point more fully explained by 'the great *Addison* . . . in one or two of his Spectators' (*TS* 1.21.71), and he jokes elsewhere about the inauspiciousness of the Shandean environment for a project of Spectatorial ambitions. There is a fragile defiance in Tristram's eschewal of Addison's fashionable urban milieu in favour of his own circumscribed world 'of four *English* miles diameter' (*TS* 1.7.10), and even in Languedoc he is 'confident we could have passed through Pall-Mall or St. James's-Street for a month together . . . and seen less of human nature' (*TS* 7.43.648). None of these connections (or comic distortions) is in itself of particular significance, but cumulatively they keep in play a jocoserious sense of Tristram writing under an anxiety of Spectatorial influence, vainly pursuing the same goal of printing himself out before death.

It has been argued before that *Tristram Shandy* is not only derivative but also parodic of dictionaries of knowledge like the *Cyclopaedia*, the original version of which Chambers was labouring to compile in the very decade (according to the implied chronology of *Tristram Shandy*) that sees Walter struggle with his *Tristapædia*.[62] Chambers had worried in his preface about the 'little measure of Time allow'd for a Performance to which a

---

[61] *Spectator*, 1: 4; 1: 1 (no. 1, 1 Mar. 1711).
[62] See Hawley, 'Sterne and the Circle of Sciences'.

man's whole Life scarce seems equal', going on to note that even 'the bare Vocabulary of the Academy *della Crusca* was above forty Years in compiling'. Ten years later he was still lamenting the 'infinite Labour' demanded of the writer of encyclopaedic works, and complaining that 'the very evil they were intended to remove has seized them; I mean, Multitude and Voluminousness'.[63] The absurdity of his dilemma (brought to an end by his death after the third edition, which left further updates, as well as a two-volume *Supplement* of 1753, to be compiled by other hands) may well have been among Sterne's inspirations. Tristram's own work is at one point proclaimed 'this cyclopædia of arts and sciences' (*TS* 2.17.141), and in the *Tristapœdia* passage Sterne reinforces the point with a complex set of connections and synchronizations between slow-moving encyclopaedic fiction and slow-moving fictive encyclopaedia. Three years and five volumes into *Tristram Shandy* we learn that 'in about three years . . . my father had got advanced almost into the middle of his work'. The glacial pace of this project puts Tristram in mind of della Casa's *Galateo*, a romance on which its author 'spent near forty years of his life' (*TS* 5.16.445–6); this in turn suggests the run he projects for his own sprawling text. With this interlocking set of *mises en abyme*, *Tristram Shandy* deftly implies the vanity of systematizing Enlightenment desires, as the vast and shifting bodies of knowledge to be digested and codified in projects like the *Cyclopaedia* endlessly outrun their vehicle.

This preoccupation with textual interminability should also prevent us dismissing Tindal's translation and continuation of Rapin as nothing more significant for Sterne than a repository of military-historical information. In the increasingly outlandish prolixity of Tindal's work (which was in its fourth decade of intermittent production as *Tristram Shandy* began), and in the relentless chase to keep up with passing time in which it embroiled its compiler, Sterne had before his eyes another extreme case of the dilemma he gives his narrator. At one point he makes the analogy plain. An earlier chapter to leave Mrs Shandy frozen in eaves-dropping posture overtly relates Tristram's organizational problems to those of Tindal's volumes (each of which would end with a badly integrated update of ecclesiastical history): 'In this attitude I am determined to let her stand for five minutes: till I bring up the affairs of the kitchen (as *Rapin* does those of the church) to the same period' (*TS* 5.5.427). Nor were such disruptions of historiographical continuity exclusive to Tindal. Even Hume is

---

[63] Chambers, *Cyclopaedia* (1728), 1: 1; 'Some Considerations Offered to the Public, Preparatory to a Second Edition of Cyclopaedia' (*c*.1738), in Robert DeMaria, Jr. (ed.), *British Literature, 1640–1789: An Anthology* (Oxford: Blackwell, 1996), 699, 698.

included in Smollett's strictures against digressions by historians in which 'the chain of events is broken',[64] and this complaint makes clear the extent to which serial history falls within Sterne's parodic reach. By identifying *Tristram Shandy* as a work 'the great humour of which consists in the whole narration always going backwards', Horace Walpole nicely catches its wry relationship to projects like Hume's, in which volumes on the Tudors (1759) followed earlier volumes (1754, 1756) on the Stuarts—a 'piece of irregularity' in Hume that made Smollett wonder sarcastically why he should have chosen 'to reverse the order of history'.[65]

As all these sources combine to make clear, there stood behind Sterne a diverse and vigorous tradition of serial writing, encompassing a variety of genres from essay periodical and encyclopaedia to historiography and fiction, and a variety of publishing modes from diurnal broadsheets and weekly fascicules to monthly magazines and annual volumes. Sterne knew this tradition well, having used (and probably owned) some of its best-known products, before starting to write and publish *Tristram Shandy*, and it continued to impinge on him as he continued to publish and write. The resulting text bears its trace in many ways and at many points. It is now clear, indeed, that *Tristram Shandy*'s parodic anticipation of Victorian serial fiction is directly rooted in Sterne's responsiveness to comparable forms of paradox and impasse in earlier serial writing. Again and again, eighteenth-century serialization had posed a central question for *Tristram Shandy*: how, if at all, can adequate closure ever be reached by a text that forgoes once-and-for-all publication in favour of indefinite ongoing production, typically in the attempt to encompass a large subject of indefinite or ongoing extent? How, if at all, can such a work ever complete its task and decisively *conclude*, as opposed to being arbitrarily terminated by force of circumstance or admission of defeat? Here were special exemplifications of the larger anxiety about the human capacity to comprehend and signify, to make one's mark before death in an unstable world, that is the central joke (and the central lament) of *Tristram Shandy*. Nowhere could this anxiety be more persistently explored than in serial form, which spreads and develops Tristram's seven-year-long story of frustration and failure over the seven years in which its presentation to the public remained an ongoing event.

It is often observed that *Tristram Shandy* becomes more straightforwardly novelistic as its volumes progress, and that a coherent story about

---

[64] *Critical Review*, 2 (Dec. 1756), 386; see Basker, *Tobias Smollett*, 108.
[65] *CH* 55 (Walpole to Sir David Dalrymple, 4 Apr. 1760); *Critical Review*, 7 (Apr. 1759), 289.

the past gets more accessible: '*Tristram Shandy* moves away . . . from mock-learning and Scriblerian satire towards a mock-sentimental comic narrative,' as Judith Hawley puts it.[66] No less important than the past-tense story Tristram tells about Toby's amours, however, is the quiet but insistent present-tense story of his own acts of telling, jeopardized as these increasingly are by chronic authorial sickness. Now the strictly literary or technical threats to completeness that dominate the playful opening of *Tristram Shandy* become, as the narrator's life-expectancy plummets, urgently corporeal. Here, in Tristram's struggle to complete his tale before interrupted by death, we find a brilliant concentration of all the questions about the capacity of writing to contain experience that serial writing inherently raises. Using the serialist's special predicament to literalize the sense of ineffability widely held in the period to vex all human art (Reynolds writes memorably of an ideal 'residing in the breast of the artist, which he is always labouring to impart, and which he dies at last without imparting'[67]), Sterne contrives a dramatization that draws for its full impact on its publishing mode—its status not as a static work but as an inexorable performance over time, the various stages and implied ending of which are quietly marked in each successive instalment. While contriving this story of parallel literary and physical defeat in ways informed by many prior serializations, moreover, he may have found precedents of particular relevance in recent serial fiction: in *Clarissa*'s incremental disclosure of decline and death, the interminability of subject matter in *Grandison*, or Smollett's gradualism in unfolding the stages of madness in *Sir Launcelot Greaves*.

Initially, the unavailability of closure, and the resulting proliferation of text, are an exuberant joke for Tristram. Even before his fantasy of an eighty-volume serial autobiography gives way to panic, however, an inauspicious context is established for this ambition. *Tristram Shandy* is a work famously preoccupied by time, by its flight, and by the pressures it exerts in a culture newly enabled to calibrate its passing in ever finer units. 'I wish there was not a clock in the kingdom,' Walter exclaims (3.18.224): quite apart from Tristram's increasingly anxious measurements of narrated time, narrating time, reading time and their various relations, the work contrives several brilliantly comic exemplifications of the passage of time and its capacity to thwart achievement. Paradoxically, it is the winding of a house clock that jeopardizes Tristram's inheritance of 'memory, fancy, and quick parts' (4.19.354), the very qualities he needs to thrive in a

---

[66] Judith Hawley, '"Hints and Documents" (2): A Bibliography for Tristram Shandy', *Shandean*, 4 (1992), 49–65 (at 55).

[67] Robert R. Wark (ed.), *Discourses on Art* (New Haven: Yale University Press, 1975), 171.

time-bound world. A newer and more stressful chronometry is in play when he rails against the 'hypercritick' who measures a narrative gap 'to be no more than two minutes, thirteen seconds, and three fifths' (2.8.119) or a soliloquy of Garrick's to have paused in mid-sentence 'three seconds and three fifths by a stop-watch' (3.12.213). Here Sterne is quick to detect the changes wrought to consciousness by a technology that was already making the minute discrimination of passing time a portable and permanent accompaniment of daily life.[68] The onward march of time is relentlessly active for Tristram, rendering ever more futile his hope of making his represented past catch up with the fugitive present. By the sixth year and fourth instalment of *Tristram Shandy*, there is something painful in his quiet joke about the two great tourist attractions (Lippius's clock and a thirty-volume history of China) that he hopes to visit in Lyon. If time would only stand still, Tristram might finish the book: 'Lippius's great clock . . . had not gone for some years——It will give me the more time, thought I, to peruse the Chinese history' (7.39.642). The joke becomes more pointed still if Sterne was remembering (along with the Peking-printed volumes that really were in Lyon) another serialized *folie de grandeur* that echoes his own: a fifty-two-part translation of Du Halde's *Description . . . de la Chine*, which, projected in 1735 and published head to head with a rival serialization from 1737, had almost ruined its publisher, Edward Cave, by the end of its halting run in 1742.[69]

The passage of time matters, of course, because it brings ageing and death to the individual, and to civilization as a whole (as Walter laments) 'decay, and . . . a perpetual night' (5.3.422). On this score, too, *Tristram Shandy* gets off to an unpromising start. On its title page an epigraph from Epictetus hints in context at the terrors of the notion of death,[70] while the preliminary dedication to Pitt locates its comic impulse alongside 'the infirmities of ill health, and other evils of life'. (Here life itself is 'this Fragment', as though doomed to be broken off, denied wholeness or completion.) Clearly there is no need to go to the *Sermons*, nor even to the desperate final stages of *Tristram Shandy*, to find in Sterne a preoccupation, however variable tonally, with what Tristram calls 'the chances of a

[68] As John Sutherland notes, state-of-the-art dials were just beginning to be marked in units of a fifth of a second, and second hands had been fitted since the 1740s with stop levers to enable users to freeze a result ('Slop Slip', in *Can Jane Eyre Be Happy?* (Oxford: Oxford University Press, 1997), 25–30 and 225–6 n.).

[69] See *TS Notes*, 481–2; Wiles, *Serial Publication*, 307.

[70] Elizabeth Carter's 1758 translation is cited in *TS Notes*, 37: 'MEN are disturbed, not by Things, but by the Principles and Notions, which they form concerning Things. Death, for Instance, is not terrible . . . But the Terror consists in our Notion of Death.'

transitory life' (7.9.589). Yorick's consumptive death displaces Tristram's birth in the first volume, and as the work proceeds Sterne shows none of the scruples that made Richardson refuse to continue *Grandison* for fear of seeming to wield 'a murdering Pen'.[71] Among his more lingering victims are Yorick (1.12.35), Le Fever (6.10.513), Trim (6.24.544), and Uncle Toby (6.24.545); among the more premature and tragicomic are Bobby ('got from under the hands of his barber before he was bald' (5.3.424)) and Le Fever's wife (6.7.507), who is killed in mid-embrace by a stray shot. '*Nothing in this world, Trim, is made to last for ever*' (8.19.684): the same could not be truer of *Tristram Shandy*.

All these problems—the proliferation of text; the passage of time; the fact of mortality—meet in the question of Tristram's own health. Struck by the limitless proliferation of matter implied by the inclusiveness of his literary ambitions, he soon devises his famous solution: 'not to be in a hurry; — but to go on leisurely, writing and publishing two volumes of my life every year;—which, if I am suffered to go on quietly, and can make a tolerable bargain with my bookseller, I shall continue to do as long as I live' (1.14.42). Here he seems in little doubt of his ability to achieve his goals, and he remains so even as he comes to see that his work will need to be 'kept a-going these forty years, if it pleases the fountain of health to bless me so long with life' (1.22.82). There seems no question at the end of this first instalment about his ability to produce the next. Yet in the context of his fleeting admission earlier of consumptive illness ('I can now scarce draw [breath] at all, for an asthma I got in scating against the wind in *Flanders*' (1.5.8)), qualifications like 'as long as I live' or 'if it pleases the fountain of health' look more significant and pressing than Tristram himself seems to see. Already, ominous notes are sounded by the implication that the text has no natural conclusion of its own, will be coterminous with Tristram's life, and will always depend for its prolongation on his prospects of health.

The ominous notes grow louder as the work proceeds. A year later the second instalment, by setting a marbled page in place of Yorick's black one (3.36.268), and by talking of the work as designed to secure Tristram's own immortality (4.7.333), plays insistently on the traditional ambition of finding in art a permanence unavailable in life. Yet at the same time the marmoreal product that Tristram seeks to leave behind him looks increasingly vulnerable. Again he talks in terms that imply the inevitable fragmentariness of his project, 'being determined as long as I live or write (which in my

---

[71] *Selected Letters of Richardson*, 296 (25 Feb. 1754).

case means the same thing)' (3.4.191). A brave face is put on the problem by the famous passage in which he finds himself 'one whole year older' than when he began the text, 'and no farther than to my first day's life'; but while celebrating the limitless publishing opportunity thus provided, Tristram also foresees its sudden curtailment. He would lead a fine life out of writing his life, he says, 'was it not that my OPINIONS'—the digressive impulse that forever disrupts his narrative line—'will be the death of me'. Now it is as though a vicious circle is at work, in which the demanding task of immortalizing oneself in writing threatens first the life to be immortalized, and thus in turn the immortalizing text. Moreover, Tristram knows as well as Defoe in *Moll Flanders* that 'no Body can write their own Life to the full End of it, unless they can write it after they are dead'.[72] As he whimsically acknowledges, at least two volumes of his work will always be lacking—or maybe more: 'write as I will, and rush as I may into the middle of things . . . I shall never overtake myself—whipp'd and driven to the last pinch, at the worst I shall have one day the start of my pen—and one day is enough for two volumes—and two volumes will be enough for one year' (4.13.342). Now he starts to prioritize more urgently, and even as he suspends the text for a year he itches to get its key sections written. The closing paragraphs of volume 4 make clear his pressing reason for this new sense of purpose. His head 'akes dismally', and he ends by mentioning the more ominous ailment that threatens the capacity of 'true *Shandeism*' to open his own 'heart and lungs': another pair of volumes will come in another year's time, he promises, 'unless this vile cough kills me in the mean time' (4.32.401–2).

Dying in mid-text, of course, has always been an occupational hazard for the narrative writer. In the seventeenth century Dorothy Osborne was disappointed when the long romance *La Prazimène* cut out *in medias res* ('I never saw but 4 Tomes of her and was told the Gentleman that writt her Storry dyed when those were finnish'd'), and the abrupt curtailment of John Chalkhill's *Thealma and Clearchus* halfway through line 3170 elicited a wry marginal note in the first edition: 'And here the Author dy'd, and I hope the Reader will be sorry.' A few years before *Tristram Shandy*, Fielding registers the same hazard in his valedictory *Journal of a Voyage to Lisbon*, where the question of whether he will live to complete the work

---

[72] Daniel Defoe, *Moll Flanders*, ed. G. A. Starr (Oxford: Oxford University Press, 1981), 5. Sterne may also have known the solution offered in a minor memoir novel from the sale catalogue, *Memoirs of the Life and Adventures of Signor Rozelli* (lot 1680). In the final sentence, with wonderful bathos, the hero receives extreme unction and 'prepared for Death, which however did not come, since I lived after that to compose these *Memoirs*'; a brisk editorial postscript then notes his death after two further months (4th edn., 2 vols. (1740), 2: 231).

becomes 'a matter of no great certainty, if indeed of any great hope to me'.[73]
Tristram Shandy is unusual, however, in making the threat of its own untimely curtailment a prominent and recurrent concern, and in using serial
production to render the uncertainty active. Where Fielding's reader can
immediately turn to the volume's end to see that, though posthumously
published, the *Journal* has indeed concluded, *Tristram Shandy's* original
reader is always kept guessing. A winter later, the appearance as promised
of volumes 5 and 6 makes clear that Tristram is hanging on; but little head-
way is made with his promised matter, and the instalment is haunted by
untimely death in the twin examples of Bobby and Le Fever. Unlike previous instalments, moreover, this one breaks off without commitment to a
specific date of resumption. Then follows an unusually lengthy pause of
three years, during which it may well have seemed that Tristram's projected eighty volumes had already met their inevitable end: by mid-1763, at
any rate, one reader had playfully drawn from the non-appearance of volumes 7 and 8 the conclusion that Tristram had now succumbed to disease,
and contributed to Robert Lloyd's *St James's Magazine* an 'Elegy on the
Decease of Tristram Shandy' (*CH* 153). When the silence was at last broken
in January 1765, volumes 7 and 8 make clear how close a call it has been.
'Now there is nothing in this world I abominate worse, than to be interrupted in a story' (7.1.576); yet it is not only the anecdote that Tristram is
telling Eugenius, but also his *Life and Opinions* as a whole, that are almost
cut off in the visit from Death that grimly kicks off this instalment.

Clark Lawlor has shown how one of the running jokes of *Tristram
Shandy* lies in its subversion of the standard contemporary assumption
that, by leaving the mind clear in its slow advance, consumption encouraged its victims to prepare for death in a serene and orderly manner. 'Indeed a certain messenger of death; but know that of all the Bayliffs, sent to
arrest us for the debt of nature, none useth his prisoners with more civility
and courtesie then the Consumption,' writes Thomas Fuller—though he
also warns that 'too often an ill-use is made thereof, for the prisoners
to flatter themselves into a possibility of an escape'.[74] Clearly Tristram
has long been failing to settle his accounts with the control of the ideal
consumptive, and now, when death civilly calls and courteously leaves, he

[73] *Letters to Sir William Temple*, ed. Kenneth Parker (London: Penguin, 1987), 131 (24–5
Sept. 1653); *Thealma and Clearchus* (1683), 168; *The Journal of a Voyage to Lisbon*, ed. Thomas
Keymer (London: Penguin, 1996), 82.
[74] *The Collected Sermons of Thomas Fuller, D.D., 1631–1659*, ed. J. E. Bailey and W. E. A.
Axon, 2 vols. (London: Gresham, 1891), 2: 386 ('Life out of Death', 1655); partly quoted in Clark
Lawlor, 'Consuming Time: Narrative and Disease in *Tristram Shandy*', *Yearbook of English
Studies*, 30 (2000), 46–59 (at 56).

flatters himself into the least appropriate of escapes. 'I will gallop,' he says (7.1.577), his verb laden with ominous irony (and the submerged pun here on 'galloping consumption'—a term in use by 1674—returns three chapters later). There is new desperation in Tristram's voice, moreover, as he now recalls his earlier proposals to write two volumes a year for forty years, 'provided the vile cough which then tormented me, and which to this hour I dread worse than the devil, would but give me leave' (7.1.575). Here again what is jeopardized, quite explicitly, is Tristram's ongoing text (now scaled down in panic by half its length) as well as his ongoing life: 'for I have forty volumes to write, and forty thousand things to say and do, which no body in the world will say and do for me, except thyself; and as thou seest he has got me by the throat (for Eugenius could scarce hear me speak across the table) . . . had I not better, Eugenius, fly for my life?' (7.1.576–7). Now a series of punning links between Tristram's flight through France and the simultaneous progress of his writing hints that little more of either life or text can be left to come. When in the following chapter he imagines himself being 'overtaken by *Death* in this passage' (7.2.578), 'passage' suggests not only the crossing to Calais but also the words he writes while crossing. When he hopes to keep 'a stage, or two' ahead of Death in his journey (7.7.585), moreover, there is yet another glance at the volume–stage analogy from *Joseph Andrews*, implying that very few further volumes can now be in prospect. As he proceeds, Tristram recognizes that Death 'might be much nearer me than I imagined' (7.10.590), envisages his own deathbed (7.12.591–2), and shifts to a scriptural register to present himself as one 'who must be cut short in the midst of my days' (7.14.595).[75]

At the end of this volume, renewed urgency marks Tristram's resumption of his story with a resolution 'that I might go on straight forwards, without digression or parenthesis' (7.43.651). When he begins volume 8 with 'a thing upon my mind to be imparted to the reader, which if not imparted now, can never be imparted to him as long as I live' (8.2.656), his confidence of beginning further volumes seems to have gone, and his anxious repetition of the phrase 'as long as I live' a few pages later (8.5.661) reinforces the threat. From that point on, the work is studded with reports of Tristram's now critical health, and with anticipations of sudden death. A 'vile asthma' torments him in the following chapter, and a broken pulmonary vessel has cost him two quarts of blood (8.6.663). A fever attacks him as he writes a chapter of volume 9, and costs another 'fourscore'

---

[75] The Florida editors note parallels here in Psalms and Jeremiah; see also Sterne's lengthy gloss on Job 14: 2, in which he plays relentlessly on Job's term 'cut down' (*Sermons*, 10.91–102).

ounces of blood—a measurement that ominously parallels the forty-year, eighty-volume project now struggling to survive. The crisis prompts Tristram, keenly aware of his own impending death, to issue a Grandisonian invitation to his readers: 'any one is welcome to take my pen, and go on with the story for me that will' (9.24.779).

It is in this final volume of 1767, beginning with the sentiment that 'time and chance . . . severally check us in our careers in this world' (9.1.735), that Sterne most clearly indicates that Tristram's life and text are now approaching their end. At one point, for example, Tristram imagines his work swimming 'down the gutter of Time' with Warburton's *Divine Legation of Moses Demostrated* and Swift's *Tale of a Tub* (9.8.754). The contribution of this passage to Sterne's serial campaign of Warburton-baiting has been finely documented;[76] but there is larger significance in Tristram's readiness to bracket his own work here with this odd couple, which have almost nothing in common except a conspicuous appearance of incompleteness. The promised third part of Warburton's five-volume *Divine Legation* (1738–41) had still not materialized a quarter of a century later (though a fragment did posthumously appear in 1788). No doubt *A Tale of a Tub* was finished as far as Swift was concerned, but not for the hack persona of the work, who merely pauses 'till I find, by feeling the World's Pulse, and my own, that it will be of absolute Necessity . . . to resume my Pen'.[77] It looks likely here that Sterne had Swift's teasing ending in mind even before his opening volumes had appeared: Dodsley may not have picked up the hint when Sterne first proposed to him 'two small volumes, of the size of Rasselas . . . to feel the pulse of the world' (*Letters*, 80), but with hindsight the echo of Swift's phrase (amplified by the reference to Johnson's work, with its famous 'conclusion, in which nothing is concluded')[78] carries a clear implication. Like *A Tale of a Tub*, this work too will end with its narrator's (as distinct from its author's) task unfinished.

More explicit is Tristram's mournful continuation of the 'gutters of Time' passage. As he apostrophizes to Jenny (whose precise identity, promised six years earlier, he has still not got round to disclosing):

Time wastes too fast: every letter I trace tells me with what rapidity Life follows my pen; the days and hours of it . . . are flying over our heads like light clouds of a windy day, never to return more——every thing presses on——whilst thou art

---

[76] Melvyn New, 'Sterne, Warburton, and the Burden of Exuberant Wit', *Eighteenth-Century Studies*, 15 (1982), 245–74 (at 273–4).

[77] Jonathan Swift, *A Tale of a Tub*, ed. A. C. Guthkelch and D. Nichol Smith, 2nd edn. (Oxford: Clarendon Press, 1958), 210.

[78] Samuel Johnson, *Rasselas*, ed. J. P. Hardy (Oxford: Oxford University Press, 1988), 122.

twisting that lock,——see! it grows grey; and every time I kiss thy hand to bid adieu, and every absence which follows it, are preludes to that eternal separation which we are shortly to make.—— (9.8.754)

Time merely 'presses upon' Tristram earlier in his narrative (5.35.474), and the change of verb at this point is laden with grim implication. Time wastes too fast, while Tristram has been wasting time, and wasting from a consumptive disease that also attenuates his text. The parallel acts of living and writing, linked throughout the work in an increasingly urgent mutual chase, are now approaching their joint extinction—and 'shortly'. At the height of the Ossianic vogue described in a later chapter of this study, the tropes of mutability and mortality used here are commonplace enough. What is not commonplace is the seven-year publishing process through which Sterne dramatizes the relentlessly declining health that first jeopardizes and now, it seems, is about to defeat Tristram's efforts to fix in print his life and opinions.

EPITASIS, CATASTASIS, CATASTROPHE

In his classic account of the ending of *Tristram Shandy*, Wayne Booth bases his argument that in volume 9 Sterne 'completed the book as he had originally conceived it' on several internal factors: the absence of the usual forward-looking serial break at the volume's end; the *a priori/a posteriori* joke that links the dedications to volumes 1 and 9; above all, the culmination of volume 9 with Toby's amours, which are trailed from the second instalment (and implicitly, Booth would have it, from the first) as the 'choicest morsel' of the work. *The Life and Opinions of Tristram Shandy* becomes 'an elaborate and prolonged contradiction of [its] title-page', its real focus being instead 'the amours and campaigns of Uncle Toby', which now—albeit limply—reach their climax.[79]

Booth's argument for closure has since been reinforced on other grounds,[80] and it might be added that his case about the long-awaited

---

[79] Wayne Booth, 'Did Sterne Complete *Tristram Shandy?*', *Modern Philology*, 48 (1951), 173, 180.

[80] Objections to Booth's case are made in Arthur H. Cash and John M. Stedmond (eds.), *The Winged Skull: Papers from the Laurence Sterne Bicentenary Conference* (London: Methuen, 1971): see Marcia Allentuck, 'In Defense of an Unfinished *Tristram Shandy*: Laurence Sterne and the *Non Finito*', 145–55; R. F. Brissenden, '"Trusting to Almighty God": Another Look at the Composition of *Tristram Shandy*', 258–69. More recently, Booth has been supported by Mark Loveridge, who argues for 'poetic closure' in volume 9 ('Stories of COCKS and BULLS: The Ending of *Tristram Shandy*', *Eighteenth-Century Fiction*, 5 (1992), 35–54), and by Samuel

delivery of Tristram's 'choicest morsel' gains weight by analogy with the structuring principles of Slawkenbergius, who retains his own best story 'for the concluding tale of my whole work; knowing . . . that when I shall have told it, and my reader shall have read it thro'—'twould be even high time for both of us to shut up the book' (4.1.325). Other, more pervasive evidence for finding closure in volume 9 has been obscured by Booth's conflation of Sterne's design and project with Tristram's own, and by his focus on the narrated time of the volume (the years 1713–14, in which Toby conducts his amours) as opposed to its time of narration (1766–7, in which Tristram is dying of consumption). Whereas *Tristram Shandy* does indeed appear to have run its course as a novel of Sterne's, it has barely got itself started as an autobiography by Tristram, and in this sense the *Life and Opinions* title page is contradicted, and its subject displaced, not only by Booth's past-tense plot about Uncle Toby's amours and campaigns, but by a present-tense plot about Tristram's decline and death. Intermittent but pervasive, this present-tense plot—an unfolding performance of terminal disease, from Tristram's troubled breathing in the first instalment to his full-blown consumption in the last—is quite as important as the plot about Toby, and even more conclusive. Booth would have seen as much had he lingered on the passage in which Toby's campaigns are trailed as 'no uninteresting under-plot in the epitasis and working up of this drama' (2.6.114). The terminology here—which returns when Slawkenbergius discusses the '*Epitasis, Catastasis . . . Catastrophe*' sequence in neoclassical aesthetics (4.317)—begs the question of what the *over*-plot will be, and what the *catastrophe* will be;[81] yet elsewhere the answer is made clear. The key passage comes when, foreseeing his own death in volume 7, Tristram pointedly resumes this language: 'I never seriously think upon the mode and manner of this great catastrophe, which . . . torments my thoughts as much as the catastrophe itself, but I constantly draw the curtain across it' (7.12.591). The catastrophe of Tristram's life, and thus of his otherwise interminable *Life and Opinions,* will be his death. This, as we know from the opening of volume 7, will be sudden and peremptory; and now we seem

---

L. Macey, who finds in it the fulfilment of Sterne's intricate time-scheme ('The Linear and Circular Time Schemes in Sterne's Tristram Shandy', *Notes and Queries,* 36 (1989), 477–9). The case for an unrealized twelve-volume plan is made by Peter de Voogd, 'The Design of *Tristram Shandy*', *British Journal for Eighteenth-Century Studies,* 6 (1983), 159–62. Closest to my own position is Melvyn New, who finds Booth's question 'answerable in the affirmative only if we understand that while Volume IX is indeed the concluding volume, the work could have admitted of additional materials before it' (*Laurence Sterne as Satirist: A Reading of Tristram Shandy* (Gainesville, Fla.: University of Florida Press, 1969), 189; see also Melvyn New, *Tristram Shandy: A Book for Free Spirits* (New York: Twayne, 1994), 104).

[81] For these terms, see *TS Notes,* 145, 316–17.

to be being told that it will happen when the curtain is down. With its newly urgent sense of time wasting and death advancing, the brisk and slender fifth instalment—almost an emblem, in its physical attenuation and galloping pace, of Tristram's condition—brings us right to this juncture.

The over-plot of Tristram's consumptive decline, then, confirms the inference Booth draws from the under-plot of Toby's amours, which is that Sterne is tacitly winding his serial up. The medical history that moves to the surface of volumes 7 and 8 precludes the possibility of many more volumes to come, and specific telltale passages in volume 9—the 'tragicomical completion' of Walter's prediction (9.2.737); the imminence of Tristram's 'eternal separation' from Jenny (9.8.754); the desperate, massive phlebotomy of chapter 24—suggest that this is the last. The subsequent non-appearance of further instalments confirms the point, and lends the blank page at the end of volume 9 a meaning quite as emphatic, in retrospect, as the black page of volume 1 (which also marks a consumptive death, as though in another version of the *a priori/a posteriori* symmetry between these volumes). Here is an ending that practises on a grand scale Sterne's favourite rhetorical figure of the aposiopesis, in which a speaker halts in mid-flow, as though unable to proceed, but usually in such a way as to imply the unspoken conclusion.[82] Now the entire serial halts in mid-flow, and the unspoken conclusion is clear: Tristram's race to prolong his life and complete its transcription has now been lost, the absence of continuation implying his sudden death—'gone! in a moment!' as Trim would put it (5.7.431)—and the terminal interruption of his text. Without any further volumes, the 'forty thousand things' he wants to say in volume 7 go with him to his grave; for it is not the explicit fact of Toby being caught by Widow Wadman but the implicit fact of Tristram being caught by death that is the catastrophe of *Tristram Shandy*, a structural aposiopesis in which Sterne deftly rounds off his serial while highlighting Tristram's failure to complete his own. As noted above (p. 140), an adroit member of the Lloyd–Churchill circle of wits had already made this inference in print in July 1763, some months after volumes 7 and 8 had failed to appear on schedule; but now Sterne's implication looks much stronger. Here indeed is a conclusion in which nothing is concluded, or one in which (to borrow another Johnsonian distinction) Tristram's life and ongoing efforts to transcribe it are 'ended, though not completed'.[83]

---

[82] A mock example from *Peri Bathous* seems relevant here: '"I can no more", when one really can no more' (*The Prose Works of Alexander Pope, vol. 2. 1725–1744*, ed. Rosemary Cowler (Oxford: Blackwell, 1986), 207).

[83] Preface to the *Dictionary*, in Samuel Johnson, *Poetry and Prose*, ed. Mona Wilson (London: Hart-Davis, 1968), 317.

Volume 9, then, evidently marks the culmination of *Tristram Shandy* as a seven-year dramatization of terminal disease, in which the frustration of human ambitions to control and fix inherently fugitive things—experience, memory, identity—is encapsulated by a story of consumptive decline, premature death, and the leaving of unfinished business. While this picture fits in with other arguments for closure that have previously been made, however, it is important to make two qualifications to Booth's influential account, driven as it is by a formalist agenda that makes him overstate the definitiveness and premeditation of the ending. The first is that, while bringing *Tristram Shandy* to implied closure, Sterne cannily stops short of making the closure explicit and binding, so tempering whatever drive towards coherence he may have had with the characteristic pragmatism of the serialist. Here Booth neglects the tendencies shared between volume 9 of *Tristram Shandy* and the endings of other serial works of the period, from Tindal's *Continuation* to *Sir Charles Grandison*, which were typically arbitrary, provisional, or accompanied by a get-out clause. Simply in generic terms, an unequivocal, irreversible conclusion of the kind Booth wants to find would be alien to Sterne's project, anticipating as it does the postmodern quality that Umberto Eco calls 'variability to infinity' or 'the infinity of the text'—that quality in which 'the text takes on the rhythms of that same dailiness in which it is produced and which it mirrors'.[84] More specifically, we cannot rule out the possibility of Sterne returning to reopen *Tristram Shandy*, not only because of the inexplicit nature of his aposiopetic conclusion, but also because of the many undeveloped nodules for continuation scattered earlier in his path. Seventy-one volumes remain to be written, after all, before Tristram's ambition will be fulfilled, their contents including (among much else) a map 'which, with many other pieces and developments to this work, will be added to the end of the twentieth volume' (1.13.40); a section 'where the instrumental parts of the eloquence of the senate, the pulpit, the bar, the coffeehouse, the bed-chamber, and fire-side, fall under consideration' (2.17.141); 'the catastrophe of my great uncle Mr. *Hammond Shandy*, [who] rushed into the duke of *Monmouth*'s affair' (3.10.198); the 'rich bale', to be unloaded 'hereafter', of Tristram's tour through Europe with his father and uncle (7.27.618; 7.28.621); the collection of 'Plain Stories' he intends to deliver once Toby's amours are written (7.43.648). Evidently enough, Sterne was treading a careful line, in ways reminiscent of the kind of 'opportunistic seriality' that William Beatty Warner has found in formula

---

[84] Umberto Eco, 'Interpreting Serials', in *The Limits of Interpretation* (Bloomington, Ind.: Indiana University Press, 1990), 83–100 (at 96).

fiction by Haywood and others in the 1720s.[85] By confining to implication his indications that the text is complete (and complete only from his own standpoint, not from Tristram's), he leaves the door to resumption ajar in case of any future need. A moribund hero, in fiction at least, could always be revived.

The likelihood of any such need was now very remote, however, and not only because the sensibility vogue had now made *A Sentimental Journey* a more promising vehicle for Sterne's writing than *Tristram Shandy*. Sterne was dying himself, and must have known it by mid-1762, when he suffered the traumatic pulmonary haemorrhage—'I was likely to bleed to death' (*Letters*, 180)—that finds its echo in volume 8. Throughout the novel, indeed, the terminal decline of Tristram's health shadows Sterne's condition, and both follow, as Lawlor has shown, the classic course of consumption as then understood.[86] Here it is easy enough to detect implied closure in volume 9, but much harder to agree with Booth that this closure marks completion of the book as 'originally conceived'. Sterne had suffered a similarly dangerous medical episode as early as the 1730s (*EMY* 61), and it is always possible that he was executing a long-held plan to use serialization as a way of rending active and dramatic a narrative in which literary ambition is choked by progressive disease. But the closeness with which Tristram's condition tracks Sterne's over the years of serialization more plausibly suggests that the relationship was causal, with the phasing and trajectory of *Tristram Shandy* developing in improvised response to the ungovernable rhythms and crises of its author's own health. In this light, *Tristram Shandy* looks very much more unstable than Booth would have it, its shape emerging not so much from elaborate forward planning as from adroit extemporization over the years, with Sterne using the contingencies of his own condition to direct the work as he wrote, published, and sickened. It would not be entirely frivolous to imagine a counterfactual scenario in which, instead of declining, Sterne grows stronger during the period of serialization, and writes not the *Tristram Shandy* we have but the alternative *Tristram Shandy* we glimpse in John Croft's 'Anecdotes of Sterne': 'Sterne said that his first Plan, was to travell his Hero Tristram Shandy all over Europe, and . . . finish the work with an eulogium on the superior constitution of England and at length to return Tristram well informed and a compleat English Gentleman.'[87]

[85] Warner, *Licensing Entertainment*, p. 116.

[86] 'The Asthma usually ends in a Consumption in lean Bodies' (John Floyer, *A Treatise of the Asthma*, 3rd edn. (1726), 175, cited by Lawlor, 'Consuming Time', 50).

[87] *Whitefoord Papers*, ed. W. A. S. Hewins (Oxford: Oxford University Press, 1898), 228.

Indeed, there is a sense in which Booth's clinching indicator of pre-structuring and closure—the transition from Toby's campaigns to Toby's amours—is also governed by contingency. These amours can begin in earnest only once Toby has been released from his war-gaming obsession by the end of Marlborough's wars at the Peace of Utrecht, an event apparently triggered in the novel by the protracted run-up to the real-time Peace of Paris (which was widely anticipated after the second instalment of *Tristram Shandy*, negotiated and signed after the third, and obliquely registered—'AND SO THE PEACE WAS MADE' (7.35.638)—in the fourth). Only then can the 'choicest morsel' be introduced in the volumes of 1765-7, its emergence depending as much on the course of international diplomacy as Tristram's convulsions depend on the state of Sterne's lungs. At the very least, these two large contingencies, public and private, regulate *Tristram Shandy*'s pace, and it may be right to see Sterne as activating his implied conclusion when he did only because one circumstance—the ending of the Seven Years War—now allowed it, while the other—his rapidly declining health—now required it as an urgent matter.

Where all this leaves us with Sterne's last work, *A Sentimental Journey through France and Italy*, is an even more puzzling question. Its second and last volume stops with Yorick no further forward in his tour than the south of France, though Sterne had earlier envisaged a work 'of four volumes' (*Letters*, 284). In a notice tipped in to several copies of the first edition of February 1768, Sterne acknowledges that subscribers 'have a further claim upon him for Two Volumes more than these delivered to them now', and promises the remainder 'early the next Winter'. A month later, however, he was dead. The result is that we can only guess whether the mismatch between title and text in *A Sentimental Journey* is just another Shandean joke about the impossibility of fulfilment, complicated further by a playful advertisement, or whether this notice is sincere evidence that a longer project was cut off. Perhaps there is a middle option, which is that Sterne, knowing the imminence of his own death and anxious not only to provide for his daughter but also to join (as he says in a letter) 'ces Heros, qui sont Morts en plaisantant' (*Letters*, 416), was perpetrating the kind of fraud that Charles Churchill wittily alleges against Johnson in his Shandean poem *The Ghost*: 'He for *Subscribers* baits his hook, | And takes their cash—but where's the Book?'[88]

One sure conclusion may be drawn, however, from the modulation out of *Tristram Shandy* of *A Sentimental Journey*, and from the door to

[88] *The Poetical Works of Charles Churchill*, ed. Douglas Grant (Oxford: Clarendon Press, 1956), 126 (*The Ghost*, bk. 3 (1762), ll. 801–2).

resumption that Sterne left ajar in both these works. His ongoing strategy for success in the faddish, unstable literary culture of the 1760s was to defer closure, generate continuations and spin-off projects, and so cultivate a mode of writing able to absorb and respond to new texts, trends, and tastes as they emerged, holding its position at this culture's cutting edge with a kind of self-renewing fashionability. The ambiguously sentimental turn in later volumes of *Tristram Shandy*, and the sideways propagation of *A Sentimental Journey* from the Maria episode in volume 9, mark the best-known case of this responsiveness to shifts in marketplace demand. Alert not only to the cultural force of sensibility in general, but also to the growing popularity of the new sentimental fiction (Sarah Scott's *Millenium Hall* (1762), Frances Brooke's *Lady Julia Mandeville* (1763), and Goldsmith's *Vicar of Wakefield* (1766) were among the conspicuous successes), Sterne reacted with a vein of writing delicately poised, in its handling of sentimental themes and tropes, between participation and parody. However, the provenance of much of the stock in trade of 1760s sentimental novels in earlier examples (the massively influential *Grandison*, with Sarah Fielding's *David Simple* and forgotten works like Guthrie's *The Friends: A Sentimental History*) makes it difficult to identify specific sentimental elements in Sterne's later volumes as simple or certain cases of improvisatory engagement with newly emerging texts. One must look in less predictable directions, and to other genres. In the remaining chapters of this book, I turn in detail to two poetic examples of contemporaneous literary projects—one public and intensely voguish, the other as yet confined to a coterie in which Sterne moved—that more plainly highlight *Tristram Shandy*'s distinctive capacity to shift, or even mutate, in mid-publication.

PART THREE

Sterne in the Literary Culture of the 1760s

5

Tristram Shandy and the
Freshest Moderns

For all the sophistication with which Sterne must have read *A Tale of a Tub*, it is hard not to feel that the hack persona in which Swift's satire is written—a deranged embodiment of dumbed-down, hyped-up, commercialized modern authorship—resembles not just Tristram but Sterne himself. The technical incompetence and preening egotism of Swift's hack feed directly (though in a gentler mode) into the character of Tristram; but, as well as appropriating Swift's satire for his own creative ends, Sterne also falls uncomfortably within its reach. Half a century's ongoing expansion in the marketplace for print had made *A Tale of a Tub* look more prescient than ever, and there are several ways in which Sterne's exuberant manufacture of fashionable print echoes the hack's strategies for success in what he calls 'so blessed an Age for the mutual Felicity of *Booksellers* and *Authors*'. Where the hack spins out his text 'from a laborious Collection of Seven Hundred Thirty Eight *Flowers*, and *shining Hints* of the best *Modern* Authors', or gleefully acknowledges 'the great *Helps* and *Liftings*' he has taken from existing works,[1] Sterne more quietly recycles the output of others, but with a degree of intricacy and intensiveness that can rarely, if ever, have been equalled. 'Sterne seems almost incapable of sustained writing that does not have recourse (or digression) to the work of others,' as Melvyn New has written,[2] and it is through this method, paradoxically, that many of his most distinctive effects are achieved. The classic instance comes with the witty regress of plagiarisms contrived at the opening of the third instalment (5.1.408), in which Tristram's earnest diatribe against plagiarism turns out to be plagiarized from Burton, who himself had partly plagiarized the passage from earlier sources. Nor is this the end of Sterne's

---

[1] Jonathan Swift, *A Tale of a Tub*, ed. A. C. Guthkelch and D. Nichol Smith, 2nd edn. (Oxford: Clarendon Press, 1958), 182, 209, 129.

[2] Melvyn New, 'Some Sterne Borrowings from Four Renaissance Authors', *Philological Quarterly*, 71 (1992), 301–11 (at 301).

silent practical joke about literary theft, because he also cribs its founding
idea from a couplet in the *Verses on the Death of Dr. Swift*—'To steal a hint
was never known, | But what he writ, was all his own'—which, self-
refutingly, is stolen from Denham.[3] As Wolfgang Iser notes of this celebrated passage, 'the Burton text shines like a palimpsest through Tristram's
complaint', and with this remark Iser glances towards the structuralist theory of intertextuality and its applicability to *Tristram Shandy*.[4] In the
terminology associated with Gérard Genette, this is a massively palimpsestuous piece of writing, one superimposing itself on multiple layers of prior
writing, yet also conferring, between the lines, a residual visibility on the
texts it reworks and transforms.

For Swift's hack, plunderings of this kind are his entitlement 'as the
freshest Modern, which gives me a Despotick Power over all Authors before
me', and this claim also indicates the obsession with novelty and fashion
that dominates his upstart text. This is an age, he reminds us, 'when a *Book*
that misses its Tide, shall be neglected . . . like *Mackarel* a Week after the
Season'—an age in which freshness is all, and books must be urgently
hawked or will rot on the stall.[5] Sterne appears to have taken the warning
to heart, assiduously nursing the voguish status of *Tristram Shandy* in the
culture on which it burst, and with it his personal standing as a celebrity
author. In part, the aura of fashionable modernity that he worked so hard
to sustain is a matter of biographical documentation rather than critical
exegesis, and indeed the premium he placed on fame and fashion is a gov-
erning theme of the most recent life of Sterne.[6] One strategy of self-
promotion was to associate himself exclusively with the A-list of the day,
and accordingly Sterne was rigorous in seeking out the most fashionable
metropolitan booksellers (the Dodsleys and, later, Becket and Dehondt),
cultivating the most fashionable patrons in the worlds of theatre, politics,
and the Church (Garrick, Pitt, and, for a while, Warburton), and employ-

---

[3] See *Verses on the Death of Dr. Swift*, ll. 317–18, and Pat Rogers's note on this couplet in
his edition of Swift's *Complete Poems* (Harmondsworth: Penguin, 1983), 854: the source is
Denham's *On Mr. Abraham Cowley*, ll. 29–30.

[4] Wolfgang Iser, *Laurence Sterne: Tristram Shandy* (Cambridge: Cambridge University
Press, 1988), 55; see also, for this term, Gerald Prince's foreword to Gérard Genette,
Palimpsests: Literature in the Second Degree (Lincoln, Neb.: University of Nebraska Press,
1997), pp. ix–xi. Iser might have added that in this case the palimpsest needs expert illumina-
tion. Though clear enough now, the play on Burton appears to have gone unnoticed for
decades, and was not recorded in print—by John Ferriar, who failed to get the joke—until
1812 (*TS Notes*, 339).

[5] Swift, *Tale of a Tub*, 130, 206.

[6] Ian Campbell Ross, *Laurence Sterne: A Life* (Oxford: Oxford University Press, 2001),
esp. 1–19.

ing only the most fashionable artists. The first was the veteran Hogarth, whom Sterne petitioned for a suitably prestigious illustration 'to clap at the Front of my next Edition of *Shandy*'; the second was the rising star Reynolds, whose portrait of 1760, once engraved, could render ubiquitous his image: 'There is a fine print going to be done of me—so I shall make the most of myself, & sell both inside & out' (*Letters*, 99, 105). Another strategy was to adopt in public the personae in which he wrote, his promotional impersonations of Tristram and Yorick in Ranelagh and St James's—and, later, his appearance in the salons of Paris as the 'Chevalier Shandy' (*Letters*, 157)—amounting to a highly visible form of performance art, through which Sterne's social existence could become an extension of his fictional text. Even the published title of his sermons (which are attributed to 'Mr. Yorick') and the name bestowed on his Yorkshire house ('Shandy Hall') were enlisted as part of the act. In this respect, the play on personal identity for which criticism so often celebrates *Tristram Shandy* is a feature not only of the text itself, but also of the life that Sterne self-consciously fashioned around it—his life as at once (as an early observer put it in the *Grand Magazine*) '*Tristram Shandy*, alias *Yorick*, alias the Rev. Mr. *St*****' (*CH* 96).

Other contemporaries suspected that Sterne was publishing attacks on himself in order to keep up his vogue, with the *Critical Review* alleging that in one anonymous pamphlet of April 1760 (*Explanatory Remarks . . . by Jeremiah Kunastrokius*) 'the author himself is here giving breath to the trumpet of fame' (*CH* 62). Suggestive evidence has recently been used to identify as just such a piece of covert self-promotion *The Clockmakers Outcry against . . . Tristram Shandy*, a bantering attack which gave new impetus to the craze it affected to deplore. 'Our manners and speech at present are all *be-Tristram'd*', the pamphlet insists, adding that 'nobody speaks now but in the *Shandean* style. The modish phraseology is all taken from him . . .'[7] Other witnesses concurred, with Boswell's 'Poetical Epistle to Doctor Sterne, Parson Yorick, and Tristram Shandy' standing out for the acuteness with which it itemizes Sterne's strategies for transforming himself from an obscure provincial figure—a man 'to Country Curacy confined'—into the toast of the London glitterati. Sterne has the smartest publisher ('Dodsley, who lives at the Court end'); the smartest public image and milieu ('By Fashion's hand compleatly drest, | He's everywhere a wellcome Guest'); the smartest marketing pitch and saturation presence:

[7] *CH* 70; for the attribution, see Anne Bandry and W. G. Day, 'The Third Edition of the *Clockmakers Outcry*', *Shandean*, 4 (1992), 153–66; also their edition of this pamphlet (Winchester: Winchester College Printing Society, 1991).

'Who has not *Tristram Shandy* read? | Is any mortal so ill-bred?' (*CH* 80–5). As Sterne put it himself at the very height of his fame, *Tristram Shandy* and trendiness were indivisible commodities, the one synonymous with the other: 'I assure you my Kitty, that Tristram is the Fashion' (*Letters*, 102).

For all this external posturing and puffing, however, it is clear that the fashionableness of *Tristram Shandy* was above all internally constructed, a feature inherent in the text itself and independent of Sterne's caperings around it. As I argue in the opening chapters of this book, novelty is the identity flaunted above all in the narrative's every move, the structural, rhetorical, and typographical peculiarities of the text combining to pro-claim its double freshness as a novel exercise in the novel form. Though af-fecting to deplore the fact that a 'vile pruriency for fresh adventures in all things, has got so strongly into our habit and humours' (1.20.66), the text is forever promising 'fresh matter' as its stock in trade (1.13.39), above all in its narrative convolutions. 'One would think I took a pleasure in runing into difficulties of this kind', as Tristram puts it in the fourth instalment, 'merely to make fresh experiments of getting out of 'em' (8.6.663). Serial-ization, moreover, enabled Sterne to subject this freshness to perpetual renewal. As *Tristram Shandy* took shape in the intervals of publication, it could move with the times, recurrently responsive to its ongoing cultural moment. Marshall Brown has identified the literary culture of the 1760s as peculiarly complex and unstable in its character, the heterogeneous output of the decade being marked above all by its unpredictability, by the sudden emergence and equally sudden eclipse of new experimental idioms, and by its characteristic rejection, vigorous subversion, and occasional surprising recasting of older forms.[8] In this context, Sterne's improvisatory serial was ideally geared to register and exploit the shifting trends of a culture in which it could re-emerge at irregular intervals, the result being to open up to Sterne's satire an ongoing repertoire of intertex-tual possibilities on which to play. Here again one might detect an echo of Swift's hack, who first censures 'a certain paultry *Scribbler*, very volumi-nous . . . [who] deals in a pernicious Kind of Writings, called *Second Parts*', but then closes his text by threatening a continuation himself.[9] For Sterne, to serialize *Tristram Shandy* was to remain forever the freshest modern, always returning to challenge or trump the latest voguish pretender to fashion and fame.

[8] See Marshall Brown, *Preromanticism* (Stanford, Calif.: Stanford University Press, 1990), pp. 1–21, and, on *Tristram Shandy*, 261–300.
[9] Swift, *Tale of a Tub*, 183.

When preparing in 1764 to return to the fray with the fourth instalment of *Tristram Shandy*, Sterne confessed to Hume that his original vogue had waned after only a winter (*LY* 93), as though sensing that by now the going rate for being famous was already down as low as fifteen weeks. Perhaps by now there is more anxiety than smugness in Tristram's reminder to his readers that they may count themselves within the category of 'any English gentleman of fashion' (7.27.616). Wary of becoming the flash in the pan that hostile observers like Johnson were anxious to dub him, he was always a vigilant observer of emerging trends that might eclipse or displace his own work. Not only that: his defensive strategy, when faced by any such challenge, was to appropriate and absorb within *Tristram Shandy* the most arresting or novel elements of the new rival, while at the same time subjecting this rival to parodic reworking, thereby shifting back in his own favour the balance of power between them. *Tristram Shandy* could mutate as it went along, taking on fresh innovatory characteristics from other texts as they emerged; but it could also retain the fundamentally parodic identity that had distinguished it from the start, redeploying its satirical arsenal at the expense of other new texts. Here the Genettian term 'palimpsest' is somewhat misleading, with the sense it conveys of over-writing (while leaving visible the trace or erasure of) a very antique source. The burden of this book is that intertextual play in *Tristram Shandy* takes place not only in relation to the learned-wit tradition that has dominated Sterne scholarship up to and including the magisterial annotations of the Florida edition, but also in relation to the brashly modern, the trendily new. Sterne freshens his ongoing text, and signals that freshness, by playing on other fresh texts, albeit in a mode of intertextuality less susceptible of annotation than the determinate, quotative mode that characterizes his treatment of Renaissance sources. Now we are dealing not with specific traceable reworkings, but with larger and rather more ghostly palimpsestuous structures: structures more like those to which Genette applies the term 'transposition', by which he means a mode of intertextuality, marked more by large analogy than local allusion, which 'can give rise to works of vast dimensions . . . whose textual amplitude and aesthetic and/or ideological ambition may mask or even completely obfuscate their hypertextual character'.[10] *Tristram Shandy*'s hypertextual character in general cannot be in doubt, but the relationship of the work as it unfolds to contemporaneous publications is much less easily pinned down than in the case of Montaigne, or Burton, or even Swift. Yet this relationship was

---

[10] Genette, *Palimpsests*, 213.

crucial to *Tristram Shandy*'s ongoing success in the 1760s, and it suffuses the text we inherit now. Most obviously, the new and modern things that Sterne assimilates in his satire are instances of that quintessentially modern genre, the novel itself. But the contemporaneity of *Tristram Shandy*'s intertextual repertoire reaches well beyond the sources outlined in earlier chapters of this book, and some of the most pervasive examples were not novels at all.

FASHION, DISORDER, AND THE NONSENSE CLUB

Take, for example, the case of the poet Charles Churchill, who briefly rivalled Sterne for scandalous celebrity in the early 1760s, partly because of the pit-bull ferocity of his satirical muse, but equally because of his shamelessly delinquent personal life (he was, like Sterne, in holy orders). As well as exploiting to the full the fame-and-fashion culture of the day, Churchill was also, with his friend and imitator Robert Lloyd, its sharpest satirical observer. In the satires of both (Churchill, Lloyd, and their 'Nonsense Club' circle present an unusually strong case for thinking in terms of collective output, as Lance Bertelsen has demonstrated),[11] modernity and novelty are the debilitating obsessions of a culture that has wilfully severed itself from tradition, and from all the values thereby entailed. The world they conjure up is radically unstable, one in which (in the words of a burlesque ode by Lloyd and Colman) 'The tyrant, Fashion, governs all'—and governs, in particular, literary success. Ministers come and go, stocks multiply or crash within an hour, and modes and manners change with every moon. But the peculiarly self-conscious poetry of the 'Nonsense Club' circle is focused above all on literary fads. 'Fashion, that sets the modes of dress, | Sheds too her influence o'er the press', as Lloyd puts it in his 'Epistle to J. B. Esq. 1757'. The result is the triumph of trendy mediocrity, of 'tawdry works . . . grac'd | With all the charms of modern taste'. In 'The Puff, a Dialogue between the Bookseller and Author', Lloyd explains more fully how to hook readers in a world in which 'Bare Merit never will succeed'. Saleable works must have surprising titles, alluring puffs, luxurious and novel material formats. Above all, they must catch (or, better, set) the mood of the moment: 'Books shift about, like ladies' dress, | And there's a fashion in success.'[12] For Churchill, 'The love of Novelty and Fashion' is in

---

[11] Lance Bertelsen, *The Nonsense Club: Literature and Popular Culture, 1749–1764* (Oxford: Clarendon Press, 1986), esp. 91–131.

[12] *The Poetical Works of Robert Lloyd, A. M.*, 2 vols. (1774; repr. Farnborough: Gregg International Publishers, 1969), 1: 121; 1: 97–8; 1: 179.

itself the only sure and stable thing, and nothing is as fugitive as literary fame: 'But Fashion so directs, and Moderns raise, | On Fashion's mould'ring base, their transient praise.'[13]

In his severer moods, Churchill finds his heroes among those who stand aloof from this febrile and debilitating literary culture. *Independence* (1764) makes the usual lament for the poem's eponymous virtue, which now has 'out of fashion grown', and bitterly contrasts patrons who once 'were Men of Sense, | Were Men of Taste', with those of the present, who now merely 'patronize for fashion sake—no more— | And keep a Bard, just as They keep a *Whore*'. In this context, Churchill celebrates an idealized poet whom 'Fashion cannot tempt'.[14] Yet there is usually as much glee as disgust in Nonsense Club writing about literary fashion, and when Sterne enters the picture—as he repeatedly does in this context—the tone is in general admiring. Lloyd is uncensorious when linking Sterne and Swift as sharing 'a fashionable turn' for indecency, and in *The Ghost* Churchill mounts what is probably the first ever formalist defence of *Tristram Shandy*'s coherence. Here Churchill singles out for praise the skill

> Which we so much admire in STERNE,
> Where each *Digression*, seeming vain,
> And only fit to entertain,
> Is found, on better recollection,
> To have a just and nice Connection,
> To help the whole with wond'rous art,
> Whence it seems idly to depart . . .[15]

In this passage, Churchill wishes that he himself could manage digression 'with half that skill', and indeed the sincerest flattery paid to Sterne in Nonsense Club satire is that of imitation. In a poem that seeks to act on its conviction that 'novelty will please the best', Lloyd looks to Sterne for guidance in how to write with fashionable spontaneity, obscurity, and innuendo:

> Like TRISTRAM SHANDY, I could write
> From morn to noon, from noon to night,
> Sometimes obscure, and sometimes leaning
> A little sideways to a meaning . . .[16]

Nor was any of this simply a pose or a joke. In its improvisatory, associative, and formally disrupted character, the poetry of the Nonsense Club

---

[13] *The Poetical Works of Charles Churchill*, ed. Douglas Grant (Oxford: Clarendon Press, 1956), 74 (*The Ghost*, bk. 1 (1762), l. 352); 22 (*The Rosciad* (1761), ll. 679–80).

[14] Ibid. 426 (*Independence* (1764), l. 510), 423 (ll. 381–2, 391–2), 413 (l. 5).

[15] *Poetical Works of Lloyd*, 2: 64, and see also 1: 8; *Poetical Works of Churchill*, 131 (*The Ghost*, bk. 3, ll. 970–6), and see also pp. 84 (bk. 2, ll. 171–4) and 5 (*The Rosciad*, ll. 61–2).

[16] *Poetical Works of Lloyd*, 2: 89; 2: 83.

must be the nearest verse equivalent to Shandean narrative ever achieved. As Bertelsen puts it when defining 'the self-reflexive process poetry of Lloyd and Churchill' in terms of its studious irregularity of thought and form, 'it is in Churchill's work that this aesthetic is given a contemporary voice surpassed only by Sterne's'.[17] Early readers immediately made this link, especially in the case of *The Ghost*, which the *Monthly Review* greeted as 'a kind of *Tristram Shandy* in verse', or again 'this Shandy in Hudibrastics'.[18] Colman and Garrick expand upon the connection in a verse epistle to Robert Lloyd, in which their own muse starts to move in wayward directions, as though

> to shew, like handy-dandy,
> Or CHURCHILL'S GHOST, or TRISTRAM SHANDY,
> Now here, now there, with quick progression,
> How smartly you can make digression.[19]

Yet this relationship between *Tristram Shandy* and Nonsense Club poetry was by no means entirely one-way traffic, and it appears as such only because, whereas Churchill and Lloyd explicitly associate themselves with Sterne's text, Sterne himself allowed the connection to remain implicit. He certainly knew Churchill and Lloyd both personally and as writers. He appears among the subscribers to Lloyd's *Poems* of March 1762, and is likely to have known some of the contents before that, either in manuscript or earlier printed forms. Two years later we hear in a letter to Churchill from Wilkes in Paris that 'Sterne and I often meet, and talk of you' (*Letters*, 212 n.), and Sterne's acquaintance with Churchill may well have been of some years' standing by then. The Nonsense Club had publicly emerged at much the same time as *Tristram Shandy*, notably with *Two Odes* (published by Lloyd and Colman in January 1760 to burlesque the formal experimentations of Gray and Mason), and it is likely that Sterne came into contact with its members, perhaps through Garrick, soon after coming to London. For years beforehand, writers of the Club had been pioneering the ostentatious unravelling of thought and discourse that we tend to think of now as Sterne's own special preserve. As David Fairer notes, William Cowper's 'An Epistle to Robert Lloyd, Esq.' (1754), in which the poet writes to divert 'fierce banditti, which I mean, | Are gloomy

[17] Bertelsen, *Nonsense Club*, 106–7.
[18] *Monthly Review*, 27 (Oct. 1762), 316; 29 (Nov. 1763), 397; see also 25 (Dec. 1761), 451, on *Tristram Shandy* as prototype for Churchill's *Night*.
[19] 'The Cobler of Criplegate's Letter to Robert Lloyd, A. M.' (1763), in *Poetical Works of Lloyd*, 97–104 (at 101).

thoughts, led on by spleen', does more than anticipate *Tristram Shandy*'s sense of being written 'against the spleen' (4.22.360). As in Sterne, the anti-splenetic train of thought goes on to scatter, and coherent syntax fragments in a chaos of dashes:

> First, for a thought—since all agree—
> A thought—I have it—let me see—
> 'Tis gone again—Plague on't! I thought
> I had it—but I have it not.[20]

Cowper's poem typifies the way in which some of the Shandean character-istics of Nonsense Club satire turn out to antedate even the first instalment of *Tristram Shandy*, and suggests something more interesting than some simple case of derivative poets clinging to the coat-tails of Sterne. The dynamic appears to have worked in two directions at once, with a kind of conversational, reciprocal influence that is most clearly dramatized in the contemporaneous serial development of *Tristram Shandy* and *The Ghost*. At the very least, both Sterne and the poets of the Churchill–Lloyd circle were giving simultaneous expression to formal and satirical moves that many writers seem to have found a logical next step for what Thomas Lockwood has called a 'post-Augustan' age[21]—moves arising not from the oddity of an individual writer (as Samuel Johnson wished to see it in the case of Sterne) but from a widely shared dissatisfaction with existing modes and structures of literary discourse.

The intimacy with which Sterne succeeded in tying his writing to the contemporaneous output of his decade is flamboyantly illustrated by his friend John Hamilton Mortimer, painter of the celebrated 'Caricature Group' (1767) in which Sterne features, and of several other Sterne-related pieces.[22] In an etching that Mortimer contributed to the second edition of a satirical poem about contemporary authorship and publishing, Evan Lloyd's *The Powers of the Pen* (1768), a malign group of braying or dozing

---

[20] *The Poems of William Cowper*, ed. John D. Baird and Charles Ryskamp, 3 vols. (Oxford: Clarendon Press, 1980–95), 1: 55 (ll. 19–20, 35–8); see also pp. 221–2 of David Fairer's *English Poetry of the Eighteenth Century, 1700–1789* (Harlow: Longman, in press).

[21] Thomas Lockwood, *Post-Augustan Satire: Charles Churchill and Satirical Poetry, 1750–1800* (Seattle: University of Washington Press, 1979).

[22] These include a portrait of the clockmaker John Ireland, who, in an inspired touch, is shown holding a copy of *Tristram Shandy*, and more than one version of the much-illustrated 'Captive' vision from *A Sentimental Journey*. See John Sunderland, *John Hamilton Mortimer: His Life and Works*, vol. 52 (1986) of the Walpole Society (London: Walpole Society, 1988), catalogue items 34 (the 'Caricature Group', on which see also *LY* 365–72), 142 (Ireland), 89–90 ('The Captive'). Item 20 in Sunderland's catalogue is Mortimer's frontispiece to *The Powers of the Pen*.

critics (Johnson, arms folded, is conspicuous among them) sit in judgement on a basketful of the latest publications (see Fig. 5). Mortimer takes
his cue here from the text by Evan Lloyd, who, though no immediate relation of his namesake Robert, was one of several satirists to lay claim to the
mantle of Churchill and Lloyd on the premature deaths of both in 1764.[23]
In keeping with the Nonsense Club spirit, his poems are shot through with
allusions to Sterne, who is represented as an ever-present figure in the
swarming, chaotically varied literary market of the day.[24] Indeed, in this
edition of *The Powers of the Pen* (which Lloyd revised soon after Sterne's
death), Sterne is seen as wittily presiding over this whole market. Bored by
old-style jesting, Jove sends Comus to earth to learn from Sterne, and then
finds himself so much captivated by 'the *Shandean* art' that he sends for the
man himself, 'And plac'd him in the Chair of Wit I Which *Comus* was com-
pell'd to quit'.[25] Mortimer concentrates this emphasis superbly in his etching, which he subtitled (with reference not only to the *Dunciad* but also to
the post-Scriblerian rise of the reviewing magazines) 'The Reviewers
Cave'. The immediate reference is to a part of the poem in which, 'Sunk
twenty Fathom under Ground, I Paper'd with *Title-pages* round, I A
Dungeon lies':[26] here the ghoulish reviewers butcher modern works of
wit and sense and flay the authors, whose distorted faces hang (Hannibal
Lecter-style) from the roof of the cave. The face to the left suggests Sterne's.
Hurled together in the basket with *The Powers of the Pen* itself are *A
Sentimental Journey*, a volume labelled 'Churchil', and another labelled
'Bagatel' (perhaps indicating Andrew Hervey Mills's obscure *Bagatelles*
of 1767). Randomly pasted to the walls are the title pages of sacrifices
from previous years, prominently including *Tristram Shandy* and 'Stern's
Sermons', which are surrounded by a range of titles including Churchill's
The Rosciad (1761), *The Apology* (1761), and *The Ghost* (1762–3), Edward
Thompson's *The Meretriciad* (1761), Wilkes's *North Briton* (1762–3),
several deliberately illegible titles, and two earlier satires by Evan Lloyd
himself, *The Methodist* (1766) and *The Curate* (1766).

With this wealth of immediate contexts and connections, Mortimer's
etching renders beautifully visual the pervasive presence of *Tristram*

---

[23] As the *Monthly Review* robustly put it, 'the Author of this Poem is one of those
numerous maggots that have bred in the remains of Churchill' (34 (Feb. 1766), 405, quoted by
Cecil J. L. Price, *A Man of Genius, and a Welch Man* (Swansea: University College of Swansea,
1963), 11).

[24] See e.g. *Conversation* (1767), 25 ('HERE *Shandy* revels in *salacious Wit*, I THERE *Wesley*
issues out DAMNATION's *Writ*'), 42 ('*Shandean* Jests, and *Love*'s salt Wit abound'), 50 ('To
laugh as *much*, tho' not so *well* as *Sterne*').

[25] Evan Lloyd, *The Powers of the Pen*, 2nd edn. (1768), 27.

[26] Ibid. 55.

Fig. 5. John Hamilton Mortimer, frontispiece to Evan Lloyd's *The Powers of the Pen: A Poem*, 2nd edn. (1768): 'Sunk twenty *Fathom* under Ground, | Paper'd with *Title-pages* round, | A *Dungeon* lies; and plac'd before | Stand *Printer's Dev'ls* to guard the Door.'

Shandy in the literary culture of the decade, and the intimacy of its relationship with the wide variety of contemporaneous publications on which
it both impacts and is impacted. It shows us Sterne not only as a competitor in the ongoing procession of claimants to literary fame (or, in the context of Lloyd's attack on the reviewers, notoriety) throughout the decade,
but as the exemplary and dominant competitor, whose writing develops in
a state of ongoing responsiveness to these other trends. Relevant in this
context (beyond the notion of Bloomian misreading) is Gillian Beer's
account of the ways in which writers 'respond to, internalize, and resist
past writing' in their arguments with prior texts, given the success with
which Beer develops a model flexible enough to register competing
currents of antagonism and attraction within a single set of literary
relations.[27] The difference is that, unlike intertextual connections such as
the Richardson–Milton and Richardson–Sidney relations described by
Beer in *Arguing with the Past*, serialization now puts Sterne in the intriguing position of arguing with the present. Alongside its many other identi-
ties, *Tristram Shandy* becomes a litmus test of tastes and fads as they
develop throughout the decade of its publication, or an optic offering new
perspectives on the diverse cultural trends reflected within it. It becomes
(to reformulate Shklovsky) the most typical work of 1760s literature.

The final section of this book explores two further sets of intertextual
connection between *Tristram Shandy* and literary fashions that developed
in the period of its serialization. These are case studies, and many others
would be possible, from the burgeoning sentimental fiction of the early
1760s to the fugitive journalism proposed by Morris Golden in his analysis
of *Tristram Shandy's* periodical context.[28] With his many partisan sar-
casms on the subject, Churchill usefully indicates the first of these connections, which lies with a body of work he found much more genuinely
pernicious than *Tristram Shandy* as an instance of voguish novelty and the
susceptibility to it of modern readers. Writing sceptically of 'That *old, new,
Epic Pastoral*, FINGAL', Churchill uses Macpherson's Ossianic fabrications
of the early 1760s not only as a surrogate target in the Scotophobic campaign that he and Wilkes were running against the Earl of Bute's Tory min-

---

[27] Gillian Beer, *Arguing with the Past: Essays in Narrative from Woolf to Sidney* (London:
Routledge, 1989), p. viii.

[28] Morris Golden, 'Periodical Context in the Imagined World of *Tristram Shandy*', *The Age
of Johnson*, 1 (1987), 237–60. I deal elsewhere with the intricate relationship between *Tristram
Shandy*, *A Sentimental Journey*, and sentimental fiction of the 1760s: see Thomas Keymer,
'Sentimental Fiction: Ethics, Social Critique, and Philanthropy', in John Richetti (ed.), *The
Cambridge History of English Literature 1660–1780* (Cambridge: Cambridge University Press,
in press).

istry, but also as an extreme case of the power of fashion and patronage to debase the public taste. 'If fashionable grown, and fond of pow'r,' he contemptuously tells his readers in a posthumously published fragment, 'With *hum'rous* Scots let Them disport their hour; I Let Them dance, fairy like, round Ossian's tomb'.[29] Here we get a sharp sense of Churchill's antagonism towards a phenomenon that had posed a double challenge to his own output, first in its diametrically different political affiliation and implication, and second in its public prominence and commercial success. With *Tristram Shandy*, indeed, the *Poems of Ossian* must go down as one of the two great literary vogues of the entire decade, and in this context Sterne's wry engagement with it can be seen as at once combative and recuperative, a blend of satirical teasing and pragmatic absorption. Sterne also found something genuinely fruitful in the Ossianic vogue for his own creative purposes, however, and his response appears to have had a serious thematic impact on *Tristram Shandy*, contributing to the growing (though always ambivalent) sentimentalism of the text, and to a pervasive sense of isolation from the past that we might otherwise think of as incipiently Proustian.[30] In a broader sense, this emphasis on loss, including the large-scale human losses of the global war that formed an ongoing backdrop to both *Tristram Shandy* and *The Poems of Ossian* until 1763, looks forward to the subject of my final chapter. Here I deal not with the emergence of new poetry but with the revival of interest, as *Tristram Shandy* was being written, in the work of a much earlier poet, Andrew Marvell, whose writing opened up for Sterne a space in which he could play (with the mingling of jest and earnest that links the methods of both writers) on warfare and its associated traumas.

STERNE AND THE OSSIANIC VOGUE

Surveying Calais in volume 7 of *Tristram Shandy*, Tristram prepares to transcribe a lengthy account of the siege of the town from the historian Rapin de Thoyras. Then he relents:

No——! by that all powerful fire which warms the visionary brain, and lights the spirits through unworldly tracts! ere I would . . . make thee pay, poor soul! for fifty

[29] *Poetical Works of Churchill*, 198 (*The Prophecy of Famine* (1763), l. 130); 442 (*The Journey* (1765), ll. 119–21).

[30] See Melvyn New, 'Reading Sterne through Proust and Levinas', *Age of Johnson*, 12 (2001), 329–60; also his 'Proust's Influence on Sterne: Remembrance of Things to Come', *Modern Language Notes*, 103 (1988), 1031–55.

pages which I have no right to sell thee,—naked as I am, I would browse upon the mountains, and smile that the north wind brought me neither my tent or my supper. (7.6.584)

In the context of a work that famously makes plagiarism an art, this is an odd enough declaration. What most struck Ralph Griffiths in the *Monthly Review* for February 1765, however, was its strange grandiloquence of tone, which seemed to recall a work already censured by the *Monthly Review*, on its appearance three years beforehand, for the 'bombast, extravagance, and absurdity' of its literary style.[31] 'Nobly said!—that flight to the mountain's top was lofty indeed!', Griffiths sarcastically writes (*CH* 162): 'Perfectly Fingalian!'

The passage is not, of course, perfectly Fingalian. Sterne may indeed have wished to bring Macpherson to mind as one very topical case of an author making his readers pay for just the commodity that Tristram here forswears: the work of another, in this case the work of Ossian, a supposed third-century bard. Perhaps he implies some wry acknowledgement, at a time when Tristram has 'ten cart-loads of thy fifth and sixth volumes still—still unsold' (8.6.663), while *Fingal* remains a bestselling success, that Macpherson and he have in a sense already changed fortunes and places. Yet no real effort is made here to catch the distinctive measure of Macpherson's prose, while the vaguely Ossianic diction on which Tristram draws is mixed with concerns of far too decadent a kind (tents and suppers, to say nothing of smiling) to have much place in *Fingal*'s world. Whatever else Tristram has in mind to revive his flagging sales, a full-blown shift into the bardic sublime is clearly not in prospect. He fails to act on his later resolution to 'go into Wales for six weeks, and drink goat's-whey' (7.29.624), and no obvious further trace of the Celtic vogue—fuelled at the time not only by Ossian but also by works like Evan Evans's *Specimens of the Poetry of the Ancient Welsh Bards* (1764)—is registered in over 500 pages of notes to the Florida edition.

Yet it remains the case that Ralph Griffiths in 1765 had ample reason to associate Sterne with Macpherson, just as Robert Burns was to do in a letter of 1783 (*CH* 260), and just as Malcolm Laing was to do in his 'Historical and Critical Dissertation on the Supposed Authenticity of the Poems of Ossian' (1800).[32] If at first sight the ardent primitivism of *The Poems of Ossian* and the playful modernity of *Tristram Shandy* seem worlds apart, a

---

[31] *Monthly Review*, 26 (Jan. 1762), 42. This long review of *Fingal* (pp. 41–57) immediately follows the review of *Tristram Shandy*'s third instalment (pp. 31–41).

[32] In Malcolm Laing, *The History of Scotland, from the Union of the Crowns*, 2 vols. (1800), 2: 407.

closer look reveals affinities that run far beyond the more obvious differences of culture, language, and genre. To examine the many historical, formal, and thematic connections between these two great literary projects of the 1760s is to see how Sterne's wry transposition of Ossianic elements in *Tristram Shandy* helped to shape his own developing emphases in ways that may have begun in parodic spirit, but became increasingly serious in tone and amplitude as he drew his work towards its implied conclusion.

There are many ways in which Sterne's *Tristram Shandy* and the sequence of Ossianic texts on which Macpherson was simultaneously at work may reasonably be seen as parallel projects. Simply as publishing processes they share similar features, jointly highlighting the hunger for novelty, openness to experimentation, and sheer opportunist vigour that characterized the literary marketplace of the day. Both (from the point of view at least of the metropolitan literary culture for which the *Monthly Review* spoke) were texts from the margins, yet both made a rapid and forceful impact on the literary centre to which their authors were simultaneously drawn. Both had protracted and strangely similar histories of production, *Tristram Shandy* accumulating in its five instalments of 1759–67 and the body of work that would be known as *The Poems of Ossian* (the umbrella title formally adopted for the 1773 edition of *Fingal* and *Temora*) in three interconnected publications of 1760–3. Both works developed, in effect, as long-running, improvised serials, creating and sustaining their own vogues, modelling and remodelling their own precedents, generating from each of their previous instalments a potentially endless succession of future matter. Both threw up in their wake a mass of secondary writing—vindications and attacks, burlesques and imitations, bogus addenda and spurious sequels.[33] Hailed at first as unfettered productions of original genius, debunked in retrospect as plagiarism or hoax, both shared the fascinating aura of sensation, enigma, scandal.

By the end of the century Malcolm Laing was denouncing *The Poems of Ossian* as a phoney confection of Milton, Young, and Pope's Homer, thereby, as he put it, 'transferring them from the third to the eighteenth century'; John Ferriar was no less dogged (and even more influential) in transferring *Tristram Shandy* from the eighteenth to the seventeenth

---

[33] On appropriations of *Tristram Shandy* in the 1760s, see Anne Bandry, 'First Reactions to *Tristram Shandy* in the Oates Collection', *Shandean*, 1 (1989), 27–52, and 'The Spurious Volumes of *Tristram Shandy*', *Shandean*, 3 (1991), 126–37; on appropriations of Macpherson, see Kathryn Temple, 'Johnson and Macpherson, Cultural Authority, and the Construction of Literary Property', *Yale Journal of Law and the Humanities*, 5 (1993), 355–87, esp. 363–4.

century, as a tissue of thefts from Montaigne, Rabelais, and Burton.[34] Both Macpherson and Sterne had by then been seen for decades as major literary names, and were ripe for revisionist attack. Both had emerged, however, in leaps from obscurity to instant fame, and from backgrounds that placed them at the very margins of the social, literary, and (in Macpherson's case) political worlds in which they would later thrive. Macpherson began as a young highland schoolmaster born and raised in a remote centre of Jacobite allegiance where the Gaelic language remained firmly rooted; Sterne as a frustrated rural clergyman, born in Ireland and now marooned 'in a bye corner of the kingdom, and in a retired thatch'd house' (1, dedication), his career in the Church going nowhere. Setting aside a series of more or less fugitive early pieces, both had made an inauspicious start with locally published damp squibs: in Macpherson's case *The Highlander*, an epic poem that '*disappeared*' (as Laing tartly put it) in Edinburgh in April 1758, ignored even by the two literary reviews managed by the poem's own publisher;[35] in Sterne's case *A Political Romance*, a literally parochial satire printed in York in January 1759, which more emphatically disappeared when all but a handful of copies were prudently incinerated (*EMY* 276–7). Setback was only a spur to both writers, however, and both now embarked on the hugely successful literary projects that were to make their names, moving rapidly to London publishers when the success of a locally published sample of their innovatory material opened the way to a larger ongoing process of related production. The first instalment of *Tristram Shandy* was published in York in December 1759 'merely to feel the pulse of the world', as Sterne told Dodsley in London (*Letters*, 80); reissued by Dodsley the following month, the volumes themselves announced an open-ended process of annual publication that was sporadically fulfilled over the following seven years. Meanwhile the *Fragments of Ancient Poetry* published in Edinburgh in June 1760 played a similar role in testing the market and generating the audience for a possible large-scale sequel. Among other surviving remains of Gaelic antiquity, as the preface declares, 'there is reason to hope that one work of considerable length, and which deserves to be styled an heroic poem, might be recovered and translated, if encouragement were given to such an undertaking'.[36]

---

[34] Laing, *History of Scotland*, 2: 377; see also John Ferriar, *Illustrations of Sterne* (1798), esp. 23–99.

[35] Laing, *History of Scotland*, 2: 407; Paul J. deGategno, *James Macpherson* (Boston: G. K. Hall, 1989), 15 (the journals being the *Scots Magazine* and the *Edinburgh Magazine* and the publisher Walter Ruddiman, Jr.).

[36] James Macpherson, *The Poems of Ossian and Related Works*, ed. Howard Gaskill, intr. Fiona Stafford (Edinburgh: Edinburgh University Press, 1996) (hereafter *PO*), 6.

It is at this point that the careers of Sterne and Macpherson start to intersect in intriguing ways. Both were lionized by literary society during lengthy visits to London, and, while their different partisan alignments will largely have confined them to different circles in the polarized political culture of the day (*Tristram Shandy* is dedicated to Pitt, *Temora* to Bute), both are known to have been paraded during the same period by the influential patron Elizabeth Montagu, who was Sterne's cousin by marriage, and a generous early sponsor of Macpherson's research tours in the highlands.[37] More significant is their gravitation towards the same publishers and printers: first the sought-after Dodsleys, who brought out the first London editions of both *Tristram Shandy*, volumes 1 and 2 (January 1760) and *Fragments of Ancient Poetry* (April 1761), as well as the first edition of *Tristram Shandy*, volumes 3 and 4 (January 1761); then Becket, who published both *Fingal* and *Tristram Shandy*, volumes 5 and 6, within three weeks of one another in December 1761. Sterne dealt directly for the printing of this third and subsequent instalments with William Strahan, the Scottish printer and bookseller. Strahan was simultaneously at work on *Fingal*, having been asked by Hume to assist Macpherson on the latter's arrival in London, and he continued to print and later publish for Macpherson well into the 1770s.[38]

In retrospect, the almost simultaneous appearance of *Fingal* and the third instalment of *Tristram Shandy* marked the zenith of both literary projects. Sterne left London for the Continent in the early days of 1762, and, though 'very hard at Work' in May of that year, as he told Becket from Paris (*Letters*, 169), he was unable to get the fourth instalment of *Tristram Shandy* published before January 1765. Macpherson retained his momentum with more success, and in March 1763 the tantalizing fragment of *Temora* first published as one of several brief makeweights to *Fingal* could re-emerge in the new guise of a full-scale epic poem. Here was a technique of linked publication that Sterne was to use when slipping into the final volume of *Tristram Shandy* a digressive chapter (9.24.779–84) trailing his forthcoming *Sentimental Journey*: not for nothing could Malcolm Laing scoff that Macpherson 'might have produced, each year, an epic poem like

---

[37] *LY* 115–16, 24–5; deGategno, *James Macpherson*, 80, 30.

[38] J. A. Cochrane, *Dr Johnson's Printer: The Life of William Strahan* (London: Routledge, 1964), 159, 46, 51; Bailey Saunders, *The Life and Letters of James Macpherson*, 2nd edn. (London: Swan Sonnenschein, 1895), 158–9 (letter from Hume to Strahan, 9 Feb. 1761). For the publishing history of *Tristram Shandy*, see the Florida edition, 2: 814–31; for Macpherson, see George F. Black, 'Macpherson's Ossian and the Ossianic Controversy: A Contribution towards a Bibliography', *Bulletin of the New York Public Library*, 30 (1926), 1: 424–39; 2: 508–24.

an annual novel, had the Temora been equally successful with Fingal'.[39] As Laing's words suggest, however, Macpherson's project too was by this time beginning to burn itself out, or at any rate to exhaust the appetite of its first audience. In the following years Macpherson contented himself with revising and reordering his material into the collected editions of 1765 and 1773, while *Tristram Shandy* capered to its jocoserious halt of 1767 with the solitary volume 9.

Becket published—or, in the case of the collected Ossians of 1765 and 1773, co-published with Strahan—all these volumes. As a staunch defender of Macpherson's integrity and an increasingly close friend of Sterne, he provides an important link between the two writers during the middle and later stages of their parallel projects. In this, however, he was far from alone. Though Sterne would have been unable to inspect the *Fingal* manuscripts that Becket later claimed to have exhibited in London 'for many months in the year 1762',[40] he would not have been able to escape the ensuing controversy on arriving in Paris that January. There he became friendly with Jean-Baptiste-Antoine Suard and intimate with Denis Diderot and the Baron d'Holbach, three of the leading French enthusiasts for Ossian, shortly after the first of Diderot's Ossianic translations had appeared in Suard's *Journal étranger* for December 1761.[41] On returning to Paris in 1764 he grew acquainted with Hume at a time when Hume was preoccupied with the question of Ossian's authenticity and actively promoting the poems in Parisian circles. If all this (as seems unlikely) left Sterne immune to Macpherson's impact during the period when the final volumes of *Tristram Shandy* were in gestation, the same can hardly be so of the closer friendship he began in Paris with the brilliant young highlander whom Boswell was to call 'the *Marcellus* of Scotland'.[42] This was the Gaelic-speaking Etonian Sir James Macdonald of Sleat, a key witness in the authenticity controversy who had quarrelled with Macpherson but was prepared to attest that he had heard his Hebridean tenant John MacCodrum 'repeat, for hours together, poems which seemed to me to be the same with Macpherson's translation'.[43] Sterne and Sleat met again at

---

[39] James Macpherson, *The Poems of Ossian*, ed. Malcolm Laing, 2 vols. (Edinburgh, 1805), 2: 264; quoted in *PO* 529 n.

[40] Saunders, *Life and Letters of Macpherson*, 249 (letter of 19 Jan. 1775).

[41] *LY* 136–9; Jacques Chouillet, 'Diderot: Poet and Theorist of the Homer and Ossianist Revival', *British Journal of Eighteenth-Century Studies*, 5 (1982), 22.

[42] *LY* 179–80, 187–8; David Raynor, 'Ossian and Hume', in Howard Gaskill (ed.), *Ossian Revisited* (Edinburgh University Press, 1991), 150–9; *Boswell's Life of Johnson*, ed. G. B. Hill, rev. L. F. Powell, 6 vols. (Oxford: Clarendon Press, 1934–56), 4: 82 n.

[43] Sir James Macdonald to Hugh Blair (10 Oct. 1763), in *Report of the Committee of the Highland Society of Scotland, Appointed to Inquire into the Nature and Authenticity of the Poems of Ossian*, ed. Henry Mackenzie (Edinburgh, 1805), app., p. 4.

Turin in November 1765, travelled half the length of Italy in one another's company, and lodged together in Naples for a further two months (*LY* 234–41).[44] The significance of this link between Sterne and one of the leading Ossianists of the day can hardly be overstated—though for sheer intimacy of connection Macdonald of Sleat is trumped by Elizabeth Draper, addressee of Sterne's *Bramine's Journal*, who rather bizarrely appears to have capped her sentimental liaison with the dying Sterne by becoming Macpherson's mistress a few years later.[45]

Sterne had no shortage of opportunity to consider Macpherson's writing, then, above all during the years in which the last three volumes of *Tristram Shandy* were planned and written. To talk in terms of these biographical connections, however, is only to scratch the surface of a complex literary affinity. More important is the question of form, and the way in which both *Tristram Shandy* and *The Poems of Ossian* are linked by their conspicuous violation, or fragmentation, of the polite registers and elegant structures of neoclassical convention. It is no coincidence that both Macpherson and Sterne earned the hostility of the leading champion of established literary decorums, Johnson, for whom *Fingal* was 'a mere unconnected rhapsody' that lacked 'the *lucidus ordo*',[46] while the dedication to volume 5 of *Tristram Shandy* (as he put it to Sterne's face) was simply 'not English, sir' (*CH* 138). It is tempting to see these objections as interchangeable, for by Johnson's criteria both works emphatically defied traditional Horatian aesthetics, while neither was written in English. In Macpherson the imitation of Gaelic verse creates an abrupt, disjointed, paratactical style, opaquely metaphorical, wifully irregular, devoid of orderly transition and explicit connection. English poetry may have been ready to move in such directions under the influence of Robert Lowth, but at the time the nearest equivalent comes only in the then unpublished madhouse experimentations of Christopher Smart. And, while Macpherson's prose swerves away from polite diction after the model (both real and imagined) of Gaelic ballad and recitation, so orality of a different kind is at work in Sterne, whose jerky mimicry of extempore utterance is similarly disruptive of the orotund, harmonious periods of Johnsonian English. Nor do

---

[44] Sleat was in Shandean decline as they travelled, having suffered 'a soar Throat' in Turin, a cough 'which still hangs about me' in Parma, 'an universal Rhumatism which confined me a month' in Naples, and eventually death in Rome, 'reduced to a mere skeleton', four months after Sterne's departure (John Ingamells, *A Dictionary of British and Irish Travellers in Italy, 1701–1800* (New Haven: Yale University Press, 1997), 622–3; see also p. 894).

[45] J. N. M. Maclean, 'The Early Political Careers of James "Fingal" Macpherson (1736–1821) and Sir John Macpherson, Bart. (1744–1821)' (diss., University of Edinburgh, 1967), app. 3. I am grateful to Fiona Stafford for this information.

[46] *Boswell's Life of Johnson*, 2: 126.

the larger structures of literary form survive unbroken in either writer, Macpherson's emphasis on the irretrievability of intact sources and Sterne's frenetic ruptures of narrative coherence effecting a similar frustration of unity and completeness. It is for these reasons, and not simply through the coincidences of printing history, that texts like *Temora* and the later volumes of *Tristram Shandy* can look so similar on the page, their ostentatious lacunae marked out by blocks of asterisks, their abrupt sentences chopped and set off by welters of Shandean dashes.

To the extent that the names of Macpherson and Sterne have been linked before, it has been from a sense that this common emphasis on fragmentation of style and form identifies them as fellow sentimentalists. When Burns named them together, he classed them approvingly as 'authors of the sentim[l] kind'; when Laing did so it was to allege the essential modernity of Macpherson's Ossian as a bandwagon-jumping participant in 'the sentimental vein' of Sterne's fiction. More recently, John Dwyer has found in Macpherson's welding together of fragments 'an uncanny resemblance to the literary techniques of sentimental writers' (he names Sterne in particular), and one that gave him a way 'to depict pathetic scenes without having to worry unduly about the potential distractions of plot'.[47] It is certainly possible to find in this shared evasion of narrative logic a redirection of focus towards vignettes of feeling, and it is easy to juxtapose passages in which a comparably sentimental emphasis comes to the fore. Consider 'The War of Caros', when 'The king's soul was sad for Comala, and his eyes could not behold Hidallan. Lonely, sad, along the heath, he slowly moved with silent steps. His arms hang disordered on his side. His hair flies loose from his helmet. The tear is in his down-cast eyes; and the sigh half-silent in his breast' (*PO* 111). Here are the very hallmarks of sentimental excess—the gesture of lassitude, the single tear, the silence of grief beyond words (and by replacing 'helmet' with 'brow' in the revised edition of 1773 Macpherson only confirms the predominance here of sentimental over-heroic values). Sterne is less terse; but, as Walter laments his own more mundane misfortunes in a volume of *Tristram Shandy* published eleven months earlier, we find an ironic elaboration of the same motifs:

he threw himself prostrate across his bed in the wildest disorder imaginable, but at the same time, in the most lamentable attitude of a man borne down with sorrows, that ever the eye of pity dropp'd a tear for.———. . . his left arm hung insensible over

[47] John Dwyer, 'The Melancholy Savage', in Gaskill (ed.), *Ossian Revisited*, 184. For Burns, see *CH* 260; for Laing, see n. 32 above.

the side of the bed, his knuckles reclining upon the handle of the chamber pot, which peep'd out beyond the valance . . . A fix'd, inflexible sorrow took possession of every line of his face.—He sigh'd once,—heaved his breast often,—but utter'd not a word. (3.29.254–5)

Here Walter's grief is mocked as well as evoked, with the characteristic double edge of all Sterne's sentimental forays; but in both texts a common interest in sentiment and sympathy evidently produces not only shared gestures, but also a shared vocabulary of sorrow, disorder, silence.

Yet there is more to fragmentation of literary form than some mere prioritization of interludes like these over the more dynamic plotting of continuous narrative; and it is here, and not only in a sentimentalism to which the relationship of both writers was at least equivocal, that we find some of the most profound and interesting affinities between Macpherson and Sterne. Fiona Stafford opens up more promising ground when she notes that Macpherson's 'concentration on the isolated poet owed as much to the literature of the mid-eighteenth century as to the classics', and when she finds in Sterne a comparable concern for the predicament of the modern memoirist 'isolated within his own perceptions'.[48] This focus on isolation is very apt, for both *The Poems of Ossian* and *Tristram Shandy* are works preoccupied by the loss of a remembered past, whether the idealized 'other times' of Fingalian heroism or the fondly recalled experiences of Tristram's youth. Both review the periods they describe from the perspective of an imagined present that by comparison seems degenerate or empty, and both document the obsessive yet finally unavailing struggles of their presiding voices to recover and transmit, in memory and language, this otherwise fugitive past. Here fragmentation may incidentally provide a means of freezing narrative progress to highlight feeling, but it serves more centrally as a presiding metaphor for the sense of disintegration and loss so pervasive in both these works.[49] At the level of form itself, it implies a view of human experience—'this Fragment of Life', as Tristram's first dedication has it—as one in which interruption, incoherence, and decay seem insuperable conditions, and in which the imperfect efforts of memory and language can only reaffirm the inevitability of separation from what is past.

[48] Fiona Stafford, *The Sublime Savage: A Study of James Macpherson and the Poems of Ossian* (Edinburgh: Edinburgh University Press, 1988), 141, 142.

[49] On fragmentation and its implications in the literature of the period, see Elizabeth W. Harries, *The Unfinished Manner: Essays on the Fragment in the Later Eighteenth Century* (Charlottesville, Va.: University Press of Virginia, 1995): Macpherson gets relatively little mention; pp. 41–55 are on Sterne.

NARRATIVES OF LOSS

Locke's account of human psychology and language as vexed by obscurity and instability has long been recognized as an important context for *Tristram Shandy*, and persuasive moves have been made to read *The Poems of Ossian* in similar terms.[50] More is at stake in this latter case, however, than some strictly philosophical loss of confidence, for the disintegration Macpherson laments is nothing less than that of a whole culture—the virtuous Celtic antiquity idealized in his *Introduction to the History of Great Britain and Ireland* (1771) and represented in his commentaries on Ossian as long since retreated to its final stronghold of highland Scotland. For a debunker such as Malcolm Laing (a modernizing Whig, and an Orcadian, not a highlander), this is a culture marked only by 'the vices of barbarians: an incurable sloth; an intemperance unrestrained except by their wants; a perfidy that disregarded the common obligations of oaths; a proverbial rapacity and the most sanguinary revenge'.[51] In Macpherson's distinctively Celtic brand of Tory civic humanism, it is a locus of pre-commercial integrity, untouched by a debilitating modernity in which heroism is enfeebled and virtue corrupted by luxury and wealth. Such perfection belongs, however, to an irretrievable past. His dissertations and annotations construct a history of internal decay barely less ancient than the Fianna itself, and he fails to suppress occasional disdain for such latterday follies as 'the ridiculous notion of the second sight, which prevailed in the highlands and isles' (*PO* 433). More recent if shadowy components of his analysis are the military and social incursions of his childhood years: most obviously the post-Culloden suppression of the Jacobite clans and cultural-political measures like the Heritable Jurisdiction and Disarming Acts of 1746–7, but also processes of longer duration and more lasting effect like the engineering projects of General Wade (whose roads and bridges prised open the highlands in the 1730s) or the state-sponsored erosion of Gaelic and promotion of English (a process in train since well before the Union of 1707).[52] Here, more even than military defeat, it is commercial modernity that lands the knockout punch—modernity of a kind that Macpherson deplored in theory as energetically as he embraced it in practice. (Not only a brilliant literary entrepreneur, he was later to become a colonial administrator in Florida, and, to his immense profit, the

---

[50] Stephen H. Clark, 'The "Failing Soul": Macpherson's Response to Locke', *Eighteenth-Century Life*, 19 (1995), 39–56.

[51] Laing, *History of Scotland*, 1: 44.

[52] Stafford, *Sublime Savage*, 16–17.

London agent of an Indian nabob.[53]) His analysis is one in which the new mobility of people, goods, and values hastens the pace of centuries-old decline, teaching the highlanders 'enough of foreign manners to despise the customs of their ancestors' (*PO* 51), and leaving the culture as a whole fragmented in ways at once symbolized and compounded by the fate of its poetic productions. Just as the ancient culture itself is now in ruins, the implication is, so the epic verse in which its values had been most fully enshrined can no longer be found intact and entire: 'The communication with the rest of the island is open, and the introduction of trade and manufactures has destroyed that leisure which was formerly dedicated to hearing and repeating the poems of ancient times' (*PO* 51).

From this perspective Macpherson seems engaged, in his complex role as translator, restorer, and forger, in some rearguard act of retrieval, salvaging the poems from 'the obscurity of an almost lost language' (*PO* 214), and from 'a few old people in the north of Scotland' (*PO* 448) in whose failing memories the verses survive in variable and incomplete states. He gathers the fragments, pieces them together, fixes them for posterity in a medium, print, and a language, English, alien to the oral Gaelic culture that produced them, but offering at least a residual afterlife in the dominant modes of the present. Nor is this simply to give the ancient culture a new environment in which, if not to live, then to echo. It is also to make the very processes of hybridization on which Macpherson blames the culture's demise cut other ways, promoting a new, Gaelic-inflected form of English that might in turn transform the nation's dominant language, however imperceptibly, into some more inclusively British tongue.

Conflicting impulses mark this ambitious project: on one hand, an impulse to fill out with confections of his own the space between fragments now known to bear some genuine relationship to authentic sources, while stabilizing in the form of a definitive text passages that have been 'delivered down very differently by tradition' (*PO* 433); on the other, an impulse to represent in all their wreckage and instability sources that, as such, bear compelling witness to the loss of the world that produced them. Macpherson's literary career might well be seen in terms of a shift of emphasis from the latter to the former impulse, though both coexist throughout. Beginning with a miscellany of brief fragments and ending with a seamless epic in eight books, the trajectory of *The Poems of Ossian* is nowhere better illustrated than in *Temora*'s slow transformation. At first the poem is barely discernible beneath the brief seventh item of *Fragments*

[53] Ibid. 181–2.

of Ancient Poetry, subsequently identified by Macpherson himself as probably not Ossianic (*PO* 156–7); then come the 'imperfect and confused . . .
broken fragments' (*PO* 479) from which *Temora's* opening alone is recovered as a supplement to *Fingal*; then comes the elaborate display of epic
unities pulled complete from the hat (though with several supplementary
fragments appended) in 1763. It is at this end point that Macpherson talks
of being able 'to reduce the broken members of the piece into the order in
which they now appear' (*PO* 215): the figure is of surgery, a restorative re-
setting of fractured limbs.[54]

That is not to speak, however, of a happy ending, of fragmentation
euphorically repaired, for loss vexes not only the transmission of Ossianic
verse but also its very content. 'The fame of my former actions is ceased;
and I sit forlorn at the tombs of my friends' (*PO* 104): even when restored
to some more or less plausible simulacrum of original wholeness, the
poetry still bears witness to the disintegration of a culture, and to the
melancholy isolation of the poet from the departed heroes commemorated in his words. In its simplest form of 1760, the Ossianic fragment por-
trays the surviving poet, 'the last of the race of Fingal' (*PO* 18), as a sightless
mourner, an aged leftover whose departed kin 'return into my mind, and
wound me with remembrance' (*PO* 14). Later poems return with renewed
obsessiveness to 'the dim times of old' (*PO* 296), yet their words are rarely
more than gloomy acknowledgements of separation from what they describe, and in this sense the enterprise of Ossian himself, quite as much as
his creator's, seems a desperate rearguard attempt to mitigate loss. In
'Oina-Morul' he likens his narratives to the flight of 'the unconstant sun,
over Larmon's grassy hill' and presents himself as one who 'seize[s] the
tales, as they pass'. Images of evanescence like this run throughout the
poems, the mists, clouds, and waves of which are much more than mere
scenery. Here it is as though the instability of language itself, and 'the shadowy thoughts, that fly across my soul', are endlessly at odds with the poet's
struggles to 'call back . . . the years that have rolled away' (*PO* 323).

In a world where the hero's highest ambition is to be immortalized in
the stones of a funerary mound or the lapidary language of a poem, and his
greatest fear the obscurity of one who departs 'like a beam that has shone;
like a mist that fled away . . . till my footsteps cease to be seen' (*PO* 88),
Ossian's predicament is severe indeed. His commemorations rarely attain
the pitch of confident celebration with which less accomplished bards

---

[54] 'To restore (a dislocated, fractured, or ruptured part) to the proper position'; 'To adjust,
set (a dislocation or fracture)', *OED*², s.v. 'Reduce', 6 and 6 b.

'raise high the praise of heroes' (*PO* 102). They retreat instead to a mode of gloomy retrospection in which to look back on the zenith of Fingalian heroism is only to be confronted by the irreversibility of its loss: 'Often have I fought, and often won in battles of the spear. But blind, and tearful, and forlorn I now walk with little men. O Fingal, with thy race of battle I now behold thee not. The wild roes feed upon the green tomb of the mighty king of Morven' (*PO* 79). Bereft of his race, Ossian can only sing into the wind, or into the ears of epigones. Already he witnesses the onset of that post-heroic degeneration to which Macpherson refers in the preface to *Temora*, which traces 'the decay of that species of heroism, which subsisted in the days of Ossian' (*PO* 211) through subsequent phases of social organization. Obsessed as it explicitly is with memorialization of the fallen, his verse suggests nothing so much as the absence of what it describes—the irrecoverability of a heroic past glimpsed only in the solitary incantations of an aged bard, and entrusted thereafter to the vagaries of memorial transmission in a declining culture and language. The dilemma is most acutely felt at the close of 'The Songs of Selma':

But age is now on my tongue; and my soul has failed. I hear, sometimes, the ghosts of bards, and learn their pleasant song. But memory fails in my mind; I hear the call of years. They say, as they pass along, why does Ossian sing? Soon shall he lie in the narrow house, and no bard shall raise his fame. . . . Let the tomb open to Ossian, for his strength has failed. The sons of song are gone to rest: my voice remains, like a blast, that roars, lonely, on a sea-surrounded rock, after the winds are laid. (*PO* 170)

The tone here is typical, and indeed it is the relentlessness of this tone that makes Macpherson, for all his popularity in the 1760s and subsequent great impact on Romanticism across Europe, unreadable in bulk today. It hardly seems necessary for him to add, as he does in a footnote about the distinctive tone of Ossianic poetry, that 'if ever [Ossian] composed any thing of a merry turn it is long since lost. The serious and melancholy make the most lasting impressions on the human mind, and bid fairest for being transmitted from generation to generation by tradition. Nor is it probable that Ossian dealt much in chearful composition' (*PO* 472). Bardic comedy, to be sure, is hard to imagine. Yet if (like Malcolm Laing) we transfer Ossian from the third to the eighteenth century, and from the hills of Morven to the vale of York, then *Tristram Shandy*—a work borne of a sense 'that every time a man smiles . . . it adds something to this Fragment of Life' (1, dedication)—becomes just what he might have dreamed up.

It is not simply that the genre of Sterne's work is in Macpherson's eyes the characteristic production of a degenerate age, in which bardic epic has fallen away, via panegyric and mock panegyric, to satire and lampoon (*PO* 519). Nor is it simply that the characters and environment of *Tristram Shandy*, when set against those of *Fingal*, so happily exemplify Macpherson's primitivist theories of latterday decadence: his theory that 'quiet and retirement . . . weaken and debase the human mind'; that 'in great and opulent states, when property and indolence are secured to individuals, we seldom meet with that strength of mind, which is so common in a nation, not far advanced in civilization'; that 'as a state, we are much more powerful than our ancestors, but we would lose by comparing individuals with them' (*PO* 500–1). Certainly, Tristram's father and uncle, a retired Turkey merchant and a retired army officer, are former cogs in the great machines of commercial and military ascendancy whose mental enfeeblement and physical impotence are central to Sterne's comedy of post-heroic vulnerability. The circumscribed world of *Tristram Shandy*—'by which word *world* . . . I would be understood to mean no more of it, than a small circle . . . of four *English* miles diameter' (1.7.10)—certainly resembles the mind-contracting environment that Macpherson deplores when contrasting the enlarged understanding of the roaming highlander with the immobility of the rural lowlander, his knowledge and experience 'circumscribed within the compass of a few acres' (*PO* 482). It would not be hard to see in *Tristram Shandy* as a whole a comic exploration of something very close to Macpherson's conviction that 'the powers of the human soul, without an opportunity of exerting them, lose their vigor' (*PO* 205).

Yet *Tristram Shandy* is of course much more than some mock-heroic exemplification of that modern frivolity and degeneration that, in Macpherson's commentaries, serve as an ever-present foil to Fingalian heroism. The work shares with *The Poems of Ossian* a pervasive and (as it progresses) a growing sense of loss, of detachment from a fondly remembered past to which the present experience of the solitary and increasingly sickly narrator stands in gloomy relation. It shares with the poems a sense of the overriding need to memorialize this past, to recover, fix, and transmit it in narrative language. And it shares with them a sense that human memory and human language can never wholly fulfil such high ambitions, that the past never can be adequately brought back or textualized in all its fulness, and that writing, no matter how much it proliferates, can in the end be little more than a melancholy trace of the absence of what it describes.

It hardly needs saying that the past that Tristram seeks to reify lacks the heroic aspect of Ossian's: that, indeed, is Sterne's point. His characters inhabit a post-heroic medium, a 'scurvy and disasterous world' in which the high deeds of epic give way to what Tristram calls 'a set of as pitiful misadventures and cross accidents as ever small HERO sustained' (1.5.8–9). It is a world of what Ossian would call little men, yet a world in which the remote chance of 'performing any thing great or worth recording' (1.19.63) seems only to intensify its inhabitants' need to record their lives all the same. Sterne's own version of the veteran warrior, Captain Toby Shandy, is the perfect example. Where Fingal's campaigns in Ireland, and especially his battle at Temora with the Irish hero Cathmor, are marked by 'instances of the greatest bravery, mixed with incomparably generous actions and sentiments' (*PO* 456), Toby's participation in William of Orange's Irish campaign of 1690–1 involves him in an inglorious past of mutual atrocities, which (as Macpherson was later to write as a historian of the campaign) 'stain the annals of the times'.[55] Where Fingal deals in heroic individual combat, Toby is entrenched in debilitating and inconclusive wars of attrition that leave international armies of tens of thousands, as he recalls, 'scarce able to crawl out of our tents, at the time the siege of *Limerick* was raised' (5.37.476). Where Fingal and his race withdraw in victory or finally fall in glory, Toby is ludicrously scarred, traumatized, and emasculated by a wound on the groin sustained from a chunk of falling masonry at the siege of Namur. Interestingly, it is only from volume 5 of *Tristram Shandy* onwards that Sterne introduces the idea of Toby serving in Ireland as well as in Flanders, and apparently in a Scots regiment;[56] it is almost as though, at the very point when *Fingal* is published, Toby's past is reinvented as a mock-heroic travesty of Fingal's own.

For all the poverty of their modern achievements, however, Sterne's characters remain no less obsessively concerned than Macpherson's with the effort to recapture, relive, and reproduce their past experience. In the absence of bardic commemoration, Toby seeks to fix the scenes of his wartime afflictions—the flux at Limerick, the wound at Namur—on the ground of his garden in scale model, controlling and displacing his memories through systematic re-enactment of later battles and sieges as gazette reports of the War of the Spanish Succession and further encounters such as the siege of Messina in 1719 reach him in his Yorkshire retire-

---

[55] James Macpherson, *The History of Great Britain, from the Restoration, to the Accession of the House of Hanover*, 2 vols. (1775), 1: 667.

[56] See note to *TS* 5.6.452. Toby serves in the regiment of David Melville, third earl of Leven (1660–1728). This was originally raised among Scottish refugees in Holland and Germany, and accompanied William to England in 1688; the regiment then served against Jacobite forces in Scotland and Ireland, and against the French in Flanders (*DNB*).

ment. Armed with a truly Ossianic ability to reconcile extravagant senti-
mentality with a relish for large-scale violence, he devotes his life and mind
to an ongoing rehearsal of warfare. Yet even these material re-enactments
prove ludicrously vulnerable to loss and decay, failing to render permanent the past they seek to fix. At one point a cow breaks in on Toby's fortifications, and partly eats them (3.38.278); the making of model mortars
leads only to the loss of an older heroic memento, a pair of jackboots that
had survived, as Walter protests, 'ever since the civil wars;—Sir *Roger
Shandy* wore them at the battle of *Marston-Moor*' (3.22.242). Trapped
within his hobby horse, Toby merely fritters away his days in the pointless
and arid exercise of traumatized memory.

   He is not alone in his absurdity, however, for in writing the history of
these mock campaigns, and in the larger struggle to fix in print his own life
and opinions, Tristram finds himself embroiled in a comparably futile
endeavour. Where Toby seeks to fix a fugitive past experience in material
form, Tristram models it in language, vainly attempting to recover, catch,
and fix in words a past that perpetually shifts beyond reach. In his hands,
the interruptions of language and fragmentations of form that most
obviously link Sterne with Macpherson seem at once the result and the
expression of conditions that make any linguistic recovery of the past, even
in the relative stability of print as opposed to oral culture, a sadly impossible task. Setting out in all confidence to transmit to posterity his life and
opinions, he sees the material to be commemorated perpetually sprawl out
of control: anything about the past he chooses to say demands the inclusion of further context and explanation, so that 'the more I write, the more
I shall have to write' (4.13.342). The work might swell to eighty volumes
and still be incomplete, and all the while, language fails in its office of conjuring in the reader's mind the ideas in the mind of its user, with the blank
page standing, appropriately enough, as the most eloquent articulation of
the problem. 'Well might *Locke* write a chapter upon the imperfections
of words' (5.7.429): here is a distinctively modern and philosophically
sophisticated version of the Ossianic dilemma, the dilemma of the aged
and solitary bard whose words, far from bringing back the days of old,
mark only separation, absence, and loss, and which, far from perpetuating
fame, must fade into the obscurity of an almost lost language.

   It is a dilemma that Walter Shandy understands well, knowing as he
does how the ruin of an ancient culture is attended and intensified by the
ensuing disintegration of its language: 'What is become, brother *Toby*, of
Nineveh and *Babylon*, of *Cizicum* and *Mitylenae*? The fairest towns that
ever the sun rose upon, are now no more: the names only are left, and those

(for many of them are wrong spelt) are falling themselves by piecemeals to decay, and in length of time will be forgotten, and involved with every thing in a perpetual night' (5.3.422). For the dying Tristram of the final volumes, the same dilemma assumes an intensely personal form. The instalment of 1765 (the first to be written after Becket's almost simultaneous publication of *Fingal* and *Tristram Shandy*, volumes 5 and 6) opens with the consumptive Tristram desperately aware, as he addresses Eugenius, of his failure to immortalize a still unwritten past as he flees from death: 'for I have forty volumes to write, and forty thousand things to say and do, which no body in the world will say and do for me, except thyself; and as thou seest he has got me by the throat' (7.1.576). He survives into the solitary volume of 1767 as some dandyish, latterday bard of the age of prose: where Ossian describes 'some gray warrior, half blind with age, sitting by night at the flaming oak of the hall, [who] tells now my actions' (*PO* 174), Tristram becomes an avowedly 'tragicomical' writer 'sitting, this 12th day of August, 1766, in a purple jerkin and yellow pair of slippers, without either wig or cap on' (9.1.737). Yet Tristram, like Ossian, is a memorialist similarly bereaved of those he remembers, and trapped in a solitary present from which the past he seeks to bring back in language only slips further away. A few chapters later we find him looking towards his own end in a truly Ossianic imagery of evanescence: 'Time wastes too fast: every letter I trace tells me with what rapidity Life follows my pen; the days and hours of it . . . are flying over our heads like light clouds of a windy day, never to return more——every thing presses on——whilst thou art twisting that lock,——see! it grows grey; and every time I kiss thy hand to bid adieu, and every absence which follows it, are preludes to that eternal separation which we are shortly to make' (9.8.754).

Many factors influenced the change in tone discernible in these last three volumes of *Tristram Shandy*, where the robust exuberance with which Tristram first confronts the impossibility of his task gives way to alternating gloom and panic as extinction approaches. One factor may have been the decline in Sterne's personal health, which threatened to curtail his own literary ambitions as much as his hero-narrator's; another may have been the advice of the *Monthly Review* and other sources that he should devote the remainder of his text to pathos. Yet there is a specifically Ossianic ring to Sterne's increasing emphasis here on the inevitability of separation from a fugitive past, and it looks likely that another factor was the encounter with Macpherson's writing that must have followed (and may even have preceded) the publication of *Fingal* in December 1761. This was the watershed month for *Tristram Shandy*, ending its life as a regular annual series and inaugurating the long hiatus in which Sterne struggled to rethink and resume his project, which returned to print only in 1765. During this period, *The Poems of Ossian*, in their insistent reference to the fragility of representation, appear to have exerted a magnetic pull on *Tristram Shandy*, bringing home to Sterne the melancholy possibilities inherent in what had begun, in 1759, as a strictly comic literary impasse. The comic edge is never entirely withdrawn, of course, and in part the wry relationship between Ossianic narratives of loss and those of *Tristram Shandy* suggests a distant and muted form of burlesque teasing. In the 1767 'Time wastes too fast' passage, however, genuine parodic distance is hard to detect, and it is entirely in keeping with the poems that Tristram's early exultation at the need to keep his work 'a-going these forty years' (1.22.82) to fulfil its ambitions should now modulate, with only nine of his pro-jected eighty volumes written, into an Ossianic sense of failure. He too is left alone as the last of his race, and as one whose imminent death will leave unperformed his increasingly desperate desire to fix in print a permanent record of all that is gone.

What is beyond question, whether we identify the relationship between Macpherson and Sterne as one of straightforward influence, mutual on-going interaction, or a parallel and largely independent pursuit of shared concerns, is that both writers have a great deal more in common than some merely fashionable appeal to the conventions of sensibility. Both might be said, like Henry Mackenzie in their mutual wake, to have formed their plans on 'the Fragment Manner',[57] and for both of them this fragmentation of form gives expression to a devastating loss of faith in wholeness or continuity as properties of the worlds they seek to describe. Both share a common preoccupation with the weight of the past, with the decay and degeneration that separate past from present, and with the struggle of their hero-narrators to recover this fugitive past in memory and language. Both are preoccupied, moreover, by the ultimate futility of such ambi-tions: their texts are laden with a melancholy sense of the instability of lan-guage and the consequent ineffability of all experience, whether individual or that of a whole culture. 'Language is only the instrument of science, and words are but the signs of ideas,' as Johnson famously puts it in the preface to the *Dictionary*, and from this point of view the mainly oral Gaelic

    [57] Henny Mackenzie, *Letters to Elizabeth Rose of Kilravock*, ed. Horst W. Drescher (Edinburgh: Oliver and Boyd, 1967), 88 (18 May 1771); quoted by Harries, *Unfinished Manner*, 1; see also Susan Manning, 'Henry Mackenzie and Ossian: or, The Emotional Value of Asterisks', in Fiona Stafford and Howard Gaskill (eds.), *From Gaelic to Romantic: Ossianic Translations* (Amsterdam: Rodopi, 1998), 136–52.

language, which Johnson elsewhere describes as having 'merely floated in the breath of the people', only exaggerates the instability of language as a whole. He might almost have been writing on behalf of his twin bugbears as he forlornly goes on to wish in the preface 'that the instrument might be less apt to decay, and that signs might be permanent, like the things which they denote'.[58]

If either work escapes the pessimism towards which its efforts at representation so strongly tend, it does so in terms of a common appeal to the reader as one whose creative involvement in the production of meaning might somehow patch up the fragments or repair the breaches with which its text is necessarily riddled. *Tristram's* insistence that writing should emulate the reciprocity of conversation, in which 'the truest respect which you can pay to the reader's understanding, is to halve this matter amicably, and leave him something to imagine, in his turn, as well as yourself' (2.11.125), is riddled in context with undermining ironies. It is in this same aesthetic of restorative readerly involvement, however, that we find Macpherson at his most confident and modern. In his *Critical Dissertation on the Poems of Ossian* (1763) Hugh Blair praises the poems for a narrative style 'concise even to abruptness, and leaving several circumstances to be supplied by the reader's imagination' (*PO* 354), and Macpherson himself makes the same emphasis. 'Nothing new, nor adequate to our high idea of kings, could be said. Ossian, therefore, throws a *column of mist* over the whole, and leaves the combat to the imagination of the reader' (*PO* 526). Macpherson, indeed, might almost be inviting the reader to draw his own Widow Wadman when he writes that 'the human mind, free and fond of thinking for itself, is disgusted to find every thing done by the poet. It is, therefore, his business only to mark the most striking outlines; and to allow the imaginations of his readers to finish the figure for themselves' (*PO* 543). Perhaps such gestures do no more than make a virtue of dire necessity, but, in the absence of any truly stable, adequate, or permanent language, whether Gaelic or English, it is in imagination alone that the past must reside.

---

[58] Samuel Johnson, *Poetry and Prose*, ed. Mona Wilson (London: Hart-Davis, 1968), 304–5 (Preface to the *Dictionary*), 749 (*A Journey to the Western Islands of Scotland*).

6

The Literature of Whiggism
and the Politics of War

TRISTRAM SHANDY, WHIG POLITICS, AND THE
READERSHIP FOR MARVELL

The odd blend of belligerence and melancholy that characterizes Macpherson's transformation of epic motifs has been linked not only to the aftermath of Culloden in the 1740s, but also to the more widespread national trauma of the Seven Years War (Macpherson's patriotism being, like Smollett's, inclusively British as well as specifically Scots).[1] As both *The Poems of Ossian* and the bulk of *Tristram Shandy* were conceived and written, the massive human losses being sustained in the war, and especially in the land war in Germany, were generating public unease of a kind that finds displaced expression in both these works. *Tristram Shandy* had been launched at a moment of national elation, as news returned of the fall of Quebec in September 1759 and the naval victory of Quiberon Bay in November. The unease had only temporarily abated with this astonishing rash of global victories, however, and the vast territorial gains accruing at the end of the war left the nation, as Linda Colley has put it, 'in the grip of collective agoraphobia'. Within a few years, a relatively small, predominantly mercantile empire had been transformed into something unsettlingly close to the failed military empires of the past—empires 'bloodily and insecurely raised on conquest', in Colley's words, and embodying in their decline and fall ominous warnings of imperial over-reach and ensu-

---

[1] See Howard Weinbrot, *Britannia's Issue: The Rise of British Literature from Dryden to Ossian* (Cambridge: Cambridge University Press, 1993); Fiona Stafford, *The Sublime Savage: A Study of James Macpherson and the Poems of Ossian* (Edinburgh: Edinburgh University Press, 1988), 74, 114; Mícheál Mac Craith, '*Fingal*: Text, Context, Subtext', in Fiona Stafford and Howard Gaskill (eds.), *From Gaelic to Romantic: Ossianic Translations* (Amsterdam: Rodopi, 1998), 66–7.

ing implosion.[2] By the close of 1760 it was widely felt that the nation's sustainable war aims had now been met in full, and that the human and material costs of ongoing conflict had become too great. It was a populist touch by George III (the king whose 'propitious reign' (4.13.342) is whimsically greeted in the second instalment of *Tristram Shandy*) to talk of the war as 'bloody and expensive' in his first address to Parliament that October—or this would have been a populist touch, had ministers not forced the alteration of his phrase to 'just and necessary'.[3] As volumes 3 and 4 of *Tristram Shandy* appeared in January 1761, however, war was still being waged as actively as ever, and the following month Sterne went to hear 'a pitched battle in the H[ouse] of C[ommons], wherein Mr. P[itt] was to have entered and thrown down the gauntlet, in defence of the German war'. In the event Pitt suffered what Sterne wryly calls 'a political fit of the gout', and in his place William Beckford, a City member of Wilkite connections, 'made a most long, passionate, incoherent speech, in defence of the Germanick war'. Beckford and the outgoing Secretary of War, Viscount Barrington, 'abused all who sought for peace, and joined in the cry for it', as Sterne continues: 'and B[eckfor]d added, that the reasons of wishing a peace now, were the same as at the peace of Utretch—that the people behind the curtain could not both maintain the war and their places too, so were for making another sacrifice of the nation, to their own interests' (*Letters*, 129).

Yet despite other references in Sterne's letters of 1761 to a rising tide of anti-war opinion—'the cry for a peace is so general, that it will certainly end in one' (*Letters*, 129)—and to the carnage involved—'I was told yesterday by a Colonel, from Germany, that out of two battalions of nine hundred men, to which he belong'd, but seventy-one left!' (*Letters*, 127)—little had changed by the publication of volumes 5 and 6 at the close of the year. It was not until February 1763, with Sterne in France and *Tristram Shandy* in the doldrums, that peace was finally established at the Treaty of Paris. In the meantime, Sterne's evident dismay at the plight of combatants may well have found an outlet in humanitarian action. Of the few books we know him for sure to have owned, one is a presentation copy of a charitable pamphlet from this period, *Proceedings of the Committee Appointed to*

---

[2] Linda Colley, *Britons: Forging the Nation, 1707–1837* (New Haven: Yale University Press, 1992), 105, 102.

[3] Geoffrey Holmes and Daniel Szechi, *The Age of Oligarchy: Pre-industrial Britain, 1722–1783* (Harlow: Longman, 1993), 242, 282–3; see also, on these phrases, Paul Langford, *A Polite and Commercial People: England, 1727–1783* (Oxford: Oxford University Press, 1989), 346.

Manage the Contributions . . . for Cloathing the French Prisoners of War, copies of which were distributed to contributors following the committee's final meeting in July 1760. Inscribed to Sterne in the hand of one of the committee's most active members, the radical Whig philanthropist Thomas Hollis, the pamphlet combines a preface by Johnson (who recommends the enterprise as one that 'alleviates captivity, and takes away something from the miseries of war') with more sentimental contributions by other hands. In a manuscript note, Hollis draws Sterne's attention to the declaration of a Cornish subscriber 'that as our victorious troops have proved an overmatch for our enemies at the fatal decision of the sword, so will our numberless subscriptions to cloath them convince the whole world, that we are as much their superiors in the gentler passions of mercy and benevolence'. Here, and in Hollis's accompanying comment that this letter 'does honor to Britain and to human nature', the incongruous blend of military zeal and pacific tenderness that Sterne embodies in Uncle Toby is made to seem a defining national virtue.[4]

In *A Sentimental Journey*, the Seven Years War puts Yorick at risk of captivity himself, and sends him in fear of the Bastille to the Duc de Choiseul—Choiseul being the minister who, in the spring of 1761, had been embroiled with Pitt in the first purposeful efforts to negotiate a peace.[5] Here is only one of many references to the Seven Years War, and to national and international politics in general, that litter Sterne's published writing. Yet scholars have had very little to say about the political dimension of either novel, and few attempts have been made to pursue into the fiction the line of enquiry opened up long ago by Lewis Perry Curtis's study of Sterne's journalism in the 1740s, *The Politicks of Laurence Sterne*.[6] Though *Tristram Shandy* is framed in its first and final volumes by dedications to Pitt, and has as its running leitmotif the whistling of

---

[4] W. G. Day, 'Sterne and French Prisoners of War', *Shandean*, 9 (1997), 136–41, quoting Johnson's preface (p. [iv]) and reproducing the end of the Cornish subscriber's letter with Hollis's manuscript comment (K2a). Day's identification of Hollis as the source of the gift is based on strong circumstantial evidence, which can be confirmed with reference to the autograph samples in W. H. Bond, *Thomas Hollis of Lincoln's Inn: A Whig and his Books* (Cambridge: Cambridge University Press, 1990).

[5] See Richard Middleton, *The Bells of Victory: The Pitt–Newcastle Ministry and the Conduct of the Seven Years' War, 1757–1762* (Cambridge: Cambridge University Press, 1985), 154–5.

[6] Lewis Perry Curtis, *The Politicks of Lawrence Sterne* (Oxford University Press, 1929). See also Kenneth Monkman's conjectural attribution to Sterne of further journalism, in 'More of Sterne's *Politicks* 1741–2', *Shandean*, 1 (1989), 53–108; 'Sterne and the '45 (1743–8)', *Shandean*, 2 (1990), 45–136; 'Sterne's Farewell to Politics', *Shandean*, 3 (1991), 98–125.

'Lilliburlero',[7] the work is generally thought of as studious in its evasions of political involvement. It has never been convincingly related to Sterne's Whig commitments and milieu, or to the context of a war that was the dominant public issue throughout the period in which its first six volumes appeared. Some of *Tristram Shandy*'s most striking passages of political innuendo have been brought together by Wolfgang Zach, whose valuable analysis forms the basis of the Florida notes at certain points; but these innuendoes are typically very localized, and resist consolidation into a larger thesis.[8] Zach points, for example, to an undeveloped foray into political allegory at the opening of the third instalment, in which Obadiah is forced to travel on foot because 'the *Scotch* horse . . . cannot bear a saddle upon his back' and 'PATRIOT is sold' (*TS* 5.2.415–16)—the reference being to the Earl of Bute's recent displacement of Pitt in the new king's ministry. More of Zach's analysis is devoted to Toby's 'apologetical oration' in defence of warfare in the same instalment (6.32.554), and he persuasively reads as a reference to the Treaty of Paris, and to the criticisms made of its leniency by Pitt and others, Tristram's whimsical exclamation in the fourth instalment: 'AND SO THE PEACE WAS MADE; | ——And if it is a bad one—as Tristram Shandy laid the corner stone of it—nobody but Tristram Shandy ought to be hanged' (7.35.638).[9] Yet here again the reference seems digressive and opportunistic, without any obvious potential for overarching explanation.

Zach's argument that the apologetical oration (in which Toby condemns the Peace of Utrecht in 1713 and wishes that war had gone on) refers implicitly to present-time debates about the Seven Years War, and about the propriety of making concessions in order to end it, has received incidental support from several scholars. Mark Loveridge has written of 'the historical analogy implicit in *Tristram Shandy*, between the contemporary Seven Years' War against the French and Toby's wars, the War of the League of Augsburg (in which he fought) and the War of the Spanish Succession, Toby's bowling-green war'; and both Loveridge and Parnell have noted that comparisons were commonplace in 1761–2 between Bute's appeasing

---

[7] On the political connotations of this 'ubiquitous anti-Jacobite song of the Williamite wars', see Katie Trumpener, *Bardic Nationalism: The Romantic Novel and the British Empire* (Princeton: Princeton University Press, 1997), 46–7.

[8] Wolfgang Zach, ' "My Uncle Toby's Apologetical Oration" und die Politische Sinndimension von *Tristram Shandy*', *Germanisch-Romanische Monatsschrift*, 27 (1977), 391–416.

[9] On contemporary debates about the Treaty of Paris as 'a bad peace', see Robert Donald Spector, *English Literary Periodicals and the Climate of Opinion during the Seven Years' War* (The Hague: Mouton, 1966), 88–129.

ministry and (as one journalist put it) 'that which concluded the ignomin-
ious treaty of Utrecht'.[10] When Tristram himself itemizes 'the many ill
consequences of the treaty of *Utrecht*' (6.31.552), he echoes not only Toby's
dislike of its conciliatory provisions, but also a contemporaneous rhetoric
in which, though fifty years in the past, Utrecht was being pointedly
recalled as 'an inglorious peace, by which we gave up almost the whole of
our conquests to a conquered and despairing enemy'.[11] The picture that
emerges is of a kind of military *mise en abyme*, in which a series of internal
reduplications sets up an unspoken but pervasive analogy between war in
the ongoing present of serialization and reading, and the two prior wars
that pervade the intertwined narrated pasts of *Tristram Shandy*. These are
the Nine Years War as fought by Toby in Ireland and Flanders (1689–97),
which is also sometimes known as King William's War or the War of the
League of Augsburg, and the War of the Spanish Succession (also known as
Queen Anne's War, 1702–13) as re-enacted in his Yorkshire garden. Most
recently, Madeleine Descargues has returned to the crux of Toby's lament
about Utrecht to find in the oration an aporetic device that is paradigmatic
of *Tristram Shandy* as a whole. By making Toby draw silently for his defence of ongoing warfare on a passage of Burton that in context is pacifist
in drift, the chapter contrives 'a deadpan presentation of contradictory
rhetorical discourses—an implicit attack on war and an explicit defence
of it—and is left without any gloss at all from the otherwise voluble narrator, Tristram'.[12] Sterne thereby concentrates into Toby's oration his larger
strategy of activating the reader's interpretative faculties, Descargues con-
tends, while also holding himself aloof from commitment to determinate
meaning.

   Probably the most sustained effort at political interpretation of Sterne's
writing comes with the spurious commentaries that sprang up around it at
the time of first publication. Foremost among these is the bogus commentary appended by Sterne himself to *A Political Romance*, in which one
reader decodes the tale as allegorizing the Seven Years War, while another
protests that his fellow exegete 'had not gone far enough backwards into
our History to come at the Truth', and relates the story instead to 'the His-

---

[10] Mark Loveridge, 'Stories of COCKS and BULLS: The Ending of Tristram Shandy',
Eighteenth-Century Fiction, 5 (1992), 35–54 (at 42); *London Chronicle*, 10–12 June 1762,
quoted by Parnell, introduction to *Tristram Shandy* (London: Dent, 2000), p. xxiv; see also
Morris Golden, 'Periodical Context in the Imagined World of *Tristram Shandy*', *The Age
of Johnson*, 1 (1987), 237–60 (at 252).

[11] *Gentleman's Magazine*, 31 (Nov. 1761), 519.

[12] Madeleine Descargues, '*Tristram Shandy* and the Appositeness of War', *Shandean*, 12
(2001), 63–77.

tory of King *William's* and Queen *Anne's* Wars' (*PR* 35). It is tempting to read the playful sense of interchangeability that Sterne develops here as heralding a comparable strategy of substitution or conflation in *Tristram Shandy*, with topical meanings thereby implied; but at the same time this commentary seems to discredit in advance, in its facile and gratuitous leaps, the whole enterprise of political decoding. Instead of any usable key to interpretation, there puzzlingly emerges 'a whole Bunch of *Keys*', which open the door on nothing (*PR* 47). The same elaborate charade returns in the earliest reception of *Tristram Shandy*, with *The Clockmakers Outcry* affecting to read Tristram's narrative as a belated exercise in crypto-Jacobite innuendo, in which 'covert attacks against our present happy establishment are glaringly evinced in his *hobby-horsical* doctrine'.[13] *Explanatory Remarks . . . by Jeremiah Kunastrokius* makes a similar association between hobby horses, Yorick's lean horse, and the white horse of the Hanover dynasty, and declares that '*Tristram Shandy* is one compleat system of modern politics', or again 'a master piece of allegory, beyond all the poets of this or any period whatever'. A key must be published to elucidate the text, this commentator insists, including its allusions to a shattering loss early in the war and the subsequent rise of Pitt:

What is the Siege of *Namur* . . . but the Siege of Fort St. Philip's in Minorca?—or, the wound his uncle Toby received there but the distress the nation was thrown into thereupon? His application to the study of fortification, and the knowledge he therein gained, means nothing else but the rectitude and clear sightedness of the administration which afterwards took up the reins of government. (*CH* 66–7)

Taken together, these and other mock commentaries imply, in the smirking absurdity of their interpretative gestures, a salutary warning about the perils of tone-deaf decoding, or of any wrong-headed attempt to systematize a text that, above all else, is perversely unsystematic.

But there is no interpretative smoke without textual fire. With something of the dizzying doubleness of their original model, Pope's *Key to the Lock* (which parodies totalizing political readings of *The Rape of the Lock*, while also insinuating that real seditious encoding is locally present[14]), these commentaries alert us to an element of *Tristram Shandy* that is genuinely comparable to, though never as simple or direct as, the stratum of political meaning they claim to expose. We must tread carefully here, and

[13] *The Clockmakers Outcry against the Author of the Life and Opinions of Tristram Shandy* (1760), 39.

[14] See Howard Erskine-Hill, *Poetry of Opposition and Revolution: Dryden to Wordsworth* (Oxford: Clarendon Press, 1996), 85–8.

in recognition of the evasiveness of the text. Sterne had none of Pope's readiness to strike bold oppositional poses, and the glancing ironies of Toby's 'apologetical oration' are characteristic not only of *Tristram Shandy* as a whole, but also of its author's pragmatic liking for the middle way. In a late memoir Sterne dissociates himself from his early journalism, writing that 'though [his uncle] was a party-man, I was not, and detested such dirty work: thinking it beneath me' (*Letters*, 4); and this same attitude is on show in his letters at the height of the war, when he looks to the influence of the new king for an abatement of partisan squabble. 'We shall be soon Prussians and Anti-Prussians, B[ute]'s and Anti-B[ute]s,' he loftily laments before the appearance of volumes 3 and 4, 'and those distinctions will just do as well as Whig and Tory—and for aught I know serve the same ends' (*Letters*, 126). As a zealous maximizer of his own circulation and sales, Sterne no doubt intended *Tristram Shandy* to maintain an ironic detachment (for all its ministerial dedications) from the partisan directness of a satirist like Churchill, and the evidence of his subscription lists is that he succeeded in finding patronage that was politically much more plural than might be expected. Though skewed towards the Whig parliamentarians with whom Sterne rapidly fell in on arriving in London, the *Sermons* subscription list of 1760 also includes Tories and others who (whether from too much principle or too little) tended to float free of purely partisan identification, such as Barrington, the Secretary of War whom Sterne heard in the Commons in 1761, and his immediate successor under Bute, whom Sterne proudly called 'my friend, Mr. Charles T[ownshend]' (*Letters*, 130).[15]

None of this is to say, however, that *Tristram Shandy* does not engage, in its own characteristically ludic and elliptical way, with the high political agenda of its ongoing moment. Inescapably, the war and associated debates form a running context in the novel, and here indeed is another way in which Sterne's serial text shows itself responsive, in its slow unfolding, to outward contingencies and conditions. Doubtless the basic topic of war was planned from the start, given that hostilities had broken out a full three years before Sterne's first approach to Dodsley about *Tristram*

---

[15] I am grateful to Melvyn New for making available to me his consolidated list of subscribers to *A Sentimental Journey* and the three instalments of *Sermons*, with his provisional analysis. On the frequently partisan nature of eighteenth-century subscription lists, see W. A. Speck, 'Politicians, Peers, and Publication by Subscription, 1700–1750', in Isabel Rivers (ed.), *Books and their Readers in Eighteenth-Century England* (Leicester: Leicester University Press, 1982), 47–68. For the complications of political identity and partisan allegiance in the 1760s, see John Brewer, *Party Ideology and Popular Politics at the Accession of George III* (Cambridge: Cambridge University Press, 1976), 39–54.

Shandy, and that military themes had in the interim become a standard part of the repertoire for fiction. *Ephraim Tristram Bates* (the story, as its title page explains, of 'a broken-hearted Soldier') was one of the promptest responses, and Sterne was not the only writer to rise to the *Critical Review*'s suggestion that the subject of this novel, though botched here, 'wou'd appear to admirable advantage handled by a man of abilities'.[16] *The Campaign* (1759) sends its hero to Flanders on a 'volunteering frolick',[17] and was imitated in 1760 by another anonymous work, *The Adventures of George Stanley: or, The Campaign*. If there is nothing unusual about *Tristram Shandy*'s campaigning theme, however, nothing matches the wit, complexity, and depth with which Sterne pursues it. Not only does the underplot that develops through Toby's campaigns in the garden set up an intricate set of parallels between the reading-time war of 1756–63, the bowling-green war of 1702–13, and, behind it, Toby's original trauma when fighting in Ireland and Flanders in 1689–97. This underplot is contrived in such a way as to invoke a third and yet earlier conflict, the Civil War of the 1640s; and it brings the memory of all three to bear on war in the immediate present, the contingencies of which then exert ongoing pressure on Sterne's serial text in terms of both pace and shape. In keeping with the intertextual dynamics of *Tristram Shandy*, moreover, Sterne makes this contextual move by way of a fashionable hypotext, using a work that evokes the Civil War to inform his story of displaced or sublimated conflict in Toby's garden, and to inform, at the same time, the studiously ambiguous, jocoserious mode in which he writes it.

Fashionable texts are not always new texts, least of all in a culture so receptive—as Macpherson, Chatterton, and Percy would all demonstrate in the 1760s—to real or fabricated retrievals from the literary past. Nor are the fashions always, like Ossian, public. To grasp the varied levels of Sterne's allusiveness, we need to remember that he was simultaneously addressing varied readerships, from the intimate constituency of 'Eugenius' or 'Jenny' to the anonymous public he addresses as 'Madam' or 'Sir'. Though *Tristram Shandy* is among the defining successes of eighteenth-century print culture, it also retains prominent features of an earlier manuscript culture, laden as it is with recondite allusions that—like the interpretatively crucial yet teasingly silent invocations of Burton—are retrievable only in the rarefied context of coterie interpretation. It is in this context that we need to understand Sterne's play on the verse of Marvell, whose elevation to the canonical prestige he enjoys today can only be said

---

[16] *Critical Review*, 2 (Sept. 1756), 143.   [17] *Monthly Review*, 20 (Feb. 1759), 189.

to have begun in earnest with the publication, in 1776, of *The Works of Andrew Marvell, Esq., Poetical, Controversial, and Political.* This was a lavish quarto edition in three volumes, edited by the Whig satirist and former naval officer Edward Thompson, and subscribed to by prominent members of the parliamentary, social, and political élites, including surviving friends of Sterne such as Garrick, Hall-Stevenson, and Wilkes.[18] Previously, Marvell had enjoyed only localized prominence as a lyric poet, and his reputation was above all political, and defined by the partisan commitment of his post-Restoration satires as opposed to the ambivalent poise of his earlier poems (some of which were not even in print). The Thompson edition did not come out of the blue, however, and the long history of its gestation, which reaches back to the early 1760s, indicates the highly political route through which Sterne is most likely to have encountered Marvell's magisterial meditation on gardens and war, *Upon Appleton House, To My Lord Fairfax.*

Thompson himself cannot be linked directly to Sterne, though he evidently had Shandean interests, moved on the fringe of the Nonsense Club circle, and was among the subscribers to the 1760 volumes of Sterne's *Sermons.* His lost play *The Hobby-Horse* was unsuccessfully staged by Garrick in April 1766, presumably with a Shandean theme, and after Sterne's death his bantering poem about Garrick's Shakespeare festival at Stratford, *Trinculo's Trip to the Jubilee, Inscribed to John Stevenson Hall, Esq.* (1769) opens with dedicatory verses to the man traditionally associated with Sterne's 'Eugenius' figure.[19] We come still closer to Sterne with Thompson's acknowledgement that much of the groundwork for his Marvell edition had already been laid by 'the late Mr. Thomas Hollis . . . [who] had once a design of making a collection of his compositions'. On Hollis's death in 1774 'all the manuscripts and scarce tracts, collected for that purpose', had devolved to Thompson, who also received by way of Hollis's heir, Thomas Brand, 'many anecdotes, manuscripts, and scarce compositions of our author, such as I was unable to procure any where else'.[20] It is likely that Thompson inherited an edition that was already substantially

[18] For the many further friends of Sterne who appear among the 146 subscribers to the Marvell edition, with other overlaps between Thompson's subscription list and those for *A Sentimental Journey* and Sterne's *Sermons*, see Thomas Keymer, 'Marvell, Thomas Hollis, and Sterne's Maria: Parody in *A Sentimental Journey*', *Shandean*, 5 (1993), 9–31 (at 23–4).

[19] For evidence about the play, see *The Letters of David Garrick*, ed. D. M. Little, G. M. Kahrl, and P. de K. Wilson, 3 vols. (Cambridge, Mass.: Harvard University Press, 1963), 1: 506–7; 1: 542. I am grateful to Melvyn New for these references.

[20] *The Works of Andrew Marvell, Esq.*, ed. Edward Thompson, 3 vols. (1776), 1: i–ii; 1: vi; see also 3: 487.

formed, and certain that the *Works* of 1776 marks the posthumous fulfilment of a project that reaches back, in its origins, to the period of Hollis's
friendship with Sterne.

Hollis, a controversial (and, for many, incendiary) radical whose political creed was enshrined above all in the republican traditions of the seventeenth century, had been drawn to Marvell by association with his
foremost hero, Milton. One hostile contemporary, the Reverend Baptist
Noel Turner, identified him as 'a bigotted Whig, or Republican; one who
mis-spent an ample fortune in paving the way for sedition and revolt in
this and the neighbouring kingdoms, by dispersing democratical works'. A
more approving twentieth-century voice, Caroline Robbins, calls him 'the
most persistent and one of the most effective propagandists for radical
Whig doctrines operating in the British Empire in the 1760's', above all by
virtue of his distribution to libraries worldwide of 'liberty books' in the
radical Whig tradition of Harrington, Locke, Milton, Molesworth, and
Nedham. (Hollis's 1,200 or so gifts to Harvard College, in the words of the
appalled Turner, 'might be said even to have laid the first train of com-
bustibles for the American explosion'.)[21] One such book, a handsomely
bound copy of which Hollis also presented to Sterne, was his own edition
of Toland's *Life of Milton*, in which Sterne might have read several approving references to the protection given Milton at the Restoration by
'ANDREW MARVEL, *who by his parts and probity made himself so much
known since that time in* England'.[22] This edition appeared in January
1761,[23] the month of *Tristram Shandy's* second instalment, and it is at about
this time that we first hear of Sterne's acquaintance with Hollis, who for all
his political austerity was an amiable figure—a kind of Yorick, indeed, who
in the words of his early biographer 'could keep a whole table in a roar'.[24]
Hollis was normally no admirer of the novel genre (he fulminates in a

---

[21] Turner's remarks appear in John Nichols, *Illustrations of the Literary History of the
Eighteenth Century*, 8 vols. (1817–58), 6: 157; Caroline Robbins, 'The Strenuous Whig, Thomas
Hollis of Lincoln's Inn', *William and Mary Quarterly*, 3rd ser., 7 (1950), 406–53 (at 412). See also
Robbins's analysis of the Hollis donations to Harvard in 'Library of Liberty—Assembled for
Harvard College by Thomas Hollis of Lincoln's Inn', *Harvard Library Bulletin*, 5 (1951), 5–23,
181–96 (the figure of 1,200 is an estimate made in 1766); also the chapter recently devoted to
Hollis in Annabel Patterson, *Early Modern Liberalism* (Cambridge: Cambridge University
Press, 1997), 27–61, and the bibliographical study by W. H. Bond, *Thomas Hollis of Lincoln's
Inn: A Whig and his Books* (Cambridge: Cambridge University Press, 1990).

[22] John Toland, *The Life of John Milton*, ed. Thomas Hollis (1761), 110–11; see also p. 116 n.
On the presentation copy to Sterne (lot 1289 in the sale catalogue), see Nicolas Barker, 'The
Library Catalogue of Laurence Sterne', *Shandean*, 1 (1989), 9–24 (at 18).

[23] Patterson, *Early Modern Liberalism*, 42.

[24] Robbins, 'Strenuous Whig', 427, quoting an undated letter of Francis Blackburne to
Andrew Eliot, Mass. Hist. Soc. Coll., Hollis Letters, fo. 113.

manuscript note to *Eikonoklastes* that young men too often neglect the 'oracle' Milton for *Sir Charles Grandison* and 'such stuff'[25]), but he evidently made an exception for Sterne. Like Edward Thompson, he had already subscribed to the opening two volumes of *The Sermons of Mr. Yorick*, and Cash lists him among the 'odd variety of people' with whom Sterne became friendly on arriving in London (*LY* 94). Hollis's manuscript diary records that the two met for dinner on 20 February 1761, and again—this time in the company of William Hewitt, a long-term member of Hall-Stevenson's Whig 'Demoniac' circle—on 21 March: 'Mr Hewett, & the Rev. Mr Sterne (Tristram Shandy) with me in the morning.'[26] If this means a visit to Hollis's lodgings, Sterne would certainly have seen the sombre 1661 portrait in which Marvell appears, as Hollis liked to see it, 'in all the sobriety and decency of the then departed Commonwealth'. Hollis had procured the portrait in mid-1760 by means of an advertisement in the *York Courant*, and later that year voiced satisfaction that 'the picture of the incomparable John Milton hangs on one side of me in my apartment, and that of the incorruptible Andrew Marvell on the other'.[27] He then commissioned Cipriani (the Florentine artist who appears with Sterne in John Hamilton Mortimer's 'Caricature Group') to make an etching from the portrait, prints of which he 'generously distributed . . . to his friends and fellow-patriots; and to some, perhaps, who were neither'.[28] It is possible that Sterne was among this motley crew of recipients, and more than likely that the two known Hollis gifts to him (both of which have come to light within the last fifteen years) are only the tip of the iceberg.[29]

Marvell's writing, however, could not be so easily distributed within Hollis's personal circle of friends, still less to the libraries of the world. He seems to have bought up and disseminated copies of an old edition by Thomas Cooke, *The Works of Andrew Marvell, Esq.* (1726), an example of

[25] Robbins, 'Library of Liberty', 13, quoting Hollis's MS note in the Harvard copy of Richard Baron's edition (1756) of Milton's *Eikonoklastes*.

[26] *LY* 80 n., 94, citing Hollis's six-volume MS diary, vol. 1, fos. 142, 149, Houghton Library.

[27] Letter of 1760, quoted in *Works of Marvell*, ed. Thompson, 1: lvii; letter of Dec. 1760, quoted in Francis Blackburne, *Memoirs of Thomas Hollis, Esq.*, 2 vols. (1780), 1: 104. Thompson also quotes the following character of Marvell as left among Hollis's papers: 'Andrew Marvell, the disciple, friend, and protector of John Milton, and like him learned, able, witty, virtuous, active, magnanimous, and incorruptible' (*Works of Marvell*, ed. Thompson, 3: 487).

[28] Blackburne, *Memoirs of Hollis*, 1: 97.

[29] Something of the scale and range with which Hollis distributed 'liberty prints' such as the Marvell portrait is apparent from his unusually specific diary entries of May–June 1762. Within six weeks he gave away more than seventy prints, to a broad spectrum of recipients including Pitt, Garrick, Smollett, Reynolds, and Hogarth (Bond, *Hollis of Lincoln's Inn*, 108).

which survives at Harvard in Hollis's distinctive emblematic binding,[30] but Cooke's edition was highly selective, and by then was extremely scarce. At some point Hollis resolved to sponsor an edition himself, and held extensive discussions on the subject with the printer William Bowyer, much of whose time between 1765 and 1767 was then devoted to the project.[31] We learn slightly more from Hollis's biographer, the radical churchman Francis Blackburne, who had been Sterne's most influential friend and patron within the diocese of York before *Tristram Shandy*. (Sterne was still visiting Blackburne in Thirsk as late as June 1767, at the height of the notoriety Blackburne earned on publishing, at Hollis's instigation, his heterodox manifesto *The Confessional*.)[32] The plan was evidently well advanced by 1765, when Hollis began recording his discussions with Bowyer 'relating to a new edition of Andrew Marvell's works, to the printing of which he seemed reluctant, from the difficulties that will attend it; animated him all I can to that end; and we are to talk further concerning it'. Progress seems to have been slow, but by 1767 he had enlisted the assistance of Richard Baron (the republican whose edition of *Eikonoklastes* had caused a furore in 1756), and an edition was projected 'in one volume quarto, to be printed by Millar and Cadell'.[33] Thompson adds that Andrew Millar (who died in 1768) even went so far as to publish advertisements for the edition.[34] Why the project then foundered remains uncertain, though it was suggested at the time that political or commercial caution, or perhaps some combination of the two, persuaded Hollis's publishers to withdraw, as they evidently did at around the time of Sterne's death.[35]

It is worth adding that Hollis and like-minded radicals such as Blackburne would not have been the only conduit between Sterne and Marvell. Although the lyric poems enjoyed little of their modern prestige, Marvell remained prominent throughout the century as a satirist, and it is not unreasonable to credit Sterne with direct knowledge of *The Rehearsal Transpros'd*, a prose satire he would have found praised in *A Tale of A Tub* as one 'we still read . . . with Pleasure, 'tho the Book it answers be sunk

[30] Bond, *Hollis of Lincoln's Inn*, 71.

[31] John Nichols, *Literary Anecdotes of the Eighteenth Century*, 9 vols. (1812–15), 2: 448.

[32] On Sterne and Blackburne, see *EMY* 235–6, and *LY* 296–7; on Blackburne's radicalism, *The Confessional*, and his involvement with Hollis, see Caroline Robbins, *The Eighteenth-Century Commonwealthman* (Cambridge, Mass.: Harvard University Press, 1959), 261, 324–5; J. C. D. Clark, *English Society 1688–1832: Ideology, Social Structure and Political Practice during the Ancien Régime* (Cambridge: Cambridge University Press, 1985), 313–14; Patterson, *Early Modern Liberalism*, 34.

[33] Blackburne, *Memoirs of Hollis*, 1: 104; 1: 361.

[34] *Works of Marvell*, ed. Thompson, 1: i–ii.

[35] Keymer, 'Marvell, Thomas Hollis, and Sterne's Maria', 21.

long ago'.[36] When Yorick enters *Tristram Shandy*'s controversy about baptism 'in a tone two parts jest and one part earnest' (4.29.389), the Florida
editors are right to note 'the long tradition by which the clergy and others
had defended the use of a tone "betwixt Jest and Earnest" in religious controversy', but they are also right to single out *The Rehearsal Transpros'd* as a
locus classicus of the phrase.[37] Within Sterne's Yorkshire milieu, at the same
time, a body of verse that was originally distributed through scribal publication must have retained its currency, not least with families such as
that of Sterne's friend and patron Thomas Belasyse, fourth Viscount
Fauconberg: Marvell, after all, had written two epithalamia for the second
Viscount on his marriage to Mary Cromwell, the Protector's daughter.
Moreover, there is some evidence that in the run-up to *Tristram Shandy*
Cooke's goal of bringing to notice lyric poetry that 'gives him no small
Claim to my Favour, independent of his other Virtues',[38] was belatedly
having some impact. In his 'Ode to Independency' of 1756, William Mason,
though setting greatest store by the controversial writings, also registers
Marvell's ability as a poet to 'strike the tender string' or write with 'plaint of
slighted Love'.[39] Several Marvell poems supply illustrative quotations for
Johnson's *Dictionary* of 1755, and it was later alleged that it was only because of his iconic status in the radical Whig pantheon that Johnson, who
'could not but have known of the merit and beauties of Marvell's poems',
had failed to have him included in the massive anthology to which he
contributed his *Lives of the Poets*.[40] Another intriguing reference comes in
a sequence of lines from Smart's *Jubilate Agno* (written 1759–63), which
brings together the names of Marvell, Mason, and Sterne's sometime
ecclesiastical ally Dean Fountayne, and also makes cryptic reference to
Upon Appleton House.[41]

That said, there is no doubt that Marvell was at his most prominent in
the intersecting Whig circles in which Sterne moved in the 1760s, from the
high-political circle of Pitt (a personal friend of Hollis, though they quar-

[36] Jonathan Swift, *A Tale of a Tub*, ed. A. C. Guthkelch and D. Nichol Smith, 2nd edn.
(Oxford: Clarendon Press, 1958), 10.
[37] *The Rehearsal Transpros'd*, ed. D. I. B. Smith (Oxford: Clarendon Press, 1971), 187.
[38] *The Works of Andrew Marvell, Esq.*, ed. Thomas Cooke, 2 vols. (1726), 1: 18.
[39] In Elizabeth Story Donno (ed.), *Andrew Marvell: The Critical Heritage* (London:
Routledge, 1978), 113; Donno's introduction, pp. 1–9, supplies a useful history of Marvell's
eighteenth-century reputation.
[40] Samuel Johnson, *A Dictionary of the English Language* (1755), s. v. 'Distrain', 'Excise',
'Nor', 'Surcingle'; *Retrospective Review*, 10 (1824), quoted in Donno (ed.), *Marvell: The Critical Heritage*, 142.
[41] Christopher Smart, *Jubilate Agno*, ed. Karina Williamson (Oxford: Clarendon Press,
1980), 115 (ll. D78–D81); see also E. E. Duncan-Jones, 'Smart and Marvell', *Notes and Queries*,
212 (1967), 182.

relled on his acceptance of the Chatham peerage in 1766[42]) to the group of polemicists and satirists associated with Wilkes's *North Briton*. Revered as an exemplary defender of national freedoms, a model of virtuous patriotism and resistance to tyranny and corruption, Marvell remained in the grip of a reputation based largely on his polemical tracts and satirical libels of the Restoration period, and shaped by the partisan agenda of his radical Whig canonizers of the 1690s.[43] That reputation evidently remains to the fore in Churchill's tribute to Marvell from *The Author* (1763):

> Is this the Land, where, in those worst of times
> The hardy Poet rais'd his honest rimes
> To dread rebuke, and bade controulment speak
> In guilty blushes on the villain's cheek,
> Bade Pow'r turn pale, kept mighty rogues in awe,
> And made them fear the Muse, who fear'd not Law?[44]

Here the awesome rhymes that Churchill celebrates can hardly refer to the delicate ambiguities of 'The Garden' or 'The Nymph Complaining', nor even to the troubled balancing act of the 'Horatian Ode' (which, having been cancelled from the posthumous *Miscellaneous Poems* of 1681, had yet to appear in any published version, and may even have been among the manuscripts in Hollis's possession). But Thomas Cooke's emphasis in the 1720s on the importance of Marvell's lyric verse, and the distinctly modern ordering of his achievement implied by the title of the Thompson edition (*The Works . . . Poetical, Controversial, and Political*), show plainly that his poetry was moving up the agenda, where it can only have complicated the stringencies of the standard Whig-republican image. In no work are these complications more fully demonstrated than *Upon Appleton House*, a profoundly political poem, yet also a poem of agonized ambivalence, and one utterly without the polemical clarity of Marvell's Restoration satires.

HORTICULTURE WARS: UNCLE TOBY AND *UPON APPLETON HOUSE*

Although it is only in the second instalment of January 1761 that Toby's bowling-green campaigns begin in earnest, the obsession that underlies them is visible in the first. Traumatized by his experiences in Flanders (and

---

[42] Bond, *Hollis of Lincoln's Inn*, 31.
[43] See Nicholas von Maltzahn, 'Marvell's Ghost', in Warren Chernaik and Martin Dzelzainis (eds.), *Marvell and Liberty* (Basingstoke: Macmillan, 1999), 50–74.
[44] *The Poetical Works of Charles Churchill*, ed. Douglas Grant (Oxford: Clarendon Press, 1956), 249 (*The Author*, ll. 87–92).

for all its comic tone, *Tristram Shandy* is riddled with anecdotal reminders of the horrors of war, from the battlefield carnage at Steinkirk to the arbitrary deaths of the Le Fever episode), Toby begins his scheme for reasons that are clearly therapeutic. Convalescing—or failing to convalescence—from the pain of his Namur wound, he finds a map of the town to study as 'a means of giving him ease' (2.1.96), and reads works of siege history so 'that he would forget himself, his wound, his confinement' (2.3.102). More and more such maps are procured, and the project gains further focus when in the third year of his confinement 'he left off the study of projectiles . . . and betook himself to the practical part of fortification only' (2.3.105). Through the long years of recuperation, it is as though scientific analysis of the mechanisms of war, and topographical specification of the damage war has done him, might bestow consoling meaning on an otherwise random disaster, or on the futility of his own small role as projectile fodder. As Tristram puts it, 'the history of a soldier's wound beguiles the pain of it' (1.25.88), and the warlike studies to which Toby then devotes his retirement promise to fix this history with psychologically necessary precision. It is Trim who proposes that the benefit thereby accruing to 'the passions and affections of his mind' (2.3.101) might also have a physical side. The trenches, bastions, and forts of Toby's obsession can be made material in the soil of his Yorkshire garden. Reenacted in the landscape itself, the wars that Toby studies on the page will afford him 'not only pleasure and good pastime,—but good air, and good exercise, and good health,—and your Honour's wound would be well in a month' (2.5.112).

The war-gaming plan of Toby and Trim drops from the narrative at this point, but Tristram's promise that 'the history of their campaigns . . . may make no uninteresting under-plot in the epitasis and working up of this drama' (2.5.113–14) is fulfilled in later instalments. This development is manifestly informed by the progress of war in the period of serialization, and specifically by the cost/benefit debate that raged in parliament and the periodical press. The letters Sterne was writing as he published the second instalment and turned his mind to the third register the debate at several points, as when he describes Barrington's defence of the war as being also 'very severe upon the unfrugal manner it was carried on' (*Letters*, 129), or when he makes a vaguer reference to 'loud complaints of —————— making a trade of the war' (*Letters*, 128). (Curtis is probably right to identify '——————' here as Frederick of Prussia, though this charge was also frequently levelled at Pitt's City Whig supporters, whose self-interested warmongering Samuel Foote was to satirize in the profiteering tradesman, Fungus, in his play *The Commissary*.) In the context of Toby's hobby, modern analyses of the statistics make arresting reading. The Seven Years War brought to sudden maturity the mechanisms of what John Brewer has called 'the fiscal-military state', and the burden of financing the war imposed unprecedented budgetary strains. The average annual cost of the Nine Years War had been £5.5 million, and this figure rises to £7 million for the War of the Spanish Succession. For the war being waged as *Tristram Shandy* was written and serialized, the corresponding figure is £18 million, which is more than double the average annual revenue from tax for the same years. Throughout the war the military budget consumed 71 per cent of public spending, and much of the rest went in servicing the national debt, which ballooned from £75 million at the start of the war to £133 million at the end.[45]

Insatiable in their appetite for resources with which to prosecute the bowling-green war, Toby and Trim parody in miniature the gung-ho profligacy of the war party, while Walter's objections have about them a discernibly Butite ring. The subject first emerges in the second instalment, immediately before the misplaced preface, when Trim is found 'busy in turning an old pair of jack-boots into a couple of mortars to be employed in the siege of *Messina* next summer' (3.20.226). (This is in 1719: in the leap-frogging chronology of the novel, the Peace of Utrecht and Toby's abortive amours are now in the past, and he has resumed his old obsession.) Walter is outraged on seeing the damage a few chapters later, not only because of the sentimental value of the boots, but because their destruction, and the money Toby cheerfully offers in compensation, typify the way in which his enthusiasm for war is making him outlive his means. His wealth is ebbing away, and Walter first draws up the inventory ('ten pounds for a pair of jack-boots?——twelve guineas for your *pontoons*;——half as much for your *Dutch*-draw-bridge;—to say nothing of the train of little brass-artillery you bespoke last week') before counselling restraint. 'These military operations of yours are above your strength', he insists: 'they carry you into greater expences than you were first aware of,——and take my word, ——dear *Toby*, they will in the end quite ruin your fortune, and make a beggar of you.' There could hardly be a defter *reductio ad absurdum* of the pro-war position than in Toby's ready reply: 'What signifies it if they do, brother, replied my uncle *Toby*, so long as we know 'tis for the good of the nation' (3.22.242).

[45] John Brewer, *The Sinews of Power: War, Money and the English State, 1688–1783* (London: Unwin Hyman, 1989), 30, 40, 114.

Armed with this comfortable rationale, Toby makes increasingly reck-less inroads on his personal resources in the following instalment, and on those of his brother and parish. He treats himself to a sentry-box 'instead of a new suit of cloaths' (6.22.538), and Tristram adds that if his artillery had consumed real powder and ammunition 'he had infallibly shot away all his estate' (6.23.541). By now Trim has stripped every spare bit of lead from Toby's house, and has even raided the church roof to procure 'no less than eight new battering-cannons, besides three demi-culverins'. Toby's appetite for state-of-the-art hardware grows insatiable, however, and leads Trim to an act that inflicts massive collateral damage on Tristram himself: 'he had taken the two leaden weights from the nursery window: and as the sash pullies, when the lead was gone, were of no kind of use, he had taken them away also, to make a couple of wheels for one of their car-riages' (5.19.451). Trim has already turned the same mad logic on every window belonging to his master, the pullies being stripped because useless without the leads, and the leads being stripped because useless without the pullies—a cycle of destructive requisitioning from which, Tristram drily observes, 'a great MORAL might be picked' (5.19.452).

None of this is in the service of any very productive cause, and by this point in Sterne's time scheme two decades have passed without the mental healing that is the purpose of the re-enactments appearing to advance at all.[46] Meanwhile, the pleasantly secluded bowling green behind Toby's house, sheltered from the world 'by a tall yew hedge . . . rough holly and thickset flowering shrubs' (2.5.113), becomes a grotesque inversion of garden retreat. Though Tristram is indulgent in his reports, nothing can alter the garden's transformation into a miry no man's land, overgrown by war and functioning now, for all the pleasure Toby and Trim take in their creation, as a standing simulacrum of mass slaughter. Nor does the mili-tary landscaping that Trim at first envisages as a magnet for domestic tourism—'it should be worth all the world's riding twenty miles to go and see it' (2.5.111)—prove at all resilient, or even safe. A tryst between Trim and Bridget comes to an unromantic end when both parties slip over the edge of a trench, 'by means of which she fell backwards soss against the bridge, ——and *Trim*'s foot . . . getting into the cuvette, he tumbled full against the bridge too' (3.24.248). The bridge requires costly replacement, and further ludicrous damage is suffered—to the organization of the

---

[46] The intricate chronology in play here is disentangled by Theodore Baird, 'The Time-Scheme of *Tristram Shandy* and a Source', *PMLA* 51 (1936), 803–20 (at 805–18). Trim proposes the bowling-green scheme in 1701; Tristram's circumcision after Trim's raid on the sash-window leads is in 1723.

narrative as well as the bastions of the garden—when 'a cow broke in (to-morrow morning) to my uncle *Toby*'s fortifications, and eat up two ratios and half of dried grass, tearing up the sods with it, which faced his horn-work and covered way' (3.38.278). As the campaigns go on, more and more of Toby's land is consumed to sustain them, and he begins 'incroaching upon his kitchen garden, for the sake of enlarging his works on the bowling green, and for that reason generally ran his first and second parallels betwixt two rows of his cabbages and his collyflowers' (6.21.535). The inroads are only halted by the Treaty of Utrecht, which Sterne introduces into the narrative before the corresponding Treaty of Paris was negotiated and signed, but at a time when he already considered, as he puts it elsewhere, 'a peace inevitable' (*Letters*, 133). In the 'apologetical oration' that Toby delivers on this occasion, his patriotic argument for continuing the war is balanced by Walter's pragmatic reasons for wishing it stopped ('*a hundred pounds, which I lent thee to carry on these cursed sieges*'), in ways that resume the parodic alignment of the Toby–Walter dispute with real-world, real-time debates (6.32.555). The same applies to Toby's mutterings about the 'private reasons' activating Queen Anne's ministers in the controversial Utrecht clause about dismantling Dunkirk (6.34.560), which mockingly echo Beckford's parliamentary allegation that Utrecht was happening again in the present day, and that certain ministers 'were for making another sacrifice of the nation, to their own interests' (*Letters*, 129).

Sterne's inability to write without resort or digression to the work of others is especially pronounced in his approach to topical controversy, and here the Burton text that underlies the apologetical oration is a prime example. Other intertexts clearly underlie the debate about war and its costs that unfolds between Toby and Walter, and if one were to search for specific instances of political journalism (as opposed to the broad terms of pro- and anti-war discourse as widespread at the time) publications such as Israel Maudit's influential *Considerations on the Present German War* (1760) might reward inspection. More interesting are the fictional precedents that exist for Sterne's oblique mode of approach to the war through the obsessions of Uncle Toby. The nearest come in the novels of Smollett. In *Peregrine Pickle*, the wounded veteran Commodore Trunnion turns his retirement house into a fully fortified garrison, and his friendship with a former subordinate looks forward to the Toby–Trim bond. 'His habitation is defended by a ditch,' Smollett writes, 'over which he has laid a drawbridge, and planted his court-yard with patereroes continually loaded with shot, under the direction of one Mr. Hatchway, who had one of his legs shot away, while he acted as lieutenant on board of the commodore's ship; and now, being on half-pay, lives with him as his companion.'[47] As David McNeil has noted, *Ferdinand Count Fathom* features a scene of fantasy war gaming, in which two imprisoned debtors move oyster shells around a map to simulate the recapture of territory that one of them (the former king of Corsica) has lost in real life.[48] As for the garden motif, there are many well-established connections between fortress architecture and garden design, some of which emerge in theoretical and material instances in the century before *Tristram Shandy*. Examples include the horticultural 'Plan of Troy' and 'Siege of Troy' laid out at Hampton Court and Kensington under William III; military conceits in the writings and designs of Stephen Switzer and Charles Bridgeman (whose development of the ha-ha was influenced by defensive trenches); and the contribution made to the design of the gardens at Versailles by Marshal Vauban, the military architect whose works form part of Toby's warlike studies (2.3.102).[49] No doubt Sterne was playing on this long tradition, which survives today in the work of Ian Hamilton Finlay at Little Sparta, a work of postmodern landscape art that maps out its creator's maxim that 'certain gardens are described as retreats when they are really attacks'.[50]

Nothing matches the complexity, however, with which *Upon Appleton House* anticipates Sterne's otherwise unique combination of all these features. The poem is nowhere explicitly cited in *Tristram Shandy*, and nowhere openly flagged by close quotation (and in this respect its relationship to Sterne's writing differs from that of another Marvellian exercise in war-torn pastoral, 'The Nymph Complaining for the Death of Her Faun', elements from which are locally reworked in *A Sentimental Journey*[51]). A more ghostly and ambient presence, *Upon Appleton House* lurks pervasively beneath the underplot of *Tristram Shandy*, enabling and informing Sterne's development of the motif they share, in which a wounded veteran, having shaped the garden to which he retires into an ongoing rehearsal of warfare, finds truly inward retirement impossible to

[47] Tobias Smollett, *Peregrine Pickle*, ed. James L. Clifford, rev. Paul-Gabriel Boucé (Oxford: Oxford University Press, 1983), 5.

[48] Tobias Smollett, *Ferdinand Count Fathom* ed. Damian Grant (Oxford: Oxford University Press, 1971), 186–7; see also David McNeil, *The Grotesque Depiction of War and the Military in Eighteenth-Century English Fiction* (Newark, Del.: University of Delaware Press, 1990), 111–12, 154.

[49] See Stephen Soud, '"Weavers, Gardeners, and Gladiators": Labyrinths in *Tristram Shandy*', *Eighteenth-Century Studies*, 28 (1995), 397–411.

[50] David Norbrook, *Writing the English Republic: Poetry, Rhetoric and Politics, 1627–1660* (Cambridge: Cambridge University Press, 1999), 289.

[51] See Keymer, 'Marvell, Thomas Hollis, and Sterne's Maria'; also *SJ* 150, 368.

find.[52] The link is tonal too, in the deftly jocoserious treatment that both texts give to the paradoxical fusion of gardens and war, mingling as they do competing strains of affectionate jest with moral and political earnest. At these levels, the relationship between *Tristram Shandy*'s underplot and the central section of *Upon Appleton House* is a classic instance of that particular mode of intertextuality (radically different from the quotative intertextuality of the apologetical oration and its liftings from Burton) to which Genette applies the term 'transposition'. This is a mode marked more by large analogy than local allusion, and one that, as Genette puts it, 'can give rise to works of vast dimensions, such as *Faust* or *Ulysses*, whose textual amplitude . . . may mask or even completely obfuscate their hypertextual character'.[53] While the relationship of *Tristram Shandy* to *Upon Appleton House* exists in the underplot alone, and is unlike the consistently strong bond between Goethe's drama and the Faust tradition or Joyce's novel and the Homeric, it nevertheless informs this teasing underplot in profound ways, and on one arresting occasion moves close to the surface.

We need to return at this point to the depredations inflicted by Toby and Trim—mutilated veterans and, in their hunger for hardware, inveterate mutilators—on the heirlooms of the Shandy family. Trim's conversion of the jackboots into mortars is crucial here, not only because of its pivotal positioning in the text, but also because it introduces a significant further conflict into the equation. As well as reintroducing the war-gaming theme in the second instalment, it adds the Civil War of the 1640s to the complex three-way analogy already established between the war in which Toby suffers his wound, the war he restages in order to heal it, and war in the time of reading. Walter is aghast because the raw materials of his re-enactments 'were our great-grandfather's, brother *Toby*', and have a military past of their own. The jackboots 'have been in the family . . . ever since the civil wars,' he laments: 'Sir *Roger Shandy* wore them at the battle of *Marston-Moor*' (3.22.241–2). The choice of battle is a brilliant touch. Fought out on the very soil that Toby and Trim now occupy (Toby's bowling green, if we are to associate the novel's setting with Sutton-on-the-Forest, would lie just a matter of miles from the battlefield site), Marston Moor was the major encounter of a conflict thought to have killed a higher percentage of the population than the Great War of 1914–18, and, with fifty thousand

---

[52] On some very fragmentary anticipations of Marvell's theme in earlier seventeenth-century verse, see James Turner, 'Marvell's Warlike Studies', *Essays in Criticism*, 28 (1978), 288–301.

[53] Gérard Genette, *Palimpsests: Literature in the Second Degree* (Lincoln, Neb.: University of Nebraska Press, 1997), 213.

combatants, was probably the biggest battle ever fought on English soil.[54] None of this counts for much with Toby, however, who delightedly presses the mortars into service. Thus is the relic and chief family memorial of this great encounter, which effectively ended the war in northern England and made the reputation of Sir Thomas Fairfax, the future parliamentarian Lord General and addressee of Marvell's poem, dismantled, erased, recycled into the mock artillery of Toby's enactments. Yet the memorial is always subsequently there as Toby's operations go on, in the sense that the very fabric of his re-enactments now materially links them to a war that, though further in the past than Toby's wars, remained much more immediately present in the national psyche. Now, in two fragments of ancient and no doubt bloodied leather, the wars of past and present meet in Toby's garden, and from that time on are forever conflated. The erasure of Marston Moor has happened, but the trace of it inevitably remains.

In this respect the jackboots-turned-mortars also offer a witty miniaturization of Sterne's procedure as a writer, for, just as Toby fashions his artillery from a relic of the Civil War, so Sterne himself fashions his underplot as a palimpsest in the Genettian sense: a text inscribed across the surface of another, the trace of which remains dimly apparent. In this case it is in the scholarship on Marvell, not in readings of *Tristram Shandy*, that the process has been discerned. In the thirty-sixth stanza of the poem (which strategically merges Fairfax's identity with that of his soldiering ancestors), the conquering general returns to his Yorkshire estate, and

> when retired here to Peace,
> His warlike Studies could not cease;
> But laid these Gardens out in sport
> In the just Figure of a Fort;
> And with five Bastions it did fence,
> As aiming one for ev'ry Sense.[55]

At this point in the poem, the garden wittily rewrites its owner's past, in ways that at first suggest nothing more ominous than (as Pierre Legouis put long ago) 'an old soldier's fad, as inoffensive as that of that sweet maniac [*ce doux maniaque*], Sterne's Uncle Toby'.[56] The evocation of the

---

[54] Peter Young, *Marston Moor, 1644: The Campaign and the Battle* (Moreton-in-Marsh: Windrush Press, 1997), p. xviii.

[55] *The Poems and Letters of Andrew Marvell*, ed. H. M Margoliouth, rev. Pierre Legouis with E. E. Duncan-Jones, 2 vols. (Oxford: Clarendon Press, 1971), 1: 70 (ll. 283–8).

[56] Pierre Legouis, *André Marvell: Poète, puritaine, patriote, 1621–1678* (Paris: Didier, 1928), 94.

garden is characteristically sensuous, with the flowers cast first as mus-
keteers who salute the general with 'fragrant Vollyes', then as regiments
that stand in order 'as at *Parade*', and then as protective sentry huts in
which 'each Bee as Sentinel is shut' (ll. 298, 309, 318). As Marvell relentlessly
extends his conceit, however, the implications become more disturbing
and, in the words of Annabel Patterson, 'we, if not Marvell's audience, are
uncomfortably aware of the resemblance between the Lord General's
"warlike Studies" and those of Uncle Toby'.[57] As the garden stanzas go on,
far exceeding their original status as affectionate whimsy, the portrait is
unmistakably of a soldier troubled in his retirement, or whose retirement
troubles the poet. Behind him lies a bloody past, not least in his Yorkshire
campaign of 1644, when a large proportion of the cavalry under Fairfax's
command at Marston Moor were lost and he himself was seriously
wounded (as he was again while besieging Helmsley, a royalist stronghold
near Coxwold, a few months later).[58] Walter does not reveal, incidentally,
on which side his great-grandfather should be thought of as fighting
at Marston Moor, but given the political traditions of the family—the
Whiggish whistling of Uncle Toby, the disastrous affiliation of Sir
Hammond Shandy to the Duke of Monmouth—we should not associate
Sir Roger with the royalist allegiance of Sterne's own forefather, Richard,
who attended Laud on the scaffold and was imprisoned by Cromwell
(*EMY* 4). Perhaps we should imagine him and his boots among the inex-
perienced and almost disastrously incompetent troops of Yorkshire
cavalry that Fairfax led in person at Marston Moor. The battle was largely
won on the left flank, and Fairfax was left isolated on the right by the
precipitate retreat of his cavalrymen (in the words of a Scottish ally, 'his
horss answered not our expectatioun, nor his worth'[59]), many of whom
were cut down as they fled in panic.

Fairfax's reputation is that of a humane warrior, and it was reported that
the slaughter of royalists at Marston Moor would have been greater had he
not intervened with an echo of Caesar's Pharsalian cry: '*Parcite civibus,
Spare the poore deluded Countrymen, O spare them*, I pray, *who are misled
and know not what they do*'.[60] Years later, Clarendon would describe Fairfax
as a man 'who wished nothing that Cromwell did, and yet contributed to

[57] Annabel Patterson, *Marvell and the Civic Crown* (Princeton: Princeton University
Press, 1978), 95.
[58] See John Wilson, *Fairfax: General of Parliament's Forces in the English Civil War*
(London: Murray, 1985), 43–55.
[59] Undated letter from Sir James Lumsden, reprinted in Young, *Marston Moor*, 241.
[60] Reported in John Vicar, *Gods Arke Overtopping the Worlds Waves* (1645), 284; partly
quoted by Wilson, *Fairfax*, 53.

bring it all to pass',[61] and six years after Marston Moor he finally withdrew in disillusionment from public life. Having absented himself from the commission that sentenced Charles I to death, he resigned his office following Cromwell's return from Ireland in June 1650, the last straw being Cromwell's determination next (as Fairfax put it) 'to make War upon . . . our Brethren of *Scotland*'.[62] In the chilling conclusion to the poem written by Marvell at this juncture, 'An Horatian Ode upon Cromwell's Return from Ireland', the poet describes a nation now seemingly locked in an unbreakable cycle of violence. Having burst on public life 'from his private Gardens, where | He liv'd reserved and austere', Cromwell has swept away the old stabilities by valour and force, and will never now sheathe his sword: 'The same *Arts* that did *gain* | A *Pow'r* must it *maintain*.'[63] Yet this is a cycle that Fairfax, uniquely positioned as a moderate parliamentarian leader who was later to become a prime mover in the Restoration, does nothing to break. In *Upon Appleton House* as much as in the 'Horatian Ode', garden seclusion marks the antithesis of public engagement, but in this context Fairfax's quiet withdrawal seems no less ruinous an event than Cromwell's explosive emergence. By walking away from public life, weeding ambition, and tilling conscience (as Marvell tactfully puts it), he is far from recapturing the virtuous austerity of Cromwell in his private garden, and the poem's playful edge is increasingly made to connote frivolity and self-indulgence. The public context, as Marvell makes clear, has ceased to be one in which retirement is a viable option. The pre-war Eden 'When Gardens only had their Tow'rs, | And all the Garrisons were Flowrs' is gone for ever (ll. 331–2), and Marvell is at his most relentless in insisting on the loss of this paradisal past. Where once 'The *Gardiner* had the *Souldiers* place, | And his more gentle Forts did trace', now, after almost a decade of fighting, the garden of England is contaminated by the mechanisms of war: 'But War all this doth overgrow: | We Ord'nance Plant and Powder sow' (ll. 337–8, 343–4). In this perspective, the military conceits of Fairfax's garden cease to be admirable exercises in wit, and look instead like hideous representations of what has actually happened in the country at large: England itself—'The Garden of the World ere while' (l. 322)—has become the world's killing field.

[61] Edward Hyde, Earl of Clarendon, *The History of the Rebellion and Civil Wars in England*, ed. W. Dunn Macray, 6 vols. (Oxford: Clarendon Press, 1888), 4: 275.

[62] Bulstrode Whitlocke, *Memorials of the English Affairs*, 2nd edn. (1732), 461; partly quoted by Wilson, *Fairfax*, 159.

[63] *Poems and Letters of Andrew Marvell*, ed. Margoliouth, 1: 91–4 (ll. 29–30, 119–20). There is a comparable emphasis in Milton's slightly earlier sonnet to Fairfax: 'For what can war, but endless war still breed' (*Complete Shorter Poems*, ed. John Carey, 2nd edn. (London: Longman, 1997), 325).

It is at this point that Marvell implies a distinct rebuke to his patron—
or articulates, as Derek Hirst and Steven Zwicker have suggested, his
patron's own mixed feelings about the rival calls of private retirement
and public duty:[64]

> And yet there walks one on the Sod
> Who, had it pleased him and *God*,
> Might once have made our Gardens spring
> Fresh as his own and flourishing.
> But he preferr'd to the *Cinque Ports*
> These five imaginary Forts:
> And in those half-dry Trenches, spann'd
> Pow'r which the Ocean might command.

(ll. 345–52)

Marvell's dependence on his patron does not preclude the possibility of
measured rebuke, and it is hard not to sense a critical edge at this point. If
so, the innuendo chimes with the judgements made of Fairfax by other
witnesses such as Lucy Hutchinson, who thought that in his withdrawal
from public life 'this greate man' had abruptly 'died to all his former
glory'.[65] In the poem, the imaginary forts and trenches of the garden now
come to seem an absurdly diminished arena, the pleasurable plaything of
a man who has chosen to cocoon himself solipsistically from a world he
might otherwise have healed to the benefit of all. (If anything lets Fairfax
off the hook here, it can only be the belated 'and *God*' that Marvell appends
to l. 346, and the compensatory compliments of the stanza on conscience
that follows.) Then comes the punishment, for as the poem goes on it
becomes increasingly evident that the sensuous escapism Fairfax seeks
to enjoy will in any case be impossible to attain. The very location of his
retirement recalls the conflict he seeks to escape, 'th' invisible *Artilery*' of
his garden seeming to point its battery at nearby Cawood Castle, 'As if it
quarrell'd in the Seat | Th' ambition of its *Prelate* great' (ll. 365–6).[66] Beyond
the garden the larger estate—normally an expression of its proprietor's
character in poems of this genre—is ineradicably coloured by visions of

---

[64] Derek Hirst and Steven Zwicker, 'High Summer at Nun Appleton, 1651: Andrew
Marvell and Lord Fairfax's Occasions', *Historical Journal*, 36 (1993), 247–69; see also Michael
Wilding's account of the poem in *Dragons Teeth: Literature in the English Revolution* (Oxford:
Clarendon Press, 1987), 138–72.

[65] *Memoirs of the Life of Colonel Hutchinson*, 2nd edn. (1808), 314–16, quoted by Wilson,
Fairfax, 162.

[66] Cawood was a seat of the Archbishop of York, and occupied as such by Richard Sterne
after the Restoration. If these lines suggest any part of *Tristram Shandy*, it is perhaps Toby's
use of diocesan property—'a beautiful wood, which the dean and chapter were hewing down'
(8.26.710)—as the backdrop for his re-enactments.

slaughter. The pastoral act of haymaking is rendered as a 'massacre', and its victims include not only the grass but also, in the kind of arbitrary, un-willed catastrophe in which Marvell so painfully specializes, an unfledged rail. Within the garden, war may be a matter of pleasure and play, but in the landscape beyond it seems to persist in all its horror, and as the poet's (and, by implication, the patron's) eye surveys the estate, Marvell seems to be evoking an early modern version of post-traumatic stress. The originating trauma is everywhere, impossible to escape. Having massacred the grass, and with it the bird,

> The Mower now commands the Field;
> In whose new Traverse seemeth wrought
> A Camp of Battail newly fought:
> Where, as the Meads with Hay, the Plain
> Lyes quilted ore with Bodies slain:
> The Women that with forks it fling,
> Do represent the Pillaging.
>
> (ll. 418–24)

These may well be the most disturbing lines in all of Marvell, at once evoking and studiously contaminating the comfortable idiom of country-house verse. Try as he might, play as he might, Fairfax proves unable to es-cape his past at Helmsley and Marston Moor. The sieges and battles stay with him, and hijack his senses with nightmarish perversions of pastoral pleasure. Just as the simulacrum of the bowling green paints itself 'upon the retina of my uncle *Toby*'s fancy' (2.5.113), so the sanguinary reality of Fairfax's experience suffuses the fields he surveys. Far from greening over the memory of war in his garden forts and trenches, he bloodies his whole estate.

THE APOLOGETICAL ORATION AND THE CRY
FOR A PEACE

The currency of Marvell's writing in the circles in which Sterne moved, from the Yorkshire of Blackburne, Fauconberg, and Hall-Stevenson to the London of Hollis, Pitt, and Wilkes, makes clear that the striking relation-ship between *Upon Appleton House* and *Tristram Shandy* goes far beyond that infinity of intertextuality that, in poststructuralist theory, inevitably reactivates prior usages of any particular word or trope, regardless of au-thorial agency or readerly expectation. Not only do the central stanzas of

the poem enable the development of the Toby underplot, which, in a burlesque debasement of Marvell's extended conceit about gardens and war,
provides the first three instalments of *Tristram Shandy* with an ironic running commentary on war in the present. The poem also allows him to play
ingeniously to a particular constituency of known readers, combining the
publicly accessible meanings of his text with a strain of implication specifically addressed to readers of Marvell in Sterne's circle, including those
Whig activists and parliamentarians for whom war was a dominant concern. It would, of course, be obtuse to identify Marvell's Fairfax as simply
the 'original' behind Toby.[67] But it would be equally obtuse to deny the wry
and delicate relationship that Sterne contrives between the two figures,
and the ambient significance for *Tristram Shandy* of this extraordinary
poem. At the simplest level, his witty transposition of *Upon Appleton
House* can be explained as a Cervantic strategy, a mock-heroic deflation in
which the conquering hero of Marston Moor is made to dwindle into a
comic monomaniac, while the scented batteries of Nun Appleton become
a churned-up cabbage patch.[68] Yet there is earnest as well as jest in Sterne's
appropriation of Marvell's theme, and at this level it is inappropriate to
think of *Tristram Shandy* as parodying a poem that, in the playful sophistication of its own procedures, inherently resists such a mode. Although
the retirement/engagement polarity that preoccupies Marvell is of little
relevance to Sterne, he clearly borrows and develops other implications
from the poem, notably those concerning the moral and psychological
status of his traumatized veteran.

Traditional readings of Uncle Toby as simply an affectionate comic creation, or as the exemplary hero of an irony-free sentimental ethics, have
been overturned by Melvyn New's influential account of Toby as being
deeply suspect in his imaginative relish for war, and as the vehicle (for all
his explicit arguments to the contrary) of anti-war innuendo in the text as
a whole. Far from exemplifying selfless and heartfelt benevolence, Toby's
war-gaming in the garden shows him to be grossly defective in fellow feeling: as New puts it in a recent restatement, it is 'purposely ironic' of Sterne

---

[67] Cash has discredited a previously suggested candidate, the eccentric former soldier
Captain Robert Hinde (*EMY* 19). Hinde's well-publicized hobby of building miniature fortifications did not begin until after *Tristram Shandy*—which may well mean that he, not Toby,
is the copy.

[68] The cabbage patch seems an especially felicitous touch: as James Turner notes, Marvell's
vision of the Fairfax garden being overgrown by war had reversed a real-life incident of 1622,
'when Master Gunner Hammond converted part of the Artillery Garden [a training-ground
in London] into "cabbage gardens"—he was eventually forced to root them up' (Turner,
'Marvell's Warlike Studies', 296).

'to describe a person who, while sympathetic towards a fly, re-enacts with pleasure battles in which tens of thousands are killed or wounded'.[69] Yet it is not impossible to reconcile New's sense of something morally problematic about Toby's enthusiasms with the traditional view enshrined in Walter Scott's *Lives of the Novelists*, where Toby is 'a lively picture of kindness and benevolence . . . with whose pleasures we are so much disposed to sympathize' (*CH* 374). We may indeed shrink from the bowling-green war while sympathizing with Toby's pleasure in it, and if so it is because the nature of this pleasure identifies him as more than physically damaged by war, and as incurably injured in the mind. Here Sterne takes a cue from *Upon Appleton House*, while extending and transforming the emphasis he finds. As in the case of Marvell's Fairfax, Toby's conversion of his garden into a simulacrum of war may at first suggest a culpable moral anaesthesia, a frivolous readiness to find private pleasure in his own fanciful reshaping of public pain. As *Upon Appleton House* develops, however, the sense of culpability gives way to a deeper sense of damage, the haunted landscape beyond the garden indicating a mind as well as a body that is irremediably battle-scarred, and unable to find true retirement. And so it is with Toby. Although his re-enactments do at last heal him physically (the decisive moment comes with 'the blister breaking' as Toby rushes to save from felling the trees behind his fortifications (8.26.710), and it is clear thereafter that impotence is not an issue[70]), they fail to cure the mental damage. Instead of proving therapeutic, the bowling-green plan becomes obsessive. Instead of restoring Toby to a full resumption of life (which, in the terms of the novel's close, means courtship and procreation), it arrests his recuperation, and renders him incapable of any alternative form of self-expression. His military hobby-horse becomes a debilitating substitute for conversation and love, a displacement activity vividly revealed as such by his immediate physical response to the garden scheme, which is to blush 'as red as scarlet' (2.5.111).[71] The 'pleasure and good pastime' that were supposed to cure him take over as ends in themselves, and, as he retreats further into his miniature world, the concupiscible Mrs Wadman sits out a decade's fruitless widowhood. Only the contingency of Utrecht releases him to any

---

[69] Melvyn New, *Tristram Shandy: A Book for Free Spirits* (New York: Twayne, 1994), 76–7; see also Melvyn New, *Laurence Sterne as Satirist: A Reading of Tristram Shandy* (Gainesville, Fla.: University of Florida Press, 1969), 164–5.

[70] See *LY* 258 and n. (citing *TS* 9.22.777; 9.26.791–2; 9.28.797); also Mark Sinfield, 'Uncle Toby's Potency: Some Critical and Authorial Confusions in *Tristram Shandy*', *Notes and Queries*, 223 (1978), 54–5.

[71] As Tristram elaborates, 'never did lover post down to a belov'd mistress with more heat and expectation, than my uncle *Toby* did, to enjoy [the bowling green] in private' (2.5.113).

healthy progression from campaigns to amours, and his diffident and botched pursuit of these amours is then followed (later in time, though earlier in the text) by a sterile resumption of the campaigns. In this sense, Toby's obsessional re-enactments indicate not only a reprehensible enthusiasm for war, but a debilitating and finally irremediable condition of which this enthusiasm is only a symptom. The victim of an originating trauma that he is endlessly doomed to act out, Toby is a fictional precursor of the shell-shocked veterans of more recent trench warfare, helplessly fixated on an unspeakable past, and left capable of expressing emotion only by whistling a sanguinary marching song, cheerfully restaging the slaughter of thousands, or mourning a treaty of peace.

The apologetical oration brings to its climax the treatment of war in *Tristram Shandy*, and indeed Tristram introduces the oration by announcing the suspension of military gardening as a major theme: 'I beg the reader will assist me here, to wheel off my uncle *Toby*'s ordnance behind the scenes,——to remove his sentry-box, and clear the theatre, *if possible*, of horn-works and half moons, and get the rest of his military apparatus out of the way' (6.29.549). In the chapter devoted to the oration, Descargues is right to note the characteristic intricacies and turbulences of the text, complicated as it is by Tristram's framing commentary, Walter's parenthetical heckling, and the quietly disruptive subtext of Burton's *Anatomy*. None of these complicating factors is needed, however, to establish the irony of Toby's apology, which unravels of its own accord. Though setting out to 'vindicat[e] himself from private views' in deploring the onset of peace, Toby circles obsessively on his own imaginative pleasures as he speaks, and ends in the ludicrous claim that the 'infinite delight' he shares with Trim in the re-enactments comes from the consciousness 'that in carrying them on, we were answering the great ends of our creation' (6.32.557). This last phrase conventionally refers, of course, to religious duty, not to the pursuit of pleasure or war, and in the context of Sterne's usage elsewhere the misapplication is hard to miss. As the Florida notes point out, when Sterne talks from the pulpit about people who fail 'to answer the great purposes of their being', he means those who neglect the commandments (*Sermons*, 23.214), and Toby's self-serving perversion of the phrase may also be measured by contrast with a representative devotional poem: 'The end of life is service; to extend | Good things to such as want, is the great end | Of our creation.'[72] The irony seems all the more pointed when we remember the warmongering way in which the Treaty of

---

[72] Nicholas Billingsley, *A Treasury of Divine Raptures* (1667), 72 ('On Bounty', ll. 5–7).

Utrecht had been invoked in the months before Sterne composed the ora-tion. As Sterne puts in the letter quoted earlier in this chapter: 'B[eckfor]d and B[arringto]n abused all who sought for peace . . . and B[eckfor]d added, that the reasons of wishing a peace now, were the same as at the peace of Utretch—that the people behind the curtain could not both maintain the war and their places too, so were for making another sacrifice of the nation, to their own interests' (*Letters*, 129). Not only does Toby's oration on the same issue share the character that Sterne gave Beckford's ('a most long, passionate, incoherent speech'); it also shows him to be prey to just the preoccupation with personal over public interest that he, like Beckford, alleges against those who seek peace.

Where to go for a less ironic treatment from Sterne's pen of war, peace, and their rival claims is not clear, but one candidate might be the dedica-tion to Pitt that Sterne added to *Tristram Shandy* in its London edition. While positioning the text in a Whig milieu through this decisive choice of addressee, Sterne's dedication pulls markedly away from the aggressive ex-pansionism that was the dominant Whig posture of the day. By presenting *Tristram Shandy* as 'written in a bye corner of the kingdom, and in a retired thatch'd house', he sounds a note that, in its 'little Englander' tone, is unmistakably at odds with the driving impulse that motivated the war. By inviting his dedicatee to take the book 'into the country' with him to beguile his pain, moreover, Sterne seems to urge the same isolationist mentality on Pitt himself. It would be an obvious anachronism to attribute to Sterne anything like pacifism, and his tone of amused detachment as he reports the 'pitched battle' in parliament about the war of February 1761 (*Letters*, 129) makes his overall attitude hard to recover. His letters do show, however, how forcefully he was struck by the human costs of the war in its latest phase ('of two battalions of nine hundred men . . . but seventy-one left!'), and in this context there seems something peculiarly double-edged about the Whiggism of *Tristram Shandy*, his decision to address it to Pitt, and its availability to other ministers of Sterne's acquaintance such as Charles Townshend, who, as Sterne wrote a month before the official ap-pointment, 'will be now secretary of war—he bid me wish him joy of it, though not in possession' (*Letters*, 130). Perhaps we should read the whole Toby underplot as participating in that 'stream' of anti-war opinion that was setting in strong as volumes 3 and 4 were being published (*Letters*, 128), or even as satirically counselling its ministerial readers against militarist expansionism. Perhaps we should see it as reflecting reservations that these ministers may even have shared, given the various hints in Sterne's letters (the lugubrious tone of Townshend's comment; Pitt's political fit of gout when called on to defend the war) that doubts about the costs of the war were beginning to trouble the minsterial élite. We need not endorse Tristram's characteristically hyperbolical claim to have laid 'the corner stone' of the Treaty of Paris (8.35.638), at any rate, to see that previous instalments had indeed been, in their usual wry and elliptical way, an intervention in the foregoing debates.

One last document of relevance here is a sermon, one of the group posthumously published in 1769, in which Sterne returns to the theme of the Civil War (this being a 30 January sermon, preached to commemorate the execution of Charles I) to urge his congregation to mend their ways through productive reflection on the calamities evoked in *Tristram Shandy* by Sir Roger's boots. Without the effort of productive reflection, the sermon insists, 'the service of this day is more a senseless insult upon the memories of our ancestors,—than an honest design to profit by their mistakes and misfortunes' (*Sermons*, 32.311). Exactly when the sermon was written remains uncertain,[73] but its rhetoric is evidently energized by war in the present. Although the 1640s are now no more than a dreadful memory, Sterne urges, and 'our history, for this last century, has scarce been any thing else but the history of our deliverances, and God's blessings' (32.307), it remains a duty to remember 'our own corruptions,—and the little advantages we have made of the mercies or chastisements of God,—or from the sins and provocations of our forefathers' (32.311). Even now, the nation has been tried by public afflictions, and has been visited above all 'with a long and expensive war', or again 'with all the devastation, bloodshed, and expence which the war has occasioned' (32.309). But lessons have not been learned: 'though we solemnly, on every return of this day, lament the guilt of our forefathers in staining their hands in blood,—we never once think of our principles and practices, which tend the same way' (32.310). Foremost among these is partisan division, as though the political rancours of the present retain at least something of the more extreme and disastrous political divisions that boiled over at Marston Moor. We must put these divisions in proper perspective, and remember, 'however we may shelter ourselves under distinctions of party,— that a wicked man is the worst enemy the state has;—and for the contrary,

---

[73] Melvyn New dates the sermon tentatively to the late 1740s because of its reference to the disastrous cattle plague of these years, in which case the war in question would be the War of the Austrian Succession (1739–48). As New observes elsewhere in his edition, however (*Sermons, Notes*, 5), we must think of all these sermons as being subject to incremental composition and perennial recycling, and in this case the apparent echo of the distinctive anti-war discourse of the Seven Years War (see above, p. 185 and n. 3) strongly suggests later revision.

it will always be found, that a virtuous man is the best patriot, and the best subject the king has' (32.311–12).

All of which seems conventional enough, and perhaps the kind of thing that any competent eighteenth-century cleric could produce in his sleep. Yet in its assertion of a grim continuity between partisan struggle and global war at the present time and the abiding horrors of the 1640s, the sermon is entirely at one with *Tristram Shandy*, and with the culminating ironies of the apologetic oration. In lamenting the peace, Toby is putting private pleasure—and private pleasure that is personally debilitating—above that great preoccupation of *Tristram Shandy*'s ending, human survival: he deplores the treaty not because of its terms on the nation, but because it ends his games with the relics of Marston Moor. It is a moment where the bloodlettings of Fairfax's war, King William's war, Marlborough's war, and Pitt's war all meet and intersect, if not with a polemical clarity that Sterne by now has taught us not to expect, then at least with a forceful ironic reminder of the evil of war in general, and of the 'devastation, bloodshed, and expence' it continues to cost.

Index